Conversations with Sonia Sanchez

Literary Conversations Series

Peggy Whitman Prenshaw
General Editor

Photo courtesy Leandre Jackson

Conversations with
Sonia Sanchez

Edited by
Joyce A. Joyce

University Press of Mississippi
Jackson

www.upress.state.ms.us

The University Press of Mississippi is a member of the Association of American University Presses.

Copyright © 2007 by University Press of Mississippi
All rights reserved
Manufactured in the United States of America

First edition 2007
∞
Library of Congress Cataloging-in-Publication Data

Conversations with Sonia Sanchez / edited by Joyce A. Joyce. — 1st ed.
   p. cm. — (Literary conversations series)
   Includes index.
   ISBN-13: 978-1-57806-951-4 (cloth : alk. paper)
   ISBN-10: 1-57806-951-3 (cloth : alk. paper)
   ISBN-13: 978-1-57806-952-1 (pbk. : alk. paper)
   ISBN-10: 1-57806-952-1 (pbk : alk. paper) 1. Sanchez, Sonia, 1934——Interviews. 2. Poets, American—20th century—Interviews. 3. African American women poets— Interviews. 4. Poetry—Authorship. 5. African American women in literature. 6. African Americans in literature. I. Joyce, Joyce Ann, 1949–
   PS3569.A468Z63 2007
   811'. 54—dc22   2006036235

British Library Cataloging-in-Publication Data available

Books by Sonia Sanchez

Home Coming. Detroit: Broadside, 1969.

Liberation Poem. Detroit: Broadside, 1970.

We a BaddDDD People. Detroit: Broadside, 1970.

360 Degrees of Blackness Coming at You. New York: Five X Publishing Company, 1971.

It's a New Day: Poems for Young Brothas and Sistuhs. Detroit: Broadside Press, 1971.

Ima Talken bout the Nation of Islam. Astoria, NY: TruthDel, 1972.

A Blues Book for Blue Black Magical Women. Detroit: Broadside, 1973.

Love Poems. New York: Third Press, 1973.

The Adventures of Fat Head, Small Head and Square Head. New York: Third Press, 1973.

We Be Word Sorcerers: 25 Stories by Black Americans. New York: Bantam, 1973.

I've Been a Woman: New and Selected Poems. Sausalito, CA: Black Scholar Press, 1978; rpt.
    Chicago: Third World Press, 1985.

A Sound Investment. Chicago: Third World Press, 1979.

Crisis in Culture: Two Speeches by Sonia Sanchez. New York: Black Liberation Press, 1983.

Homegirls and Handgrenades. New York: Thunder's Mouth Press, 1984.

Generations, Selected Poetry: 1969–1985. London: Karnak House, 1986.

Under a Soprano Sky. Lawrenceville, NJ: Africa World Press, 1987.

Wounded in the House of a Friend. Boston: Beacon Press, 1995.

Does Your House Have Lions? Boston: Beacon Press, 1997.

Like the Singing Coming Off the Drums: Love Poems. Boston: Beacon Press, 1998.

Shake Loose My Skin: New and Selected Poems. Boston: Beacon Press, 1999.

Plays

The Bronx Is Next. Drama Review 12 (Summer 1968): 78–83.

Sister Son/ji. In *New Plays from the Black Theatre: An Anthology*, ed. Ed Bullins. New York:
    Bantam, 1969.

Dirty Hearts. Scripts 1 (November 1971): 46–50.

Malcolm Man/Don't Live Here No Mo'. Black Theatre, no. 6 (1972): 24–27.

Uh Huh: But How Do It Free Us?. In *The New Lafayette Theatre Presents*, ed. Ed Bullins.
    New York: Doubleday, 1974.

I'm Black When I'm Singing, I'm Blue When I Ain't, unpublished, but performed at the
    OIC Theatre, Atlanta, Georgia, April 23, 1982.

Contents

Introduction

In his *Blackness and the Adventure of Western Culture*, George Kent gives his definition of the *sensibility* of a writer. He asserts that writers have "characteristic emotional, psychic, and intellectual response[s] to existence" (Third World Press, Chicago: 1972, 17). Of course, three ways of examining a writer's sensibility are through examining his/her creative work, exploring a writer's biography, and reading his/her autobiography. A fourth method of deducing an author's sensibility emerges as a combination of creative work, biography, and autobiography. I am referring here to interviews or conversations with a writer. While the interview process documents a dialogue between the interviewer/critic and the writer/interviewee, the writer controls the interview, despite the nature of the questions the critic asks. The writer has the advantage of filtering through his/her emotional, psychic, and intellectual reservoir in order to critique his/her work, to create an image, to correct misconceptions, and to call attention to overlooked or undervalued issues or subjects. The interview can provide the reader with a more accurate perception of who the writer is and with a view of how she/he views his/her purpose as an artist. Sonia Sanchez's responses in her interviews, perhaps, reveal aspects of her sensibility that we may overlook in reading her poetry. The sensibility we discover in the interviews collected here provides a clearer understanding/interpretation of Sanchez's poetry, despite contemporary literary theoretical views that attempt to devalue or erase the influence/role of the author.

An observation of the interviews/conversations with professor, poet, playwright Sonia Sanchez reveals a feminine, a political, and an intellectual sensibility that decided at the very beginning of her literary career to use her talent and her energy to challenge global multifaceted injustices. Ranging from 1979 to 2005, the conversations collected in this edition illuminate Sanchez's ideas toward her creative work; her teaching as a university professor; her activities as a community activist; her work as a feminist;

her involvement in the institutionalization of Black Studies; the diversity of her creative imagination, revealed in her poetry, her plays, her children's stories and plays; her work with younger poets and hip-hop artists; her travels; her stage productions of her poetry; and her many awards.

As early as 1979 in an interview with Anita Cornwell, which appears in *Essence*, Sanchez talks about how she became a writer, her writing habits, as well as how she balances being a mother and a writer. In the years of interviews to follow, in her reading of her poetry before audiences as well as in her poetry, Sanchez explains that as a child she had difficulty communicating with those around her, and thus her stuttering resulted from these experiences. In one sense, Sanchez's stuttering represents the beginning of her artistic career as a child. In at least two subsequent interviews—D. H. Melhem's interview in *Heroism in the New Black Poetry: Introductions and Interviews* (1990) and David Reich's interview with her in *World* (1999), Sanchez addresses the connection between her stuttering and her poetry. In her conversation with Melhem, Sanchez explains that poetry was her first genre: "I think the first art form was poetry. I first started to write poetry when I was a little girl in Alabama. As a child I stuttered, and I was what Black people called 'tongue-tied,' too. . . . I was a very introspective kind of child as a consequence of that, and I started to write these little things on paper, and someone finally told me, 'That's a poem.'" To David Reich Sanchez adds, "I think I started stuttering because of the great loss of my grandmother, who died when I was six. She was a pivotal person in my life, a woman who came to my father's house and picked me and my sister up and said she would take care of us because my mother died trying to give birth to twins. They all died— she died, and they died in her."

Sanchez's responses are very important because they illuminate a poetic sensibility, though the talent is innate, that emerges from the shock and pain of loss, in this case the loss of a mother and a grandmother. Not only does the stuttering play a role in Sanchez's finding her talent at writing poetry, but also her poetry reveals that she has structured stuttering into the form of her written poetry and into her dramatic readings of her poetry. Continuing to show the relationship between stuttering and emotional trauma, Sanchez has the mother and wife of the drug addict in the prose poem "After Saturday Night Comes Sunday" stutter as she has difficulty talking to her addict husband after she learns that she has no money to buy food for the babies because he bought drugs with all the money they had in the bank. Perhaps, an even more important way in which Sanchez's stuttering reflects her poetic sensibility is that we can see a linguistic and typographical similarity between Sanchez's representation of stuttering on the printed page and the typographical innovations to American poetry characteristic of the poets of the Black Arts Movement.

Despite the fact that poets such as Sanchez, Amiri Baraka, Eugene Redmond, Ishmael Reed, Nikki Giovanni, Askia Touré, Jayne Cortez, and others have been writing poetry, which defines the merger of their politics and creativity for over thirty years, James Edward Smethurst's recent *The Black Arts Movement: Literary Nationalism in the 1960s and 1970s* (2005) emerges as the most comprehensive text that connects the literary and political activity of the Black Arts Movement to the Black left, to Black nationalism and, most importantly, that describes the presence and activities of the Black Arts Movement in Chicago, Detroit, Los Angeles, Oakland, Washington, D.C., and Atlanta. Sanchez then is a prime mover in a national literary movement that challenged the Euro-American literary status quo. Although Sanchez's association with the Black Arts Movement appears as subtext in all the conversations in this collection, in her interview with David Reich in *World*, she addresses the fact that she, Baraka, Touré, and "a bunch of other poets from the Black Arts Movement" went into bars in Harlem to read their poetry because their goal was to take their poetry to the people. In response to India Dennis-Mahmood's request that she define the Black aesthetic in *Feminist Teacher*, Sanchez echoes Stokely Carmichael (Kwame Ture) and Charles V. Hamilton's *Black Power* when she defines the Black aesthetic exclusively by negating the stereotypical concept that Black physical features are synonymous with a lack of physical beauty and a lack of intelligence. She says the Black arts poets "subverted" the whole idea that Black is "terrible" and chanted "Black is beautiful." This assertion that "Black is beautiful" translates in her poetry and in her interviews into a concentrated focus on Black speech and Black music as poetic form (to paraphrase Stephen Henderson's *Understanding the New Black Poetry*) and with a study of those writers who she felt had mastered the precision of poetry. The interview with Annie Finch represents Sanchez's detailed focus on the precision of the poetic form. In fact, a cross-referencing of all her interviews illuminates that Sanchez believes that poetry is not poetry without meticulous attention to craft.

In a 1985 conversation with Herbert Leibowitz, Sanchez boldly gives her criteria for good poetry. She cites the value of structure, vivid imagery, beauty, and the "walking" of style and content together so that they are fused, and she holds that a poem is indeed rooted in race and gender. Thus a poet's experiences, implied by Sanchez, are inherent in the poet's "sharpened tools of craft." A mere glance at an annual series of texts called *The Best of American Poetry* for any given year reveals the consistent names of Langston Hughes, Gwendolyn Brooks, and Amiri Baraka. These texts exclude an entire history of Black poetry because the tradition of African American poetry differs from Euro-American poetry in its continual denunciation of racism and/or in its innovative changes in poetic form. Similar to the literary establishment's rejection of what it refers to as protest literature in the 1930s and 1940s, the poetry of the Black Arts Movement continues to suffer from the misconception that it is more political than it is artistic.

Always aware of the literary establishment's criterion that political poetry is not artistic or aesthetically crafted, Sanchez in her conversations with her interviewers consistently addresses how and why she writes and the influences on her poetry. In a 2003 interview with Kadija Sesay, Sanchez dispels the myth that political poetry is not well-honed poetry. Sanchez indicates that she revises some of her poems at least nine or ten times. In a later conversation with Jennifer Jordan (*BMa: The Sonia Sanchez Literary Review*, Fall 2002), Sanchez discusses at length the writing process in her second book-length poem *Does Your House Have Lions?* She explains that she keeps her writing pad beside her bed and woke up one night with the lines of the title in her head and that the rhyme royal form was stimulated by the fact that she was teaching the form to a graduate class in creative writing at the time.

Following in the tradition of Gwendolyn Brooks's "The Anniad," also written in rhyme royal (a seven-line iambic pentameter stanza, rhyming *ababbcc*), Sanchez demonstrates the merger of a European poetic form with a Black communal, personal context, illustrating another characteristic of her sensibility as an artist: her ability to use form to distance herself emotionally from painful, personal or political subjects. In *Does Your House Have Lions?* the poet uses the voices of her African ancestors to address her family's alienation from her dead brother who died of AIDS and to assuage the pain of his death for her, her sister, and her father. Though in her readings, Sanchez frequently cites Chinua Achebe and Ngugi wa Thiong'o as sources for her use of

African words in her poetry, her conversations with writers of color throughout the Diaspora reveal a list of literary influences from American writers—both Black and White—to Central and South American writers, who have influenced her sensibility.

Some might argue that Sanchez's sensibility as a writer began with her grandmother who told the other adults to "just let her be" as the poet enjoyed jumping from high places as a little girl. Yet, Sanchez speaks frequently about her discovery of the Schomburg Library, which contained books written by and about Black writers exclusively. A more recent conversation with Sascha Feinstein details the poet's first entrance into the library and her meeting the librarian Jean Hutson, who directed the poet to Zora Neale Hurston, W. E. B. Du Bois, and Booker T. Washington. Sanchez acknowledges having heard the music of poets, such as Langston Hughes, Countee Cullen, and Paul Laurence Dunbar before she left the South. In her interviews with Claudia Tate, D. H. Melhem, and Herbert Leibowitz, she cites Alexander Pushkin and Gwendolyn Brooks as influences. Yet, in tracing the development of Sanchez's poetry from *Home Coming* (1969) to *Shake Loose My Skin: New and Selected Poems* (1999), we find that her poetry indeed reflects her comments to Melhem to whom Sanchez says she reads Latin poets, African poets, Federico García Lorca's poetry, and the poems of Euro-American writers. She makes it clear that the influences on her work extend beyond the provincial. These multicultural influences manifest strongly in the poem "MIA's" in *Homegirls and Handgrenades* (1984) and impressively in "At the Gallery of La Casa De Las America Habana. Dec. 1984," "Picture No. 2 Roberto Malta: Chile: Sin Titulo," "3 × 3 shigeko: a Hiroshima maiden speaks," and "Africa Poem No. 4," all collected in *Under a Soprano Sky* (1987). Like Black Arts Movement poets Jayne Cortez and Amiri Baraka, Sanchez, too, traveled to Cuba and emerges as heavily influenced by the love of Cuban people and the lyricism of Nicolás Guillén's poetry.

A cross-referencing of the presence and consistency of the poems in which Sanchez celebrates Malcolm X, Sterling Brown, Martin Luther King, Jr., Margaret Walker, Gwendolyn Brooks, Marcus Garvey, and others with the interviews in which she pays tribute to these political and literary figures illuminates a communal artistic sensibility that views itself as part of a continuum. A major goal for the writers of the Black Arts Movement, though they were well-read and traveled widely, was to perfect those aspects of the Black literary tradition that they saw as indigenous to a displaced

African people, who created their own language and used their tonal memory to transform African music into blues and jazz. In addressing her conception of a poem about a young sister "who went down on [a] brother in the middle of the dance floor" in public, Sanchez proposes in a conversation with Larvester Gaither in the *Gaither Reporter* that the young woman demeaned herself because "she didn't carry her ancestors with her, she didn't understand. She was ahistorical." Here the poet echoes Marcus Garvey's contention that a people without knowledge of their history are like a tree without roots. In other words, the poet's psychical and intellectual sensibility illuminates that she views her art as a means of transforming minds, especially the minds of Black people.

Yet, Sanchez's interviews, like her poetry, demonstrate that if we fail to appreciate her intellectual complexity and her emotional growth, we fail to understand how she transformed herself as a poet and as a human being, searching for the meaning of that humanity. While her earlier poems and interviews challenged the multifaceted injustices that stifled Black lives, her later interviews have begun to highlight the need for planetary, humanistic harmony. When Sanchez chants in poems, such as "Improvisation," asking Blacks, Jews, gays, Whites, teachers, communists, and others to come together in a struggle to achieve world peace, she reaches out to a more diversified audience than she did in the late 1960s, 1970s, and 1980s. In her 2002 interview, Jennifer Jordan asks Sanchez to talk about what some refer to as multiculturalism in Sanchez's recent poetry. Sanchez responds by pointing out that we all come from Africa and "from our loins have come all these different races." She says that she purposely includes "the idea of freedom and liberation for Asians and Latinos and Whites and gays and lesbians and Muslims and Jews and everybody, Africans and everybody." If read very carefully, Sanchez's further comments indicate that a plutocracy has used 9/11 to convince all the groups she names above to fear "terrorists." When she implies that what we must learn on the planet is how to avoid manipulation and how to live in peace, she connects her earlier appeal to a Black audience to the interconnection among peoples regardless of their race and geographical location.

The stereotyping of Sanchez as a poet who speaks exclusively to a Black audience has its source not only in the political fervor of the 1960s and 1970s, but also in the fact that Sanchez was one of the three original Black professors for the first Black Studies Program at San Francisco State

College (now University). In my interview with her in *Black Studies as Human Studies: Critical Essays and Interviews* (2005), Sanchez, along with two other Black Arts Movement architects Askia Touré and Amiri Baraka, provides answers to the history behind their invitation to become the first Black Studies faculty, giving their definition of Black Studies, explaining the nature of the courses they taught, citing the weaknesses and strengths of Black Studies, and providing their visions for what should be the future of Black Studies. Sanchez repeats here the story that she reveals in many of her interviews: FBI agents visited her home and harassed her because the government saw her teaching W. E. B. Du Bois, Paul Robeson, and Marcus Garvey as subversive.

Having taught at Rutgers Livingston College, San Francisco State College (now University), Amherst, the University of Pittsburgh, the University of Pennsylvania, and Temple University, Sanchez in her interviews suggests that she immensely enjoys teaching. It is clear that her philosophy as a teacher is no different from how she views her role as a writer. In Sanchez's on-line conversation with Cheo Tyehimba, the convergence of her role as a writer and her philosophy as a teacher is remarkably clear. When asked to define her teaching philosophy, Sanchez again cites the FBI agents' visit to her home. She says here that the agents' questions made her realize that she was "teaching sociology, economics, the culture of a people." Her subtext here is that the agents' real concern was that she and other Black Arts Movement writers as well as Black Studies teachers were empowering Black people by teaching Black history.

Although Sanchez worked as a professor for over thirty years, her advice to young people extends far beyond the classroom. She functions regularly as a judge for nationwide poetry contests, and she has formed allegiances with young contemporary hip-hop artists, such as Mos Def, Rakim, and Talib Kweli. She also works closely with Ursula Rucker and Lamont Stepto, very skilled poets, who were once her students at Temple. In his conversation with Sanchez in Derrick Gilbert's edition of *Catch the Fire!!!: A Cross-Generational Anthology of Contemporary African-American Poetry* (1998), young poet and university professor Tony Medina asks Sanchez what advice she would give to young poets. Sanchez's advice reflects the path she has followed in her own career: She advises young poets to study their tradition, to acknowledge the source of their creativity, to remember that they are connected to a tradition that comes out of struggle. One of the ways in which Sanchez teaches the connection between the art of poetry and politics is her work as workshop leader with the students who attend Cave Canem, a poetry retreat, instituted by poet Toi Derricotte for young poets. Some of the participants from Cave Canem were present for the event entitled "Lucille Clifton and Sonia Sanchez: A Conversation" (Eisa Davis, *Callaloo*, Fall 2002).

Sanchez explains in this conversation that she first met Lucille Clifton at Morgan State University in 1973 and that they later met at Margaret Walker's home. In addition to Margaret Walker and Lucille Clifton, Sanchez speaks very lovingly of her friendship with Audre Lorde and Toni Morrison. The consistencies of the attention she gives to women's issues in her interviews corroborate this same focus, which appears repeatedly in her poetry. *Like the Singing Coming Off the Drums: Love Poems* (1998), a beautiful collection of haiku poetry, manifests the particularly femi-nine characteristics of Sanchez's poetic sensibility. In the interview with Zala Chandler in *Wild Women in the Whirlwind: Afra-American Culture and the Contemporary Literary Renaissance*, Sanchez lists a throng of Black women writers with whose works she became familiar only after her college years because of the nature of the American educational system. She says she can "feel" the influence of a host of women writers such as Phillis Wheatley, Frances Harper, Nella Larsen, Jessie Fauset, Zora Neale Hurston, Ann Petry, Margaret Walker, and Gwendolyn Brooks.

In my "Interview with Sonia Sanchez: Poet, Playwright, Teacher, and Intellectual Activist," one of my goals was to ask Sanchez to connect her choice of women writers for her course on the Black woman at the University of Pittsburgh to her work as a feminist and to the everyday realities of Black women's lives. Her response is detailed and at times original. She takes the reader back to the Moynihan Report, talks about what she terms a diarchal Black culture, and analyzes Moynihan's ignorance or neglect of the effect slavery has had on the Black family and especially on the inti-mate relationships between Black men and women as well as on the Black man's self-perception. One of the most consistent aspects of the history of Sanchez's conversations is her inclusion of a mention of her children. Just as pictures of the poet flanked by her twins appear on a number of her book covers, she talks frequently in her poetry readings and in her interviews about how she wrote when her children went to bed, how she would take them to the park so she could write while they played, and how she traveled with them. Her integrating her children into the rhythm of her life manifests not only in her dedicating poems and books to her sons and to her daughter, but we learn also from her interviews that she wrote children's books, such as *It's a New Day* (1971), *The Adventures of Fat Head, Small Head, and Square Head* (1973), inspired by her conversations with her sons; and *A Sound Investment* (1980).

In " 'This Thing Called Playwrighting': An Interview with Sonia Sanchez on the Art of Her Drama," in the Spring/Summer 2005 issue of *African American Review*, Sanchez explains that she has written two children's plays—*A Trip to a Backwoods Farm* and *Malcolm Man/Don't Live Here No Mo'*. While her poetry and her readings of her poetry are enjoying increasing national and international visibility, Sanchez's plays have not yet received the critical attention they merit. Thus Duke University Press's forthcoming publication of Jacqueline Wood's edition of Sanchez's plays will be a valuable contribution to the study of Sanchez's canon. In the "Interview with Sonia Sanchez: A Panoramic View of a Writer," Sanchez at length explains the rationale behind or conceptualization of her plays. Her play *I'm Black When I'm Singing, I'm Blue When I Ain't* solidifies a connection between Sanchez's focus on the intricacies of women's lives and her deeply ingrained appreciation of music. The play presents a woman who has multiple personalities, identified with Billie Holiday, Bessie Smith, and Nina Simone.

While most of Sanchez's readers are familiar with her spellbinding readings of her poetry and while in other interviews she has frequently talked about her father's being a musician and thus her having grown up around music and musicians, her conversation with Sascha Feinstein in *Brilliant Corners: A Journal of Jazz and Literature* emerges as an engaging overview of Sanchez's knowledge of Black music. Through her chanting and lyrical performances, she says she tries "to make people hear that which they ignore. I try to make people hear that which they would rather not sing." Sanchez's use of her voice to accentuate meaning in her poetry and stimulate feeling in her audience continues the tradition of the Black Arts Movement poets, whose goal was to write poetry with the stylistic innovations peculiar to the vernacular and music of the Black community. In her conversation with D. H. Melhem, Sanchez reveals the first poem she wrote "to be sung" was "A Coltrane Poem," which appeared first in *We A BaddDDD People* (1970).

Though Sanchez very rarely reads the typographically virtuosic "A Coltrane Poem," in July 2004 she performed her poetry at Atlanta's National Black Arts Festival to the accompaniment of pianos, drums, a bass, a trumpet, electric and acoustic guitars, an organ, percussions, a keyboard, background vocals, and with dancers. She has subsequently repeated this production at the Tribeca Performing Arts Center in New York City. Therefore, Sanchez's most recent stage production entitled *The Full Moon of Sonia* reflects the twenty-first century representation of the development of the Black Arts Movement. In "Interview with Sonia Sanchez: Poet, Playwright, Teacher, and Intellectual Activist," Sanchez makes this same connection, explaining how her performance brings together poetry, blues, jazz, spirituals, rap, and thus the diversity of the cultural aspects of the Black community. Sanchez has moved from reading her poetry in the bars in Harlem to reading/performing it to wider audiences, who can purchase the CD, recorded from the musical orchestration of her poetry.

Because mainstream American poetry has elitist, limited definitions of poetry and because we too frequently do not use the word *intellectual* to refer to creative artists, especially Black women creative artists, in my interview with Sanchez, which appears last in this volume, one of my major foci was to ask Sanchez questions that would illuminate her highly intellectual sensibility. My approach is rooted in the fact that regardless of the nature of the questions asked of Sanchez in other interviews, she appears to have a set of responses that gives the interviewer and reader the pictures of her and her work that she wants historicized. Yet, not so subtly hidden under the consistencies in Sanchez's responses to interview questions in this volume is a measured, deeply ingrained intellectual awareness of how she is perceived as a woman, as a Black woman, as a poet, as a playwright, and of her role in challenging or destroying the anti-humanistic attitude toward Black art, Black women, Black people, and other people of color. The interviews disclose that a conscious aspect in the development of her interviews is her growing understanding that a destruction of injustices on our planet is impossible without including all ethnicities into a conversation about the need for a more spiritual approach to social, political, economical humanistic harmony.

The interviews collected in this volume, with the exception of a few grammatical and spelling corrections, are reproduced uncut and unchanged and cover the years 1979 to 2005. The interviewers represent a diverse gender, racial, and generational group interested in Sanchez's work. While Sanchez has published sixteen books and though we have a journal—*BMa: The Sonia Sanchez Literary Review*—devoted exclusively to Sanchez's work, the critical attention given to her work has been slow in coming. My goal as interviewer/critic in the last conversation collected in this volume was to interrupt Sanchez as little as possible. Over the years, I have found that she is an excellent critic of her own work. Thus I allowed her the space and time to develop her ideas.

It is my hope that this collection of interviews will stimulate more scholarly books and essays on Sanchez's work, focusing on the diversity of her creative imagination and on her indelible place in the history of African American, American, and world letters. It is my desire that this volume serve as a resource reference for those scholars, students, and everyday readers who are familiar with her poetry on the printed page and for those who encounter her poetry for the first time through her dramatic readings. Because Sanchez speaks repeatedly about teaching poetry, I think creative writing teachers will find the interviews collected here especially enlightening.

I want to thank profusely Quincy Jones, my friend, ex-graduate student, and poet; Mary Middlebrook-Longs; Rujuta Chinkolchar-Mandelia; and Nicole Barcliff for their invaluable assistance with this project. Without their gracious generosity, I would have suffered considerably. I give a special "shout out" to Quincy Jones. I also want to thank all those interviewers who granted their permission to use interviews, especially Ms. Mary Tate, Claudia Tate's mother. With pleasure, I acknowledge the patience of my husband whose company I missed the many hours I spent working on this manuscript.

I want to thank Seetha Srinivasan, director of the University Press of Mississippi, who responded very positively to my request that the press produce this collection of conversations with Sonia Sanchez. And, of course, this book would not exist without Sonia Sanchez. I thank her for allowing me to come into her home, for giving me at least two days of her time, for all of her generosity, time, and assistance in sharing interviews that she had, helping me to locate some of the authors of those interviews, and especially for sharing her delicious microbiotic food with me.

JAJ

Chronology

1934	Born Wilsonia Benita Driver on 9 September in Birmingham, Alabama, to Wilson L. Driver and Lena (Jones) Driver.
1935	Mother dies.
1940	Grandmother dies.
1943	Moves to Harlem from Alabama.
1951	Graduates from high school and enters Hunter College.
1955	Receives a B.A. degree in political science from Hunter College.
1956	Studies poetry as a graduate student with Louise Bogan at New York University.
1957	Daughter Anita is born in New York.
1962	Contributes to the *Minnesota Review*.
1963–65	Teaches at the Downtown Community School in New York City.
1965	Travels to Mexico.
1966	Contributes to *Afro-American Festival of the Arts Magazine* and to *Transatlantic Review*.
1967–69	Teaches at San Francisco State College and helps found the first Black Studies Program.
1968	Twin sons Morani and Mungu are born in San Francisco; the play *The Bronx Is Next* is published.
1969	*Home Coming* is published; the play *Sister Son/ji* is published; *Liberation Poem* is published; *We a BaddDDD People* is published; travels to Bermuda; contributes to *For Malcolm: Poems on the Life and Death of Malcolm X*.
1969–70	Teaches at the University of Pittsburgh.
1970	Contributes to *Black World*.
1970–71	Teaches at Rutgers University.
1971	The play *Dirty Hearts* is published; *360 Degrees of Blackness Coming at You* is published; *It's a New Day: Poems for Young Brothas and Sistuhs* is published; travels to Jamaica and meets

Amy Garvey, wife of Marcus Garvey; reads at the University of the West Indies; records *A Sun Lady for All Seasons* with Smithsonian Folkways Recordings.

1971–73   Teaches at Manhattan Community College.

1972   The play *Malcolm/Man/Don't Live Here No Mo'* is published; *Ima Talken bout the Nation of Islam* is published; receives honorary doctorate, Wilberforce University.

1972–75   Member of the Nation of Islam.

1972–75   Teaches at Amherst College.

1973   *The Adventures of Fat Head, Small Head, and Square Head*, a children's book, is published; *A Blues Book for Blue Black Magical Women* is published; *Love Poems* is published; *We Be Word Sorcerers: 25 Stories by Black Americans* is published; travels to China.

1974   The play *Uh Huh: But How Do It Free Us?* is published.

1976   Moves to Philadelphia.

1976–77   Teaches at the University of Pennsylvania.

1977   Begins teaching in the English Department at Temple University.

1977–78   Conducts poetry writer's workshop at YM/YWHA, Philadelphia.

1978   Travels first to Cuba and meets Nicolás Guillén. *I've Been A Woman: New and Selected Poems* is published.

1978–79   Receives a National Endowment of the Arts Award.

1979   *A Sound Investment*, a children's book, is published; granted tenure at Temple University.

1980   Brother Wilson Driver, Jr., dies, 8 June; contributing editor to *Black Scholar*.

1982   The play *I'm Black When I'm Singing, I'm Blue When I Ain't* is performed at the OIC Theatre in Atlanta, Georgia, on April 23.

1983   *Crisis in Culture: Two Speeches by Sonia Sanchez* is published.

1984   *Homegirls and Handgrenades* is published. Promoted to full professor at Temple University; recipient of the Lucretia Mott Award from the organization Women's Way in Philadelphia; travels to Canada; conducts writer's workshop at the Afro-American Historical Museum, Philadelphia.

1985   Recipient of an American Book Award from the Before Columbus Foundation for *Homegirls and Handgrenades*.

1986   Travels to Australia. *Generations, Selected Poetry: 1969–1985* is published.

1987   *Under a Soprano Sky* is published; appointed as Laura Carnell Professor at Temple University; receives honorary doctorate from Trinity College; Afro-American Historical and Cultural Museum Award; travels to Nicaragua and meets Ruben Darío at the Poetry Festival; National Hispanic Heritage Week Award, presented by the Philadelphia Federal Executive Board's Hispanic Employment Program Council.

1988   Recipient of the state of Pennsylvania's Governor's Award for Excellence in the Humanities.

1989   Recipient of the Peace and Freedom Award from Women International League for Peace and Freedom (WILPF); recipient of the Paul Robeson Social Justice Award from Bread and Roses; travels to Norway with James Baldwin and meets Octavio Paz; Distinguished Poet in Residence, Spelman College.

1991   Adopts John G. Whittier and Rhoads Middle School; contributes to *Poètes de New York Mosaique.*

1992   Receives the Frances Harper Award at the First Annual Black Women Scholars Conference; receives Mayor's Arts and Culture Award for Literary and Performing Arts; Zala Writer in Residence, Newcomb College.

1993   Receives Special Recognition for Outstanding Service to Humanity from the National Association of University Women, Philadelphia Branch; honorary doctorate, Baruch College; recipient of Roots Award, Pan-African Studies Community Education Project (PASCEP), Temple University.

1993–94   Recipient of a PEW Fellowship in the Arts.

1994   Became Lifetime member of the NAACP; Service to All Mankind Award, LSH Women's Program.

1995   *Wounded in the House of a Friend* is published; receives the Reader's Choice Award from the *Philadelphia City Paper*; receives Parent's Day Award from Lincoln University; Samuel French Morse Poetry Judge; invited to the White House as an Outstanding Community and Professional Leader for discussion of issues confronting America; Master Artist in Residence, Atlantic Center for the Arts, New Smyrna Beach, Florida;

performs "Stay on the Battlefield" on CD *Sweet Honey in the Rock: Sacred Ground*; included on DVD of *A Furious Flowering of African-American Poetry*, 1994; performs song/poem "Sometimes I Wonder" on CD *All That and a Bag of Words* with D Knowledge (a.k.a. Derrick Gilbert).

1996   Receives Contributor's Arts Award from the Gwendolyn Brooks Center, Chicago State University.

1997   *Does Your House Have Lions?* is published; appears on Sinbad's *Vibe Show*.

1998   *Like the Singing Coming Off the Drums: Love Poems* is published; reads poetry on the television program *The Cosby Show*; receives honorary doctorate from Temple University; honor citation from City Council of Philadelphia; inducted into the Germantown Historical Society Hall of Fame.

1999   *Shake Loose My Skin: New and Selected Poems* is published; recipient of the Langston Hughes Poetry Award from the City College of New York; retires from Temple University.

2000   Reads poetry on Russell Simmons's *Def Poetry Jam*; father dies, 30 November; recognition of honor from the Senate of Pennsylvania; performs "When URE Heart Turns Cold" on CD *The Rose That Grew from Concrete* with a group of poets, actors, and musical stars who come together to join Afeni Shakur (Tupac's mother) in a discussion of Tupac's poetry; reads "Wounded in the House of a Friend (Set No. 2)" on CD *Our Souls Have Grown Deep Like the Rivers: Black Poets Read Their Work.*

2001   Received the Robert Frost Medal from the Poetry Society of America; recipient of an Otto Award; distinguished minority fellow, University of Delaware; visiting professor, Howard University; sister, Anita Patricia Meza, dies, 1 October; receives citation from the Pennsylvania Legislative Black Caucus; presented key to the city, Wilmington, Delaware; ceremony for mural of Sonia Sanchez, located on the corner of Diamond and Carlyle Streets, Philadelphia, sponsored by Philadelphia Mural Arts Program.

2002   Honorary doctorate, Ursinus College; receives the Phillis Wheatley Award from the *Black Review of Books*; conducts writer's workshop for Poet's House in New York City.

2003   Visiting Professor, Bucknell University; receives Litterarum Humanarum Doctor, from the Starr King School for the Ministry; travels to Italy; contributes to *Furori: Tra Poesia Civile Passioni Personali.*

2004   Recipient of the Harper Lee Award for Alabama Distinguished Writers; recipient of Atlanta's National Black Arts Festival's Living Legend Award; records CD *Full Moon of Sonia* with VIA International Artist and performs *Full Moon of Sonia* with Amiri Baraka, Amini Baraka, T. C. Carson, Toshi Reagon at the Black Arts Festival; performs *Full Moon of Sonia* at the Tribeca Performing Arts Center, Manhattan, New York, with Oscar Brown, Jr., Billy Childs, T. C. Carson, Toshi Reagon, Amiri Baraka, Amini Baraka, and others; receives honorary doctorate from Haverford University.

2005   Reads poetry on Russell Simmons's *Def Poetry Jam*; receives Avatar Award for Artistic Excellence from Philadelphia's Arts and Business Council; visiting professor, Bucknell University; receives Leeway Foundation Social Justice Award; teaches as visiting professor at Columbia University; included on DVD *Furious Flower II;* Contributes poems to CD *Poetry Speaks to Children,* Sourcebooks, Inc.; performs poems on CD *Monnette Sudler: Meeting the Spirits.*

2005–6   Art Sanctuary of Philadelphia sponsors "A Full Year of Sonia," a year of poetry readings, poetry workshops, and poetry/musical performances, highlighting Sanchez's career as a poet, community activist, and her participation in the Black Arts Movement.

2006   Performs poem "Humbled," with Ursula Rucker on CD *Ursula Rucker: Māāt Mama,* !K7 Records.

Conversations with Sonia Sanchez

Attuned to the Energy:
Sonia Sanchez

Anita Cornwell / 1979

From *Essence*, July 1979, 11. Reprinted with permission from the author.

> . . . *i want my body to carry my words like*
> *aqueducts.*
> *i want to make the world my diary*
> *and speak rivers . . .*

Born in Birmingham, nurtured in New York, poet Sonia Sanchez now resides in Philadelphia's Germantown section. An associate professor of English at Temple University, Ms. Sanchez has been widely published in literary journals and reviews. She has written two plays and eleven books of poetry and prose. She is also a single mother of twins. In the following interview, Sonia speaks about the challenges and rewards of writing and mothering two children.

AC: How did you become interested in writing?
SS: I stuttered as a child, and sometimes it was very hard to communicate with people. So I started to write. I distinctly remember a holiday—George Washington's birthday—when we were out of school. I was sitting in the bedroom writing a poem about George Washington crossing the Delaware. Of course it was in rhyme.

My mother called me to the kitchen because I hadn't done the dishes properly. While I was rewashing the dishes, my sister went into the bedroom and found my poem. She came out to the kitchen, stood in the doorway—I can still see her till this day—and started reading the poem. The she said, "What is this junk you're writing in there?"

I reached for the poem, but she pulled it away and finished reading it to everybody in the kitchen. They all laughed. I don't really remember it as cruel laughter, but I was a very sensitive little girl. So I was very much upset, and after that I began hiding my poems. I doubt if anyone knew I was still writing.

AC: Did you get involved in writing when you went to Hunter College?
SS: I did take a writing course there. I remember one of the stories was about my father and some of the trials he had gone through. The professor wrote on it, "Things are not that terrible." And he gave me a C+. So I wrote this story about the mirror beginning to talk to me. Don't you know the professor wrote on it, "I'm mighty pleased. This is what I'm talking about!" Of course, that wasn't my reality. I dropped the course.

About two years after I left Hunter. I went to New York University and took a course with Louise Bogan, the poet, who was teaching there in the evening. Some of us from that year's course decided to meet together in Greenwich Village and start a workshop. I belonged to that workshop close to three years, until I had found enough of my own voice to start writing poems that were distinctly Black. The group wasn't ready to deal with them. They became self-conscious. So it was time to move on.

At that point I met Imamu Baraka in the Village, and he took some of my poems. He knew the people at the *Liberator*, and my work began to appear there in *Soulbook*. I was also getting published in the *New England Review* and the *Minnesota Review*.

Then I went to California and began publishing regularly in *Soulbook* and *Journal of Black Poetry*. Of course I had more than enough material for my first book, *Home Coming*, which finally came out at Broadside Press in 1969. At that time, also, my play, *Sister Son/ji*, was published in a collection called *New Plays from the Black Theatre* (Bantam Books, 1969). My second book, *We a BaddDDD People*, came out in 1970, also from Broadside Press.

AC: How do you write?
SS: Well, sometimes a line comes and I'll write it down. Then sometimes a feeling comes, and I'll write down lines of what I feel, okay? Then I'll leave it until later on that night.

Usually I work from about twelve midnight until three-thirty or four o'clock in the morning. I'll read it aloud. Then I'll start fussing at those things that obviously don't work.

Very often I'll pick up a favorite book and read. I read something I've read before, or I'll read a poet that I like.

Sometimes it's none of these things. Sometimes I actually see something that moves me or makes me angry or whatever, and then line by line just pour out from God knows where. Whenever people compliment me after a reading or tell me they enjoyed one of my books, I'll say, "Thank you so much." But inside I'll say to myself, "It's not just me." Everything that you or I could write has been written before; there's that energy there in the universe for us to pull from. Many of us just become attuned to that energy.

AC: How do you balance being a mother and a writer?
SS: For example, my twins, who are ten now, were born in San Francisco on January 26; two weeks later I was back in the classroom. It wasn't easy but I had to do it.

I've had the usual problems that women have with baby-sitters. Mine have been somewhat more intense because I've had to do a lot of traveling. Of course, some of that was relieved by my Aunt Sarah, who lived with us for a couple of years. But I was still involved with going out to work, then coming home and doing all the things the stay-at-home mothers do.

It's not particularly easy, you know, trying to raise children by yourself. When I see women out there doing it, I have to say "Hey, I *know* what you're going through."

I always try to get evening classes. If my children get sick, I can stay home with them during the day. Then I can always get a baby-sitter for the evening.

AC: How do you balance your work with the rest of your life?
SS: My writing plays an important part in my life, but I never let it get out of balance. I've always adjusted to the fact that I do have the children. They didn't ask to be born, you know? They mean a hell of a lot to me. Not only do I love them, but I like them.

I don't frustrate them with the idea of my writing. I arrange it around them. I've done ten books that way.

Sonia Sanchez: An Interview

Herbert Leibowitz / 1985

From *Parnassus: Poetry in Review*, vols. 12 and 13, nos. 2 and 1 (1985): 357–68. Reprinted by permission of the author.

(This interview took place on April 30, 1985, in New York City.)

Herbert Leibowitz: Do you think there is a feminine sensibility which differs conspicuously from that of the male?

Sonia Sanchez: Yes. Women are quite different from men in what they feel and think and how they view the world. I use feminine imagery which is drawn from ancient cultures. I use words like Olokun—she is the goddess of the sea—so that people understand when we're talking about the sea that we're talking about women. I use Oshun and Yémaya who are the female riverine goddesses. Some of these goddesses use bells to announce, resoundingly, their teachings. From the pine tree to water reflecting water, a lot of my poetry expresses what it means to let people taste and feel sweetness and power running together, hate and love running together, beauty and ugliness also running together. My poetry has talked about what it means to be a woman ironically, too, in portraits of women who have been violated, as the earth has been violated. I try to focus attention on injustices, on wrongs, but I try to do it in a way that is both sharp and loving. Black poetry often incorporates "playing the dozens," that bawdy and tough talk about family and love and race. Americans never had people talk to them in this fashion, at least not out loud. What some of us women poets did was come out with a sprinkling of curse words to needle the finicky.

HL: Do you think there's a language which belongs to women, to black women poets?

SS: Sometimes. Sometimes. It depends on the subject matter, on whether the poem happened to be cerebral, political, lyrical, or just moving somewhere else.

6

HL: Do the young women on the street play the dozens in the same way that the young males do?

SS: I think it's less violent with women. We hear it and understand it but we play it less, of course. It was a way of getting attention, of bringing black culture into poetry. You can't criticize the poetry unless you understand the culture. And if you don't understand the culture, you don't understand Sterling Brown or Gwendolyn Brooks or Margaret Walker, their use of blues, poetry, and folk poetry, and black language. In the same way, I can't criticize the poetry of other ethnic groups in this country, not unless I first study their histories. Just because people are what I call "American-made" does not necessarily mean that they can be quickly analyzed. My generation and perhaps the generation coming after me did not play the dozens in such a violent way, but young women in the schools today are as "bad" as some of the young men. (I mean "bad" in the good sense.) They have no compunctions against saying and doing what they damn well please.

HL: How does black dialect and the vitality and humor of street talk get into your poems?

SS: That happens from listening and talking and speaking, not just as an adult but as a little girl. Not, interestingly enough, as an Alabamian, not those eight years in Alabama. My memory is very quick on that because when we came to New York City I remember we didn't have a southern accent—you know how people expect you to have a southern accent? Well, we didn't—and we had not even eaten chitterlings. We spoke very tactfully, very properly, no street talk. My father was a schoolteacher in Alabama. But we learned street talk because everyone else outside the house spoke it. I learned it consciously. I made mistakes initially and people would laugh. And it was hard for me because I was a stutterer as a young girl. And I didn't stop stuttering until I came out of high school at sixteen; I would memorize how I was going to say things, so when the words came out they came out right. I'd listen very carefully and I'd never say anything unless I repeated it twenty times in the sanctity of my room, in the sanctity of my head, and going down the hallway; then I would come outside and burst right out with it.

HL: You have a very good ear for street talk.

SS: My stepmother, who was a very interesting woman, spoke what I call black English. I remember coming home from school and carrying on dual

conversations with her. In school, they were pulling us to get beyond ourselves, beyond our "defects." But I used to listen to the students who would
not conform in class, the hip kids. I would walk with them sometimes and
think, "That's really a great way of saying it." But above all, I remember my
grandmother, who also spoke in black English. She was not an educated
woman but I remember listening to her imagery. I didn't stutter when my
grandmother was alive, only after she died (I was about six). It was a kind of
self-protection, I think. No one bothered me once I began to stutter; people
would say, "Oh, she's strange, a quiet one. Give her food and leave her alone."
So I sat and read and wrote and no one really intruded. But when my grandmother was alive and spoke, I remember taking her words sometimes and
repeating them. "Why?" she would ask. "Because I like to float into words,"
I answered. Now that was a child's way of saying that her words were beautiful and couched in interesting similes and images. I could really see them
floating. And she was so permissive and loving that she allowed the imita-
tions. She knew I wasn't mocking her. She gave me that language. Now I hear
some little kid out in the street acting tough and sassy and speaking black
English, and I'll stop and talk to him and say, "Isn't that pretty?"

HL: Black kids invent metaphors with ease?
SS: Their metaphors are unbelievable. I taught one of the first courses in
black English at San Francisco State. The English Department was wondering
what in the hell I was going to do. I shrugged. "I know how the students will
greet me, how nervous they'll be in the classroom. I'm going to let them
understand that black English exists alongside standard English and that it's
fascinating." I didn't know how to teach it initially. I had to fight through it,
to come home and even battle myself, but that was a very exciting class. My
students were able to release a part of themselves without shame or guilt.

HL: When did you write your first poem?
SS: In Alabama, after Momma died. I must have been seven. I was sitting in
the corner and I had a real "Live" stepmother—I had three of them—who
was really classic, mean like in the fairy tales. She came over and grabbed
what I was doing and read it to someone (I believe it was her sister) who said,
"That's a poem!" My first real poem as such, if you can call a ten-year-old's
scribblings poems, was about my grandmother, memories of her that began
to come back in a very sharp fashion in New York. We were not accustomed

to living in a small apartment, or to a bedroom window that faced a blank wall. I began to suffer from claustrophobia. The poem was about Mama and how she let me run; I ran with the boys instead of playing with dolls. She allowed that. I could come home with my dresses torn and she'd say, "Don't put those on her, she's not a fancy girl." I've never worn frilly things; I've kept my style to this day. If I see little girls dressed in pinafores, I collapse. So the first piece I wrote was about that. I don't have it anymore. You get older, and see that it's terrible and throw it out. But the Schomburg—I'm giving my papers to the Schomburg Collection—they get upset about things like that. The first poem I ever published, in the *New England Review*, was again about the South. Once an aunt and I were on a segregated bus on which blacks could only sit at the back and whites up front. When it got very crowded, blacks had to move to the last seat and when it got jammed, they had to stand up. That day the driver stopped it and said, "Get the hell off." Well, she wouldn't get off. You know how tall I am now, you can imagine at that age how little I was. I was also very thin. I was holding on to her. This bus driver came towards her and she spit on him. There was an uproar and so she was rushed out of town under cover of darkness.

HL: Why did you choose poetry instead of prose?

SS: I don't know. Perhaps because of the fun with words I had with Momma. I've always been trying to recreate that. I did it in a streetwise manner in New York City where I spent all my years from nine on. We spent time playing dozens, and tripping people out. The poems were my way of protesting: how could you let me grow up in this country and not tell me about black history? How could you make me feel so inferior? Playing with words, as I used to, was like going outside and running and jumping over walls and getting cuts that are still with me. I was running into words because I thought they were so inventive and beautiful. My grandmother was a deaconess, and the Sisters would have meetings on Saturdays at our house. I'd go behind the couch or sit under a table and listen. That's where I learned how to watch people. My grandmother would become very emphatic about a particular kind of woman she respected or despised and to this day I identify people from what she said to me.

HL: In *Homegirls and Handgrenades* you do have several long pieces that are not exactly short stories, not prose, but prose poems. You seem to have

moved quite comfortably into vignettes that remain poetic. Everybody's favorite seems to be " 'Just Don't Never Give Up on Love.' "
SS: That's one of my favorites also.

HL: How did it come to be written?
SS: It really is unbelievable. One morning I went out to the playground with my twins. I saw this old woman who was not eighty-four, but ninety-four; no one would believe that someone ninety-four could be that lucid. I'd come outside to read a book and write a review for a journal. When I got up on her, she was nodding in the sun, and she opened one jaundiced eye. My whole body movement said, "Don't bother me, old woman; I have work to do." I sat with my back to her and opened the book I'd been assigned to review. Anyway, as I watched the twins go back and forth, I suddenly felt this nudge and it was she. She actually had slid across from her end of the bench to the middle. I turned and began to stutter—I reverted—because I didn't know what she wanted or what she was saying. Looking at me, she said her first words in black English, and I responded: "Look, woman, please don't talk to me, I have work to do, I'm so far behind that people are screaming and it's my fault." But she was very persistent, as older people are, and kept talking. When I said something abrupt like, "Yeah, that's nice," she laughed. I stopped, then put my book down, and looked at her because this old woman really laughed, and she said, "You've got some kind of spunk about you, after all. Come on, sit close to me." She had been married five times, though she talked about two marriages. The first man was beautiful, but he would have killed her if she hadn't left him. Afterwards I hugged her and the next day there she was and we talked again.

HL: Which writers were the important influences on your work?
SS: When I first started to write in school I had to read the usual people— Longfellow, Whittier, Scott—and I knew I didn't write poetry like them. I never read any real modern poets until I was in college. And then I found a black woman in the library on 145th Street who gave me Langston Hughes and Pushkin, which was fascinating. I'd come in and she'd say, "You're always in the poetry section. You should read this man because he was a black man." And then she said, "Have you read Robert Browning?" She began to redirect me, handing me, interestingly enough, some of the Latin poets I'd never touched, and though I didn't quite understand some of their

imagery, I still read the poems. I didn't understand Pushkin completely but I read him.

Louise Bogan was a very important influence. I studied with her at NYU. One of the first things she said was: If you're going to write poetry, you must read it aloud. None of us believed that. I was one of the first people who had to read aloud in that class, and as I read the damn poem, Bogan, in her droll, distant fashion, remarked, "Did you read that poem aloud, Miss Sanchez?" The rest of the students looked at me as if to say: I'm glad it's you. I was literally caught, and I started to fake it. Bogan just looked away and commented, "Well, I hear some problems in the poems." But she never rewrote any of the content, and I felt safe on that point.

At that time of course I didn't write anything that really said anything about being black or being a woman because no one wanted to bring her face or sex to anyone's attention; that was naughty, especially if you were a woman who declared "I'm a woman." People would say, "Please, you shouldn't be writing poetry if you're a woman. Or if you're black, by god, you shouldn't be writing poetry at all." So I never referred to it. But every now and then something would creep in. Usually I'd write a mild little poem about something that was happening in the South; the civil rights struggle was intense. And a poet in the workshop said: "We don't want to hear that at all." It was really rough.

HL: How did Bogan respond to your poems?

SS: I never came out and asked: "Do you think I can write?" She remarked drily, "There are some people who can write and others who can't. I would say that you can write if you work and study form." Then I began to read her work and I saw her structures. This classical woman poet was shaping a lot of us. Though some resisted form as too rigorous, I did not because I thought that my sprawling work needed form. To this day, I teach my students the villanelle, the sonnet: I preach all the exercises and discipline that Bogan gave to me. I began to move, to see how form can work, can demand a certain kind of response. That was very important for me. I realize now that she was not necessarily interested in her students. She was not a woman who'd open up to you, but she was honest and fair. That was what I needed.

HL: It sounds fortunate to have had so rigorous a mentor at the foundation of your career rather than somebody who was permissive. What other poets exerted an influence on you?

SS: Neruda and Lorca for their imagery, their showing that you could pile image on image and still make people understand. Langston Hughes, Gwendolyn Brooks, Margaret Walker. At the Schomburg Collection, I met Jean Hutson, the curator, who told me that the library was devoted to books about black folk. My reaction was, "You must be kidding." I had just gotten out of Hunter College and hadn't read anything by blacks. She gave me an entire library; that's where I first read W. E. B. Du Bois, Claude McKay, and Zora Neale Hurston. One day I turned to Jean Hutson and said: "I'm going to have my books in here," and she looked at me as though thinking that I was a rash young woman, but now she tells my students, "This is the young woman who vowed that one day she'd have her books in here," and she hugged me. After I read these black writers, I knew I was on the right track. They nurtured me. Later on I greedily read a lot of women poets: Atwood and Piercy, Brooks and Walker, Dickinson and Bogan. Then I began to buy books of poetry—that's the one thing I would spend money on—and write in the margin, to indicate the things I liked and disliked. I also read aloud. Bogan really insisted that a poet must read her work aloud. She said, "You will not always have people with you who will tell you whether something's good or bad, but your ear will."

HL: Could you talk about Neruda's importance to your writing of political poems?

SS: My early poetry was introspective, poetry that probably denied or ignored I was black. I wrote about trees, and birds, and whatever, and that was hard, living in Harlem, since we didn't see too many trees, though I did draw on my residual memories of the South. People kept saying to me, if you write a political poem, it will be considered propaganda—an ineffective and poor poem—but I read Neruda and saw that he didn't deny the personal. In the early sixties I became aware that the personal was the political. Even my loneliness was never just my own but a much larger loneliness that came out of a society that did not encourage blacks to learn for the sheer joy of it, to expand beyond drinking a bottle of beer at the end of the day and watching the idiot box. I may show you a picture of an alienated and hostile person, but there are reasons for it, and lessons to learn, too.

HL: You call your latest book *Homegirls and Handgrenades*. A hand grenade is very explosive, destructive. Do you intend us to think that poetry is in some way like a grenade?

SS: The hand grenade can also explode myths. Take the poem about the Amtrak ride. It really happened. A young/old/black man bopped on at Newark; he had a mobster's look. I immediately put my shopping bag on the seat, warning him that I didn't want to be bothered. He looked away but sure enough, he sat right behind me and began to talk to a middle-class white man. I heard this man inhale, from unease, you know, and I felt that the young old man heard it also. They had a conversation that I had to record because myths exploded there. It finally ended with the man not taking in those uneasy breaths and the black man saying simply, "I've been trying to deal with the problem of how non-work makes you less of a man in this country" and then they said goodbye and smiled at each other. That's what I mean: hand grenades are the words I use to explode myths about people, about ourselves, about how we live and what we think, because this is really the last chance we have in this country.

HL: Were you stereotyped as a political poet?
SS: Writing has been a long, tense road of saying what I wanted and needed to say. When I gave my book *Love Poems* to a friend, she said, "God, I didn't know you wrote love poems." But in every book of mine there's been a section of lyrical pieces. If you describe me, as some critics do, as a lyrical poet, I say yes, I am, but I'm also a hard-hitting poet and a political poet because this is a lyrical world and a terrible world, too, and I have to talk about that.

I have also been deeply involved in Philadelphia with what they call the literacy campaign. I go to older men and women who are learning how to read and read the poems aloud and discuss them. Once someone said to me, "I read that because it was about me, and I read it well." This person actually said good, I read it good, and I felt that she did read it good. "If this is poetry," they say, "I like poetry." And the whole point is to bring poetry to a larger audience, something I've tried to do for a long, long time.

HL: Are you conscious of writing for a particular audience?
SS: No—but I know my audience, if that makes sense. From the beginning I've had a black audience, women, and students, black and white. Now because of what's happening in this country, that audience has widened. I get letters from people saying "I understand what you're doing because I feel the same thing." What I felt as a woman, as a black woman, had to get translated to other women, too.

HL: Ishmael Reed made a comment recently that he wished Alice Walker had written about strong black men rather than unreliable males in *The Color Purple*. Is there a conflict between black male and female writers?
SS: America doesn't allow two or three major black writers to exist at the same time. You know the business: when Baldwin came along he had to kill off Wright, and when Ellison came along he had to kill off Wright, also, because Wright had maintained that position of power. Whether you have genius or not, if what you're saying sells, then by golly, by gee, they'll elevate you. Alice Walker is a talented woman. She's one of the nurtured, so therefore black success could happen.

HL: Nurtured by?
SS: By the establishment, by her publishers, purposely, so the flowering happens. Ishmael and some of the other writers are perhaps announcing: we, too, have something to say and it's not necessarily getting the play it deserves.

HL: Not reaching the same wide audience?
SS: Ish should understand that there's a different movement happening: a special interest in what women are saying, a lot of support of women writers now. Some black women writers are creating characters that reflect the negative aspects of some black men. The problem is that there's no balance in the marketplace. For that we shouldn't fault the writer; instead we should understand the need to provide progressive images. But black writers, male and female, have to maintain a sense of themselves, politically and as writers. I never look up to see who's better or worse. When I finish a reading and people come up and hug me, not because I've been sassy and smart but because I've prodded them and insisted that they think, and they say, "You've made me go another step." I know why I write.

My work, really, has always been motivated by love. In the sixties, the country had to be shocked with the horror of how it had raised Negroes who hated themselves, who were bent on wiping themselves out, intent on not seeing themselves, on being invisible. So I have a poem about Norma, who had a genius for language. I saw her on 145th Street years later, with tracks on her damn legs. What in the hell could she have done? Can you imagine what her four little girls, involved in that drug scene, see and know? She said they're going to be different, but of course I knew they weren't going to be different. This is what, finally, I'm talking about in my poems.

HL: What is your argument when somebody, not only a conservative, says that poetry transcends gender, that ultimately a poet has to be judged on the variety and brilliance of the language rather than on the question of being male or female, black or white?

SS: That time has not arrived. So the poet must educate people, which is what a lot of us are doing. If someone says, I am this, because my hair curls when it gets in water, there can still be beauty in the work. There can still be brilliance in the language that informs. Exhorts.

HL: Isn't there an implicit bias that such a poem favors content over style?

SS: For many of us our change in style was synonymous with a change in content. This forged a new and exciting creation, movement.

HL: Mallarmé's comment to Degas that poems are not made out of ideas but out of words is a favorite piety of modernism. Perhaps the twentieth century has gone too far in the direction of purity of language and we need the pendulum to swing back more toward substance.

SS: Good poets write all kinds of poems. Women poets today might make a political statement about what it is to be Hispanic or black or Jewish, whatever; their poems give me an understanding of their pain, their joy, their determination to be what they are, what they want to be. This amplifies poetry as opposed to narrowing it.

HL: What are your criteria for deciding whether poems are good?

SS: Is it well structured? Is the imagery vivid? Is there beauty in it? I might say something smartly, but the poem must have another leap and another bound to it so that style and content can walk together, can become fused. When a poet relies only on the crutch of "I'm this or I'm that" and does not bring us the sharpened tools of craft, we have to look up and protest. Some people think that the poem should not have a race or gender; it should be weightless. Whether you're Wallace Stevens or Audre Lorde, you bring what you are to the poem.

HL: Where does the criticism of your work come from? From black critics?

SS: Mostly black critics. Black women critics have done some of the best work to date. But every audience I read to becomes a profound group of critics. Their reactions affect the work, affect me. When I write, I tune in to the collective unconscious, and there I hear voices, lines, words, I hear music. For a long time I rejected the music because I felt I couldn't sing, I'm not a singer, but now in some of my pieces, I do sing. In the Martin Luther King poem, I chant. When the chant first came out, I literally shook, I said what the hell, how can I do this? But I wrote it out. When Biko was killed in South Africa, the women had come out singing *ke wa rona, ke wa rona,* so I wrote that down, with some other words around it, to chant. It was frightening to me but I just did it. I wrote that poem for the University of Pennsylvania's celebration of King's forty-sixth birthday. As I stood up to recite it, I said, I will just say *ke wa rona:* Malcolm, *ke wa rona:* Mandela, *ke wa rona:* Martin, you know, and they will know what that's about. Forces had come to me while I wrote it and I did exactly what they wanted me to do.

HL: When did the African influence enter your poetry? I take it you're fascinated by African religions.

SS: There were some phenomena I could not explain, like the collective unconscious, but I wanted to. When I read *Flash of the Spirit,* the Egyptian Book of the Dead, I laughed. That's the person I talked to, that was Yémaya. I was born on the ninth month and the ninth day and one of the numbers for Yémaya is nine. I was bringing into the arena of poetry the sense of another sensibility, another way of looking at the world, another life force. If I touch you, I give you a life force, also. To those who record desolation and say you can't do anything about it, I'm affirming that a person can do something, I'm saying yes. In other words, I'm taking what might be considered a metaphysical concept, this collective unconscious, and using my relationship to it to change real things.

Interview with Sonia Sanchez

Zala Highsmith-Taylor / 1990

From *Wild Women in the Whirlwind: Afra-American Culture and the Contemporary Literary Renaissance*, edited by Joanne M. Braxton and Andrée Nicola McLaughlin. New Brunswick, New Jersey: Rutgers University Press, 1990: 353–62. © 1990. Reprinted with the permission of the author.

Highsmith-Taylor: Who are some of the women in your early life who have influenced and inspired your work?

Sanchez: I was born in Birmingham, Alabama. And there are a couple of relevant things that happened to me in the South. My mother died when I was one year old. And my grandmother came and got my sister and me because she had decided to raise us "correctly"! (My grandmother was a deaconess in the A.M.E. Zion Church.) She meant so much to me as a child. That is why I offer her a letter in my new book, *Under a Soprano Sky*. I end that letter with, ". . . and I BE, Mama!" You see, my grandmother was a woman who spoiled us outrageously, who dared to just let me "be." I played hard as a child—usually with boys. I would come in the house real ragged from my hard playing, and people would cluck their tongues, shake their heads, and say, "You know, this girl just ain't gon' be!" But Mama would always respond, "Just let her be! Just let her be!"

The realization of who you are, I believe, is necessary for any artist—or anyone else for that matter—who is concerned and involved with liberation. You must be able to understand what it means to "be." And you cannot "be" unless you understand your history . . . the history of all the "Mamas" of the world, who always wanted something better for you . . . who would always stand up for you, risk dangers for you. My grandmother was tough and spiritual enough to never let white people touch me. If they attempted to touch my sister or me, she would always respond, "Don't touch them! These are mine. Don't take the power from them at all!"

Of that period in my life, I also remember that Mama used to have the "Sisters" (church women) over to her house each Saturday to talk, to cook for

17

the Sunday dinners, to heal each other, etc. And these sessions were really important to me. I knew that those women were transmitting knowledge to me . . . wisdom to me that I would keep all my life. And I can remember looking at them and thinking that I want to be just like them. I wanted to be like them because I saw and heard power there. I heard an awareness there. I heard a people very much assured.

These were very important days for me. And I didn't really realize how important until I was asked by an editor of a magazine to write about my empowerment as a Black woman. The editor wanted me to write about my empowerment in terms of my professional life and my success as a writer. But, to their dismay, I could not do this. Many years ago I might have been able to make a statement about empowerment in those terms. But that would have been before I understood the connections. You see, I don't see myself as being empowered because of a certain job or status. I see myself as being empowered because of my grandmother, and people like her. It has really been that kind of transmitting that has given us the power. My power may have gotten manifested in a different kind of politic than that of my grandmother. But nonetheless, it was the same power . . . the same energy that had been infused in me, that had been given to me by my grandmother.

What this means, simply, is that I don't speak alone anymore. I don't speak singularly—for myself. I speak for the many, many women who, though physically dead, remain spiritually alive through me. And I speak for those women here on earth with me, like me. And I speak for the women yet to be born.

My grandmother died when I was six years old, and, after that, I had a lot of other experiences with people in the South—extended families—that were not necessarily good. But that foundation that I had with Mama proved to be so important because it kept me sane, actually. I think it's significant to mention that after Mama's death, I had started to write poetry, these little ditties, because I had started to stutter and found it difficult to communicate with people. I used to be tongue-tied and a stutterer, which was fascinating. Because I couldn't communicate well I retreated to books and to writing. And I spent a lot of time in solitary.

Highsmith-Taylor: Who have been some of the Black women who have really inspired you in the literary tradition?

Sanchez: I have been inspired by most of the women writers who have come before me, because I recognize that they have accomplished under the greatest of odds. I remember stumbling upon Zora Neale Hurston in the sixties, and I would end up talking endlessly about her. I thought that *Their Eyes Were Watching God* was one of the most beautiful books that I had ever read. I also stumbled upon Nella Larsen's and Jessie Fauset's books, and admired them. And I was very impressed with the Black women poets of the Harlem Renaissance, though I was always disturbed that their only work that seemed to be printed in anthologies were love poems. But I knew that there had to be something beyond that. It wasn't until years later that I found out that, of course, they had other works—works that were not put into these anthologies. For example, Georgia Douglas Johnson wrote a lot about the killings of Black people in the South, and what it meant for that to be happening. I always knew that there had to be writings like hers, but sometimes one has to stumble upon them while doing research. Like I'd stumble across early plays written by Black women that dealt with (what were then) controversial subjects like a woman having a child though she wasn't married. The play would show how there would be a community of women supporting her. There were several works about women supporting women or about the plight of the Black woman. Often you'd look up and wonder why you were never exposed to these works before—works like those written by Frances Ellen Watkins Harper, an abolitionist Black woman who began to write about what it was like for a Black woman in slavery. And of course when I started to teach, I went back into some even earlier literature like that of Linda Brent, who also discussed the slave woman's condition.

Often these works would be very painful, but they inspired me, nonetheless. Because I have developed a very basic understanding about the treatment of Black women and the view that America holds of Black women, I could read these works with compassion, and be inspired by them. I could see the connections between them and me. I can understand what it means to be a Black woman trying to be strong, trying to be woman, trying to be holy, pure, trying to just be "self" in the midst of a society that says that Black women are whores, in the midst of a country that would have a president—Jefferson—who in his notes would make a statement that Black women are stretched out with orangutans. And as a result of this understanding, I know why the forces that have propelled me through the years have always made me feel the necessity to be correct . . . to be righteous. If I did something that was a violation of my people, I would have dreams. I would dream about Black women crying—crying because I had done wrong. I don't walk "correct" because I want to be super righteous. I simply want to say to the world—through my actions—that Black women, having endured, are certainly women who should be revered . . . respected on the stage of history. And that is why I cannot produce a work or walk on a stage as if I am a whore, a harlot. I can't slide on a stage like "Here I am, baby." I must walk on stage saying, "Yes! This is me." I am coming with a whole host of women, unsung heroines, unsung women we will never know. I see them in my dreams. I hear them in my dreams. I walk with them everyday. If I want to do something dumb and stupid, they hold me and say, "Look! You can't do that!" That's why I can answer your questions with names like Phillis Wheatley, Frances Ellen Watkins Harper, Jessie Fauset, Nella Larsen, Zora Hurston, Ann Petry, Margaret Walker, and Gwendolyn Brooks. I can say them because I can truly *feel* history.

One of the things that I've attempted to do in my lifetime via these women and via the women whose dreams I cherish—whose screams I cherish also—is that I will never again involve myself with what I call secondary consciousness. I will never again see myself, see other Black women, see Black men, and Black children secondarily, through the eyes of the oppressor . . . the slave master. I will never again see my kinky hair, my big nose, or my big lips as something horrible. I don't want the bluest eyes. I don't want the long, straight blonde hair. I maintain that I will never in my life walk secondarily again—or even appear to have any secondary views. If you approach me, you must approach me on an equal level. If I see your stuff is incorrect, is racist, then I will tell you. And when I hit the stage, I know that I am just as tough as anyone there. People aren't accustomed to that kind of behavior. That is a legacy that we've gotten from Malcolm, from Fannie Lou, from Du Bois, and from Ida B. I am aggressive; I will not deny myself. I will not be one of those people talking about they need to get some training on how to be aggressive. To them, I say, all you have to do is come into a sense of yourself, announce that you are an African and intend to "be." That is some automatic aggression. And you will see that in order to defend yourself, you will have to move in an aggressive fashion. Because the moment you say that you're not sure of who you are, people will slap you down, will attempt to slap you to the right and the left, tear you up! So yes, it's the Gwendolyn Brooks and the Margaret Walkers and the Ann Petrys and all the others that kept me very much rooted. And that's important.

Highsmith-Taylor: Can you talk about some of the recent movements of
Black people during the sixties, the seventies, the eighties and tell us what
impact these movements had on you, and what messages you were giving
during this time.

Sanchez: To have discovered oneself in the 1960s—probably the late fifties
but definitely manifesting itself in the early 1960s—was almost like being
reborn, I would say. It was like waking up each morning and discovering
a new part of yourself. For the first time in your life, you did not have to be
concerned about your nose, or your lips, or your hair. You could just get up
in the morning and comb your hair and be pleased. You did not have to get
involved in a whole lot of makeup and eye shadow and you name it. You did
not have to be concerned about the right shade of makeup, ensuring that you
didn't come out too light, or too dark, or too black, etc. You could be your
natural self. What a relief from a peculiar kind of bondage that was there,
that we were involved in. It means that we now had more time to do some
things with our heads, with our brains.

One of the first things that some of us said in some of our work in the sixties was that we were Black. And that in itself was a hard word for many of us
to say because in our history, the word Black meant something negative. I can
remember that when I first got on the stage and proclaimed that I am a Black
woman, it was very difficult for me. And it was also difficult for the people to
respond to that. I mean, sometimes people would ask what do you mean by
all of this "Black" stuff? This Black woman stuff? And, again, it was Malcolm
and the Muslims who brought that terminology to the forefront. (I'm not
a revisionist, you see. I can't revise history. I can't revise that. I'm not saying
that people have to then go and like Muslims or dislike Muslims. I just want
to be correct and give credit where credit is due.) Yes, Malcolm kept saying
that we're Black men, we're Black women, we're Black people. And that really
stirred the imagination in the same fashion that Marcus Garvey did when he
asserted that Black people are Black, are African. Malcolm made the same
impact on writers in the sixties that Garvey made on writers in the Harlem
Renaissance period. Garvey made poets say, "What is Africa to me?" He made
people begin to talk about "my Black self." People really began to respond to
him—many people who might never have responded before. All the way
from Countee Cullen, to Claude McKay, to Langston Hughes, writers
responded. Well, in the same fashion, the climate of the sixties was all aglow
with the words of Malcolm and other people who were saying positive Black

things and being very much the activists. The poets of that day could not just stay introspective. This was a period when we called white people a lot of names and cussed them out a lot. But it was also a period when we began to say that we had to move beyond cussing out white folk, and start to do the work that we needed to do for our survival. It was a period when we felt the necessity to write about our internal contradictions, and we often juxtaposed the public image and the private image. For example, I'd often write about the Black woman as woman, as mother, as activist. We also wrote about the problems that existed between Black men and Black women. And we were forced to say sometimes that we were tired . . . just plain old simple tired! Tired, you see, because there were some really depressing things happening sometimes. In addition to the intense attack by the state apparatus, there were a number of internal contradictions. Things like the whole drug scene, where people were on the stage talking about being Black and then walking off the stage to get high. Yes, there were things that could make for great depression. But, on the other hand, there were also things that were happening that would make you feel good—seeing people opening up before your eyes, almost like flowers, and coming to the realization that, indeed, they were Black, and indeed, they were political. It was beautiful to see people recognize that they *had* to be political if they were to survive, to live, to "be."

Those were the kinds of things that one saw happening in the sixties. There was anger, there was love, there was confrontation, and there was us saying to America, "You're racist! You're racist!" We were informing people about racism. And the people took up the call because they were able to personalize the message.

Our work in the seventies was about empowerment. We couldn't just keep on saying that America is racist, America is racist. We had to start talking about what we were going to do about it. We were saying that if this country is racist, then what do you do? Do you just sit down and cry? Do you go home and lower the shade and drink your wine? Do you shoot skag? What do you do? The message was that you must begin to take over schools. You must begin to make the churches be responsive to new times. You must go to school and get more of an education so that you can then go into our community public schools and teach or go into the universities and teach. You must continue to struggle and make sure that African American history is taught, that African American culture is taught, that Black Studies is taught, that Black Women's Studies is taught—so that we don't have another generation of Black students coming through life thinking that their people have contributed nothing to the world.

The poetry of the seventies is poetry that talks about work and also about memory. I wrote the book *A Blues Book for Blue Black Magical Women* in 1973, and I realized that the book was really about the use of "memories." I believe that's very important to us. We can find lessons in the memories. Through writing that book, I began to go back and look at some of the things that had happened to me. And I offered that book as something to be informative for Black women. The book says, simply, let me tell you, show you a picture of a woman who came from the South as a little girl, and grew up knowing nothing about herself. She came to a place named New York City, and thought it was just hip to be a carbon copy of a white person. It's about a woman who moved to the Village, ate brie cheese and drank white wine, etc., imitating people. And then all of a sudden this woman hears Black people begin to talk a certain new kind of new way, a way that gave her a sense of self, a way that touched her and put her on the wings of history. It is about male and female relationships, and what it means to be put on the earth—having had your tradition of initiation stolen from you, leaving you with no idea of how you're suppose to choose the "proper" man or define the "proper" relationship. Yet you attempt to do so anyway, only to find out that there is hurt in store for you. The man you choose to love cannot even love himself. So how is he going to love you? And then I talk about this woman finally moving on to the realization that she has got to love herself before she can even think about getting anybody who could love her. And maybe she would end up by herself. As long as you have love of your people, the love of your children, you are not alone. As long as you have your activism, your memories of people who have gone before you—who have propelled you— you are not alone.

That book was a blues book. I attempted to speak about both the political part of us and the personal. I wanted to show that they are so intertwined. I wanted us to know that in order for us to be effective political people, we must be in control of the personal.

The seventies also was a period when many of us were fighting with the forces that would rewrite the history of the sixties. We had to come up against people who said that the sixties were wild, unimportant days. Folk who said that "Black thing" was just a fad. We were up against forces that said that we should stop being angry. After all, they would say, you people have got everything now. You have made it. We gave you affirmative action, and you have more Black people in college now than ever before. You have more people in medical school, dental school, and law school than ever before. And we even let you be "beautiful" they would say. We figured out some better formulas for you to be able to have hair that slings once again. So you can cut loose all that "natural" stuff. We started to hear slogans like "We've come a long way, baby." Yes, we had to fight all of that nonsense in the seventies. There had to be some of us who said that we would not be moved. We would not be tempted by the glitter. There were some of us who sincerely never saw the sixties as a fashion. It was a new-found understanding, a new-found spirit. A spirit that was to be worn proudly. Black spirit. Beautiful Black spirit. You see, there were those of us who would continue to deal with the world politically. Nothing would change that.

One of the pitiful things that happened during the late seventies was that you had an emergence of a group of Black people who got so carried away with themselves that they started to act as if there is no history to their work, their development. They started patting themselves on the head and back saying simply that, "I'm here without anybody." You had young writers not even saying anything about the people who had come before them, people who had helped to produce some of them. That was amazing—and amusing too. Such violation of the African tradition. Such violation of the connections! You must always show the connection. You must always be responsible. Certainly, you can say that we've done some terrible things to each other. But in the end, you must show us as products of this imperialist, racist, oppressive place.

The seventies also was a period for many of us to say, "So now that we have the consciousness, let's implement some of the skills that we had learned in the sixties." Some people want to put down the seventies. But I don't think that we should do that. It was a time of some real learning, some real organizing. Some people want to say that what happened in the sixties became disintegrated in the seventies. But that's not true. Nothing disintegrates fully. There were people who learned what they learned in the sixties and went on to implement it. They continued to be political, and they joined or started organizations that in a very real sense began to speak to what is going on in this country. For example, many Black women's organizations were started. New welfare rights organizations were started. Black mothers organizations were started. New student organizations were started on various campuses, etc. Remember, we had learned how to organize in the sixties. We had held organizing seminars, and now a lot of that has come to fruition. There are people out there who have some serious skills, and they are organizing.

Another important thing that happened during the seventies was that we began to develop a world view—a view that allowed us to see ourselves and see the connections beyond America. And as a result of a lot of mistakes, it was also a time when we began to be more critical of this thing called "Blackness." It wasn't enough to just have Black skin anymore. We began to see the necessity of asking some hard questions about what a person's "Blackness" meant in terms of how they saw America. We learned, for example, that we needed to have been asking questions like: Where do you stand on the issue of racism and sexism in America? How do you view imperialism? Do you like capitalism? How do you view change, revolution, etc.? These are critical questions now. We need to know who are our friends and who are our enemies.

The eighties caught us in a peculiar dilemma. You see, America had a tremendous campaign to counter our energy that was exhibited in the sixties and seventies. So we arrived in the eighties with people saying things like: "We've arrived!" or "There's no need for people to say anything about racism or sexism any more" or "The only thing that we really need to do is make money." There was a belief that if we could only achieve economic power, then we would be all right. These views, of course, fly in the face of history that teaches us that in America, even Black men and women with money get lynched, get beaten. There is a growing mood at all levels of America that says that they can treat us any old kind of way again. It's a time when there is increased racist terror and violence, e.g., police brutality. It is a time when we are no longer walking around with a posture that says, "Don't touch me! I may be dangerous." It is a time when we don't have the organizations needed to say that there will be an equally violent response to the murder of our people. Therefore, we have a lot of work to be done in the eighties to counter all of this. To young people who tell me that they want to be rich and famous, I say, "You'd better have a militia." Because that's what it's about— real power! Being rich without real power means nothing.

Highsmith-Taylor: Where do we go from here?
Sanchez: I am very optimistic. I am optimistic because I can see a win. You see, I understand the dialectics of people's movements. I understand that

there are progressions and regressions. What are four years, eight years, twenty years in terms of a whole lifetime? In terms of the lifetime of the universe? It is but a tiny speck in history. I can see beyond the year 2000. I can see a period when you won't have oppression. You won't have people exploiting people. Granted, there will be a lot of people dying before we get to that point. Some will die because they don't have the strength or the ambition to stay alive. They really don't understand that there can be a better day. Their vision is too limited. And there will be people who die because they will come up against the activities of the oppressors. But you see, these oppressive monsters are carrying out their activities because they are a dying breed. During the end of this century, they will try to murder a lot of people in order to stay in power. But when you see that there are more people who have begun to understand history and who refuse to be exploited, then you understand that the time of the oppressor is numbered. Yes, they are killing many, many people in Africa—via germ warfare (AIDS), via starvation and famine created by the oppressor's violation of the earth, via military violence, etc.— but that's a part of it! That's the pain before the victory. We will be victorious! Their days are numbered. This belief comes from my political understanding.

At the same time that I offer this political understanding, I must offer a sincere belief that in addition to the necessity for us to be political, we must be spiritual. We must have spiritual sources that we rely upon. We must call upon our residual memories. We must call upon our ancestors. And they will propel us through all the crap we currently face on a daily basis. Our spirituality will keep us from becoming cynical, from becoming bitter, from becoming harsh. Our politics combined with our spirituality will keep us from becoming like the people that we are now trying to replace.

Yes! We must hear the voices and have the dreams of those who came before us, and we must keep them with us in a very real sense. This will keep us centered. This will help us to maintain our understanding of the job we must do. And if we do the job we must do, then we will win.

Form and Spirit: A Conversation with Sonia Sanchez

Annie Finch / 1994

A version of this interview was originally published in *AWP Chronicle*, vol. 31, no. 5 (May 1999): 5. The full-length interview published here is printed with permission from the author.

Note from the Interviewer:

I interviewed Sonia Sanchez after a magnificently dramatic poetry reading at the University of Northern Iowa, where she had been flown in for the day as a distinguished visiting writer. After the reading, Sanchez was surrounded for nearly an hour by enthusiastic young poets and readers from the local African American community and the university's English Department. She had time, warmth, and attention for everyone. After most of the fans had drifted away, we let our planned hour's interview lengthen into a two-hour conversation in the empty auditorium while two or three stalwart audience members listened in. This conversation remains one of my most blessed memories as a young poet.

AF: In *A Blues Book for Blue Black Magical Women*, you describe three visions that you had during a period of emotional change. One of the voices says, "You are a singer, but you have not listened to the songs." Does this refer to something that happened to your poetry when you changed the way you were writing?

SS: I think that whole section is really speaking to the fact that many of us grew up in America and had no history of ourselves at all. I'm speaking specifically of young women who moved towards womanhood without anyone bringing them through that whole process, so they'd grow up and just be, just all of a sudden be there. So that section is speaking to the voice saying, "You write this poetry and you're not even aware of your history; you sing these songs and you really don't know from whence they come; you have no real history here." You're really moving and writing and living out of a void, which is what I think most of us were doing in this country. And that's why there was such a run towards information about ourselves in this country. This is the motion and movement of most African American women in this country: you don't know any of your history, you read books that are given to you, you don't search for books that could tell you other truths. You move as a free woman but look at you, your body is a monument to slavery and is dead, you're still enslaved by the way you wear your hair, by the way that you dress, by the way that you act. Like most women, our motion is always towards men; whether we feel comfortable in what we wear or not, that's what we wear. If we don't define ourselves, we're doomed to failure.

AF: Did you find books that did teach you truth after that?
SS: The black history books. A man by the name of Micheux had a bookstore on 125th Street right across from the Hotel Theresa, and Mr. Micheux gave me all of these black historical books, the black poets, the black writers, and I said to him, "I can't afford these books, I can't afford to pay for these books," and he said, "Don't worry, you'll repay us by passing it on, and repay me by coming to my bookstore and doing readings for me when you get to be known." I thought that was farfetched, but eventually I did that.

AF: What books did he give you?
SS: He gave me some books by Du Bois, he gave me some books by Walker, and many others. He was like the second part of a triangle.

   Jean Hutson was probably at the top of that triangle; she was the curator of the Schomburg Collection. When I had gotten out of college and was going to grad school, and I stumbled upon the Schomburg at 135th Street, the guard there told me, "All these books are by and about black folk," and I said in a very smart fashion, "Yeah, there probably aren't many books in here, then . . ." He told me, "You need to go talk to Miss Hutson." Miss Hutson was a quiet, unassuming woman who was the curator of the Schomburg. The guard directed me to her and I said, "This man tells me that this is a library that has only books by and about black folk." And she said, "Yes, that's right dear." I looked at her as if to say, "I don't believe it."

The old Schomburg had a long table on the first floor where all the scholars would come and read and write. She sat me down with three books, *Their Eyes Were Watching God* and *The Souls of Black Folk* and I think *Up From Slavery*. The first book I started to read was *Their Eyes Were Watching God*. I thought I'd be thrown off by the Black English in there. I read about a third of the book and I stood up and I walked over to her and I said, "This is really a great book!" She said, "Yes, dear," and I walked around the table just mumbling to myself, "How could I be educated and I haven't read this book? How could they say I'm educated?" So I came back and sat down and read another third, and I stood up again, and I walked around the table again, mumbling, and came and sat down; I finished the book, and I got ready to stand up again, and one of the scholars beckoned to her and said, "Miss Hutson, will you please tell this young woman to stay seated!"

I came back and sat down, and I read and read for one week. At the end of the week I told her, "I'll be back;" and then I said, "I'm going to have a book in here one day." And Miss Hutson said, "Yes, dear." She tells that story now, as only Miss Hutson can tell it, with great amusement. She is part of that triangle, because she fed me books then, and started me to read black history books, and black philosophy, and also literature.

AF: Did you read Phillis Wheatley then?
SS: Yes, at that time I read some of Phillis Wheatley's poetry. The third part of that triangle was a woman in the library when I was in high school. I used to go to the library every day, and one day she said to me, "Do you like poetry?" And I said, "Uh huh." I didn't tell her I wrote poetry though. And she said, "The next time you come I'm going to have some books for you," and she started to feed me books. I don't know if they were the library's books or her own personal books. She gave me Pushkin, and the music that was there was unbelievable, and she gave me some anthologies of what they called at the time "Negro poetry."

AF: James Johnson's collection?
SS: Yes, probably it was that; I'm almost sure it was that. And I'm almost sure it was also Sterling Brown's collection. And there I came across what I called the formalists, the Black formalist poets.

AF: Dunbar, Cullen?

SS: Yes, all of them, from Hughes to Dunbar. And then I remembered that I had heard people quote Dunbar in the South, because at assemblies they would recite Dunbar. But I remembered also that we as young people striving to speak "the correct English" were somewhat startled by him and rejected him; we backed away from him, saying, "We don't want that stuff." They would always bring someone in who would recite it, and we would sit there—unless it happened to be funny and then we would respond to it. We were not into so-called "dialect poetry," because we were moving to another level, and you have to almost become educated to understand what that poetry is about.

AF: You have a prose-poem where you quote Wheatley, "for black history month/February 1986"—you quote from her poem "On Being Brought from Africa," "remember Christians, Negroes black as Cain / may be refined . . ." I wonder in what spirit you quoted that, and what your response is to Phillis Wheatley, because I know that in the sixties a lot of people rejected her. I wonder if your attitudes have changed towards her.

SS: I never formally rejected any poets per se in the sixties. But some of the older poets who were alive at the time rejected us initially, because they couldn't figure out where we were coming from; Sterling Brown said to me once, years ago, "Sonia, when we first heard you and Baraka and Larry Neal, you scared us half to death."

AF: That's when Gwendolyn Brooks changed her style . . .

SS: Exactly. So their response to being scared was either to ignore us or—not so much Sterling, but let's say, Dr. Arthur Davis—to write an essay about the New Black Poets as such. But I know Dr. Arthur Davis now; we're dear friends, and he has said to me, "You were right." He was able to change and see that his initial response was an initial response of the time; there was a meeting. There was an intersection.

AF: Can you read some of your new work-in-progress, the elegy to your brother?

SS: Think of short and black
    thin mustache draping thin lips
    think of country and exact

thin body, underfed hips
watching at this corral of battleships
and bastards. Watching for forget
and remember. Dancing his pirouette.

And he came my brother at seventeen
recruited by birthright and smell
grabbing the city by the root with clean
metallic teeth. Commandant and infidel
pirating his family in their cell
and we waited for the anger to retreat
and we watched him embrace the city and the street.

. . . And a new geography greeted him.
The Atlantic drifted from off shore
to lick his wounds to give him slim
transfusion as he turned changed wore
a new waistcoat of solicitor
antidote to his southern skin
ammunition for a young paladin.

AF: I noticed a lot of Gwendolyn Brooks influence here—early Gwendolyn Brooks, like "The Anniad."
SS: Right, yes,

AF: The "think of," and even the word "paladin" . . .
SS: "Paladin," I pulled "paladin" . . . Actually, it was so weird, because I got up and wrote part of that during the time I was teaching her, and I looked at it and I said, "Gee, this is probably the influence because I'm teaching her." Then I started to take it out, but I left it because it worked, because it worked. I realized I had the word "paladin," and I had "think" at the beginning of the lines: "Think this, think that . . ."

AF: "Think" and the rhythm, the same rhythm.
SS: But the rhyme royal has that rhythm, so anyone who writes the modern day rhyme royal is going to end up almost . . .

AF: But you did it in tetrameter and so does she, and most people would do it in pentameter.

SS: Exactly.

AF: Was that where you got the rhyme royal idea for this poem, from her?

SS: Well, at the time that I woke up in the middle of the night and wrote the first stanza, I was teaching that poem, "The Anniad," to my grad students and to my literature class too, so it was all over me. And I had been talking to Gwen about it also, because I had some questions about it. So I called her and I was talking to her about this piece. And so I think it just was all in my psyche at some point.

And so in the middle of the night, I woke up and wrote these lines, and I looked at it in the cold morning air and I thought, "What is wrong with you?" Then it was just this one little stanza. And then when this thing began to continue, I would say, yes, there was a great influence there, primarily because I was teaching it, getting involved with it, making my students get involved and understand and see all the layers of it. And then for some reason, every time I am writing about something painful, I always retreat in some kind of strange way to formal work.

AF: Does that happen to you more now than it did in your earlier books? It seems as if your work is getting a little more formal in the last ten years or so.

SS: I've always written some formal things. I just never published it, because of the times; in my journals, I have a lot of work that is in form but that was chosen out. Sometimes—at least for the early books, the Broadside Press books—you'd send the manuscript and they would choose the poems that were going to sell. Because you've got to realize that we've sold more than one hundred thousand copies of our books in our time. That's poetry. That's amazing, in this country; that's amazing.

AF: Yes.

SS: People don't realize; when people say poetry does not sell, I always crack up, because Haki [Madhubuti], Gwen, Baraka, we've sold hundreds. That's a lot of poetry. That was the whole point of selling our books for $2.50 and $3.00 and $4.95 at most, because we wanted to make sure that people had access to our books. So it's amazing that we have done that,

that we were able to sell hundreds of thousands of copies of our poems.
I love it.

AF: Do you think that their choice of free verse then, and not publishing the
formal verse, helped it sell better?
SS: Well, one of the things we were talking about is making poetry accessible
to everyone, and free verse certainly does allow for that. But at the same time,
I always wrote the haiku and the tanka and then I started publishing it, when
I took control over what I wanted to put in my books. But I think also there's
always the formal—what I call the formal lyrical poem—that even in *Home
Coming*, you see. You just have to go and find it; it's there. I remember at one
point, when I had a lot of lyrical things, people said, "We want some of the
hard-hitting stuff that you do." Which I did, and so I did it. But always, in my
notebook, the lyrical poems are all there.

AF: And the blues?
SS: And the blues. They've always been there.

AF: The blues you didn't publish until about your third book or so?
SS: No, the blues was published in the second book. The third book was the
children's book, I think, so the second book had to have had "In the night, in
my Negro dreams," the blues—that's in *We a BaddDDD People*, I think.

AF: What about the sonku?
SS: That's mine; that's my form. I made that up.

AF: Why did you make it up?
SS: Because I have all my students make up a form, to let them see that they
can create any form—the haiku was created by someone, the tanka was created by someone, the cinquain is American . . .

AF: Adelaide Crapsey . . .
SS: Yes, Adelaide Crapsey—so I say, "If she can do that, why can't you." So
I don't even pose it to them. What we do is, I teach the haiku, the tanka,
the cinquain, and I say, "Make up your own," and it's a natural thing.
I don't say to them, I *think* I want you to. I say, "Make up your own form
of syllabic verse," and they do it, because you don't give them a chance to

not do it, to fail. And they've come up with some fantastic forms, some of the students, especially a lot of what I call the artsy students have come up with fantastic forms, and then they will do paintings around it, or do calligraphy and whatever, or they will mount a show—they'll do things like that.

AF: Does the sonku do things for you that the haiku and tanka don't?
SS: Well the sonku—I like the sound of the sonku, and quite often the sonku also requires some kind of lyricality. I think because of the sound of it.

AF: It's 4-3-4-3, isn't it?
SS: I think that's what it is. Yes. [laughter]

AF: Are you thinking of the ballad stanza when you do that? It reminds me of that in a way.
SS: Well not really, but when I teach the ballad sometimes the students can't hear it, or they can't do the ballad stanza, so I break it down in syllables, and that way they can hear it. Someone said to me once, "Why do you do that?" and I said, "Look, I want them to learn anyway you can get them to learn, and 4-3-4-3 is easy to learn, it really is."

But I've never thought about that [with the sonku]. I was playing with a form, and for some reason that's how it came out. And then I looked at it, and I was trying to change it to a variation of 6-3-6-3, and I will probably still do it. I want to use something with 6-3-6-3, because I'm the ninth. My birthday is the ninth day of the ninth month, so nines have followed me a great deal, and I was trying to do something that would be a nine also. It's one of the things that I have in my journal to do, that I haven't done yet.

AF: In your statement on form in the anthology *A Formal Feeling Comes*, you describe the importance of form in your teaching of poetry to undergraduates.
SS: Yes. If you do that with grad students they say, "Well I just want to talk theory, I really don't want to do this, I'm a grad student and I should have had all this." But every now and then I slip in some exercises for them also, though quite often they're so far gone that it doesn't work. I do have a number of independent people, I do their thesis, and in the

privacy of that year of study, I make some of them deal with form, and
something happens to their thesis and it gets tightened up. I use form to
tighten the work, and I use it because they might want to be like some
of us and deal with it, and write it quite often. One guy was so pissed at
me that he said he'd never take another writing class, and then he did
a sonnet sequence for his final. He said, "I started writing it, and I just
couldn't stop." So you never know what you tap sometimes, when you
teach form.

AF: In the last sentence of the prose-poem "don't ever give up on love" you
say, "black woman echoing gold . . ." and then it ends, "carrying couplets
from the sky to crease the ground." That is so mysterious to me. What do you
mean couplets there? Why couplets?
SS: Well, that's a good question. The refrains, when we sing about black
women, you know? Quite often, they are two-legged, you know—they are
two lines, and I wanted to talk about this woman who was carrying our history as she walked away. And a lot of our history comes from the two lines
that you get in blues, the two lines that you get in ballads sometimes, you
know, the refrain, also, that's repeated. That's what I was alluding to at that
particular point. I know that sometimes I do some difficult lines; I always tell
students that you don't have to know everything a poet means, but if you get
the music of it and the gist of it, then you've gotten it.

AF: Have you always had songs in your poetry, or chants, or things that were
made to be sung or chanted?
SS: I have. I never used to sing them, as I said this afternoon . . .

AF: But did you sing them to yourself as you wrote them?
SS: Yes. That's how I knew they could be sung; that's why I would put in the
margin, "to be sung." But I never had the strength or the nerve to do it for a
long time.

AF: Have they been set to music formally, by other people?
SS: Yes. There's a man and woman team in Paris, France, who have set
some of my blues and, interestingly enough, the haiku, to music. I always
thought the haiku should be done; I could hear the music for the haiku. In
fact, I have a reading in Oakland, California, next week with a bass player,

and I'm going to read some of the haiku to him and then see how he can respond to it; I can hear almost like one long note behind it. The piece to my brother was done to the tune of a jazz piece. Each time, by coming in on the first accent like that, it worked outrageously with jazz, because of how you accent it . . .

AF: The trochaic rhythm . . .
SS: Exactly, exactly.

AF: In the poem "Sequences," you parody "Billy Boy": "Where have you been . . . etc." Do you quote songs like that in other places too?
SS: Yes, I have; I would take little children's rhymes or the nursery rhymes that we learned. I do that in *Blues Book* also, someplace along the way.

AF: I remember, where you repeat, "I'm hiding and I won't come out."
SS: Yes, I do the games in there, too, that children do. And also, in a couple of the very rough poems to America, I do that, like in the John Coltrane poem, where it says, "are you sleeping, are you sleeping, brother John, brother John?" It's like a little refrain there, and it's repeated a couple of times. Of course it's my response to Coltrane and "My Favorite Things," but it's also counterpoint; I do something and then all of a sudden I stop it, and do that little chant: "Are you sleeping, are you sleeping, brother John, morning bells are ringing, morning bells are ringing." It's paying respect to Brother John—everyone called John Brother John—but it's also to emphasize that he's not really dead, so I say sleeping instead, to bring back the whole idea of life and death at the same time. I also use the song in the sense of Frere Jacques, the Brother John—making it holy—because the point was that Coltrane was holy to us all. When people asked did you pray, you'd say yes, I play Coltrane. And they weren't being facetious either—because of just how mystical his music was, and how his music kept a lot of people alive at a time they wanted to be kept alive.

Blues Book was written in 1972, published in 1973. In that book, I brought in the whole idea of children's games: "five, ten, fifteen, twenty, twenty-five, thirty 'thirty-five' forty whatever." A lot of people do it now—but then, as I researched and went back into the childhood of little girls, I realized that no one had brought in the games that they played, and the songs that they sang.

I like this book a great deal; it's heavy with the ideology of the time in a lot of places, but there's a lot here that I like . . . the idea of bells, the feminine imagery there, and what the bell means in different religions—to announce things, that a black girl is born—the idea of the "double dutch days"—what I'm trying to bring up is the whole sense of little girls being outside playing hide-and-go-seek, and playing hide-and-go-seek with the family and the world and the country also; like the chanting there: "No matter what they say, I won't come out."

AF: I wanted to ask you about your attitude towards iambic pentameter. I noticed this line in *Blues Book*: "if I had a big piece of dust/to ride on I would gather up my pulse"; there are other iambic pentameters hidden in the book, but this one is the only one I saw that was really out there. It seems to be almost saying that the iambic pentameter was like your pulse; I wondered what you would feel about that?
SS: I think people don't place things on pages unconsciously. A lot of poets get away with things, saying they were unconscious, but when I go back and hone things down . . . that was a long line, and I understood that and knew it also. It had a lot to do with my understanding that we do speak in iambic pentameter. People always say they don't understand it, and when people try to teach it, they say it's too difficult or whatever. But if you listen to people speaking, that's how they speak, really. And what I was trying to show there too was not only that's how I speak, but that's how I breathe also . . .

AF: Have you ever had any ideological problem with iambic pentameter?
SS: I've never had any problems with any kind of poetry. I've never said to people, "I would never write this and never write that." That never came from my mouth. I've always said, even in the midst of heavy ideology, that I've always read all poets. And that's not backtracking; that's true. I've always said it, because I understand the need for poets to read everyone.

AF: Did you apprentice yourself to a poet?
SS: No; I wish I had.

AF: Who would you have?
SS: You'd probably think that the first person I would say would be Langston Hughes, but it wouldn't be. It probably would have been someone like Gwendolyn Brooks or Margaret Walker.

AF: Did you read Margaret Walker early on?
SS: Yes, I did. I read her in the anthologies.

AF: What about your relationship with Louise Bogan? Could you tell some of those stories about her again?
SS: [laughs] People are always surprised that I studied with Bogan. When I was in college, I took a writing class and I was wiped out by this man who was concerned about the work that I was writing. . . . He asked us to write a piece about a parent, something not in step with what the parent was always doing, that was out of character in a sense. So, my father came home from work one day, and he slammed the door, which was unusual for him, and he was furious because a white man had patted him on the head, and he knew that that was a very negative thing, right? He was furious, so he brought the fury home; my father did not curse, but he did a curse word at that point. I remember that I was startled by it. I remember that I was trying to get the whole feeling of the feelings that this man had because this man patted him on the head, and he was so angry about how could he do this kind of thing. So I did this piece about my father, who is a man who was raised in the South, so therefore he knew his place in a sense, and he never reared up about anything or got angry about most things. I did this portrait of my father coming in slamming the door, and ranting and raving. And this professor gave it back to me with red all over it, saying that he did not understand this piece, that why would this man be upset about someone patting him on the head? I got a C plus on that.

The second thing was that we were asked to do something on another parent showing some emotion. I wrote about my stepmother who was a southern black woman who was afraid of New York. New York frightened her, so she would only go to 125th Street for shopping. She would not go downtown, because it meant navigating those subways and a lot of traffic. Because we were younger, and we had to go to school, we navigated everything, and we wanted to go downtown, to the movies, etc. She couldn't find something that she needed on 125th Street, so she asked us to take her downtown to Macy's, mind you, which was a store for all people. It wasn't Best & Co., it wasn't Lord and Taylor, it wasn't Saks Fifth Avenue, it wasn't any of those other stores that perhaps if you went in as an African American they would follow you around the store forever. So Patty and I took her there, and she found what she wanted, and she brought it to the counter. But this woman was waiting on people, and when she finished waiting on the other people, she just stood there, and I said to my stepmother, "Go on, give her what you have," and Jerry was just waiting for the woman to recognize her, to come towards her, because she knew her place, my stepmother did. And I remember looking and thinking to myself that my stepmother was fearful of this confrontation. And that woman knew what was happening, so she waited on twenty million people and then finally she turned towards my stepmother and said "yes." She took what my stepmother had and put it in a bag and gave her the change on the counter. She wouldn't touch her hand or anything, and wouldn't say "here." I saw all that as a child, and understood it as a child, and was thinking to myself, "I'll never let no one do that to me." And I was really angry at my stepmother for being. So this piece was about her ostensibly, but it was about me and the anger that I felt towards her too, because the fear that was oozing out of her, I didn't want it on me. I knew that it was possible that parents can pass that fear from mother to child, from father to child, and I was wise enough to understand that that fear could be passed on to me, so I didn't want it. So I did this kind of complex piece, and the guy gave it back and said, "I don't understand, in this day and age, anyone being afraid to go downtown to Macy's," and it was all over in red . . . C plus. Well, you know, I was not a C plus person. So we had a conference, and this man said to me, why don't you do something more imaginative. What he was really saying was he didn't want to be bothered with that, because it might make him think too much. So I was furious, but I went home and I'm sitting in my bedroom and I looked in the mirror, and I pretended that something came out of the mirror and started talking, pure crap, so I wrote this piece about how some image came out of the mirror and started to talk to me, and I got an A minus on it, and he said, "This is what I mean." And I stopped writing. I wrote for his class, pure crap, but I stopped writing.

AF: How long did you stop writing for?
SS: Until I went in Bogan's class. Because I went searching outside of Hunter [College] and would go into these classes, and these men were all teaching classes, no women were teaching, and they just walked all over you like you weren't really supposed to be there, and I was paying money to take these classes at some of the Ys and wherever, and I knew that they didn't want me there. The men didn't want me there at all, the other students didn't want me there, so after a couple of sessions I would leave. I was going to NYU at that time, and I looked in the catalog, and I knew Bogan's work, because we had

to read it in college in these anthologies, and so I actually went and sat by the door, because I figured this would be the same old thing. But the first night I read some of my work, and she asked me to hand it to her, and she commented on what was incorrect, and she thanked me for it, and I went and registered for the class and stayed there, and studied with her.

AF: She didn't mess with you, is how you put it before.
SS: She didn't mess with the me in there. She messed with what was wrong in terms of form, in terms of non-form, in terms of how it could be said maybe a little bit better than that, etc. . . .

AF: Was that a free verse piece?
SS: That was a free verse piece, right; and then she taught us some forms. She made us get a poetry handbook, she made us get a rhyming dictionary also, the first rhyming dictionary I ever got—I got a huge rhyming dictionary— and [Babette Deutsch's] *Poetry Handbook*, which I use now and my students do. And we had to go in there, and she'd choose a form; she would write something on the board and then she'd tell us to get the rest of it out of the book and come in with the form. And when we read we had to come up front, in front of the class, and read things aloud.

Bogan told us two or three things. One was that you must learn how to read your poetry aloud, because you must train that ear, because the ear will tell you when something is right or wrong. And then of course you must read every poet who is walking on the planet Earth, period—OK. Well, you listen to the professor, but you really don't always follow what they say. Well, I had written this poem, and it was my time to come up and read it, up in front of the class. Well, when I started to read the poem, my ear actually did tell me; I went "oops," because I heard some things that were wrong; I went "oops, oops," but to myself. But I looked at the students looking at me, forty some strong, and they heard it also, and they looked at me, thinking "I'm glad it's you and not me," because Bogan said, "oh, may I see that please," in her very formal voice. I handed it to her and she said, "Did you read this poem aloud?"

AF: When you wrote it.
SS: Right, when I finished it. Now my brain clicked: "If I tell her yes, and I didn't hear this, then would I be in more trouble than if I tell her no?" So I finally said, "No, I didn't," because I thought it was better for her to think

that I hadn't read it aloud than that I had read it aloud and not picked up on it. But I was hearing it all along what was wrong; it was very obvious what was wrong there. So she said, "Well, if you had read it aloud, you would have heard the following . . . ," and she dissected that little sucker left and right. I'm looking at the students looking at me and they're sitting there smiling, "I'm glad it's you, and not me." [Laughter]. And that was the last time I did that. It was a hard lesson, but from then on I read everything aloud. Yes, I did; make no mistake about it. And she was right. She said, "I can't guarantee you that your ear will be trained in one semester, but I can guarantee that if you keep doing this it will finally be trained, and you will hear that which is right and that which is wrong in your pieces. But you have to train it; you have to read it aloud and make your ear pick up those things that you don't ordinarily see when you're just reading it silently, or just writing it. And it's true, you know. You really do. You do have to train that ear.

And Bogan taught us a third thing; many professors don't teach you this, but she considered herself a writer: she taught us how to keep a notebook for sending work out. She said something like, if you keep doing it regularly, every few months you send to the journals, they'll get to know your name, and it was true, because after a year, I started getting notes from some editors saying, "We'd like to see some more of your work." I get a lot of my students to do that, to send their work out.

So she taught us to train the ear, to read a lot of poetry, and she taught us how to send the work out too. And that was important, a simple thing like that. And she made some of us send some work out. I was just as frightened as could be, I was so nervous. But I did that in her class; I started sending the work out, and it paid off.

AF: Was it a workshop where the other students would comment too, or was it just her?
SS: It was a workshop where we all commented on each other's work. Oh yes, she required that. Eight or nine of us came out of that workshop, but only one other person that I know of kept publishing. Bogan taught me something else; she said, "There are a lot of good writers; a lot of people have talent. Some people don't do anything with it, though. But do you have the strength to keep pushing and keep writing and keep pushing?" A number of the people in that workshop were very good, but they didn't push themselves, or they didn't have the drive to push themselves.

AF: You had the drive.

SS: I think so. My maiden name is Driver, which I think is very significant. And I was named after my father, Wilson. They put an "ia" on it, "Wilsonia," and I think the most significant thing in Wilsonia is "will." In fact, the sisters named me. They expected a boy, and so they had no name for me. The only name my father had for me was Wilson, since he wanted a boy, and so the sisters said that's alright, they made up a name for me, and so they named me Wilsonia Bonita. It's fascinating how families and members of families and just sisters in the church will name you.

AF: How did you continue your education in poetry after Bogan's workshop?

SS: While I was in her workshop, a guy by the name of Fred Stern came over and got what he called the best people out of the workshop, about eight or nine of us; he said, "You, you, you, you: we are going to meet in [Greenwich] Village." And we met in the Village for three years, every Wednesday night, and the only requirement was that you had to bring a poem.

But you can get stifled in a workshop. What happened is that I started to publish in that workshop, and then, other people weren't publishing. At some point I knew that I had grown beyond the workshop, that it was time to leave the workshop. We used to go to some of the little jazz joints in the Village. We went into the Five Spot one night and Baraka—Leroi Jones—was sitting there, and he says, "Hey, Sanchez, someone said you're a poet. I'm editing an anthology coming out of Paris, France; would you send me some of your work?" And that was the first time I was called a poet. From that time on I began to say, "Maybe I am this poet."

AF: Did you write in form at all, after Bogan's workshop?

SS: Yes. I did a number of sonnets. Some of the sonnets to my father were things that were done for her class, that I reworked in some of my books. And I began to experiment. . . . She didn't teach us the haiku. That was something I came upon in Japanese poetry, and also since I was reading Richard Wright; I saw his haiku also. So I took that upon myself, as a form that I thought was really very important. But I have done, in journals, blank verse that has never been published—mostly the sonnet, and blank verse— and also the blues always, the blues, I've always brought the blues with me—and ballads, when I wanted to tell a story. I picked up the haiku and

tanka on my own. And the prose poem I picked up on my own, and after
I did it, I said, "I know this exists before me, I know that I'm not inventing
this," and I went searching for the whole idea of the prose poem. I also did
concrete poetry. I was fascinated by concrete poetry for a while, and so
I would make designs and whatever.

AF: Is any of that published?
SS: That's all in my journals. No, the concrete poetry is not published. At the
time I was discovering, reading everyone, all the poets, and I would then do
what other people had done, just to see how it felt and how it seemed.

AF: You have used the haiku often. What is your attraction to that form?
SS: I fell in love with the haiku form, and I knew just what I wanted to do
with it. I thought it would be almost cliched to always try to do the nature
haiku, that is so rampant in haiku, because I thought that probably that
would be almost impossible, to capture that kind of beauty. So what I
decided to do was to make my haiku, and my tanka, either with some
thought, or some beauty, or some love—an idea that in a sense would be
almost surreal sometimes, that would make you stop *in nature*, you know,
stop and look. So therefore my connection for my haiku with nature is
that it makes you stop and connect with another human being or an idea, so
that's the connection with nature; to stop in time, and you leap across time,
and that's the connection with nature.

AF: So that's what you want to do, you want to make a connection.
SS: But I also want sometimes some of them just to be beautiful, so
therefore that also would reflect nature, and some are just so harsh, like the
haiku, "If I had really known you, I would have left my love at home"—that
is so hard, and so harsh. That's what I mean, because you see, the beauty of
the haiku the way they used to do it in the old days is not only the nature
connection, but also it is that very surreal thing that goes beyond nature,
that goes into nature. It goes in and you know that there are lives in
between our own lives. That's what I try to do too. Sometimes there are
double meanings and triple meanings there too, which means that you know
there is life between the poem and the lines, which means that if you really
understand your life, our lives, there are lives in between that we don't always
see, because we limit ourselves. I'm struggling with this because I don't

usually talk about it. I might write about it, but when you talk about it
sometimes, people look at you in a very strange fashion. I always think that
we are always out there as poets sometime, someplace, but that's what
I attempt to do with it.

AF: There are moments like that, and there are people like that, that are just
alive the way poetry is alive when it's alive.
SS: I feel that poets are so helpful in the world, because they help people to
connect in spite of themselves, and they help people to love in spite of themselves, if it's just loving the poem or the line, if you can make people connect
and love a line or a word or whatever, you've helped them to stay connected,
to life and beauty, which means they will be a much better human being. So
I think poets have a role to do that, to continue to do that, to keep people
human, finally.

AF: Do you think there is any connection between form and poetry? Is there
anything about form that helps poets . . .
SS: I think Bogan posed a question in the classroom once, and I pose the
question in my own classes too: "Will form make this poem come out in a
different fashion, take a different form? I'm not being facetious now; will the
very fact that you're doing a villanelle shape that poem in a special way, a
different way than if you were doing it in free verse? It's true, I think it does.
You teach the form, and you make other things happen.

AF: And if poets are doing this, if they are making people connect in spite of
themselves, then is there anything about form that helps poets do that?
SS: Well, I think that poets connect to every kind of poetry. You might burst
on the scene writing free verse, because that's the period you come out of.
But you're connecting to prior times also, and so I think that at this point
I'm connecting to a prior time. I think that's the only reason why I'm doing
that piece on my brother in rhyme royal, because it came out of the night, it
came all written, one stanza, so that something, someplace that is making
you do this poem and because I don't think that I would have done it
consciously. And I think that we do connect for instance, and I think that
that's happening to me at this point in my life and I find it very interesting.

I was in the Friends Society recently [in Philadelphia] doing a reading for
them, for Black History Month. The building is an old building with seats

going all the way up to the ceiling almost. I walked into this building, and I had a feeling similar to what I felt when I was at the African meeting house, where I really heard Douglass and people and smelled the blood, and I sat down and I was shaking because you could just hear it. Well I sat down here and I was not shaking, but there was something here. I said "Gee, there's some force in here." I stumbled from the beginning to the end of the poem, I stumbled; I went wild, and I said out loud, That's very strange, I haven't read that piece for a while, but I have never read it in this fashion. There was something bothering me, there was some force in that room, and in the piece "don't never give up on love," when I had to speak in the old woman's voice, it wasn't my voice. Then a scream that I knew wasn't my voice came out, and it said, "Help me, help me, help me," and by that time everyone in the audience was entranced, because they didn't know what was going on, and I didn't know either, but anyway, to make a long story short, the logical thing was to say "I'll help you," and that's what I said. I said, "Don't worry, I'll help you, go in peace, go in peace; I'll help you." And then, whatever was there left, and one of the women [in the audience] said she saw a blue haze, a blue over my body. Something did happen in that room evidently, and I'm saying all that to say that at this time in my life I am making connections that are very real. There are connections, I think, with the past.

AF: You're using a form like that to go back to the past.
SS: Um hum.

AF: I asked about form because I have thought sometimes that form, because it uses repetition, accesses different parts of people's minds, different parts of their brains, and connects them in a different way.
SS: It could very well be. It probably has a lot to do not just with the brain, but it probably has a lot to do with the entire body, when we really look at the body. We always want to be hooked in with the brain because we think that's the highest level of intelligence, but I think the soul and the heart probably are even more so, and I think that quite often, form will make us retreat to the soul, and to the heart, and to the spirit.

We always want to believe that the form is being dealt with on what we consider the highest level of intelligence, and that is the brain, the intellect— but I think that contrary to that, we have to concentrate so much sometimes on the form that the form becomes very much involved with the body and with the soul and with the spirit. Because people don't understand the spirit and the soul, they want to relegate them to an arena (and I'm not being negative now) of probably free verse, because that's free-form; but the soul and spirit are formalized, they are formal things. They're blues, they're spirituals, they're haiku, they're tanka, they're all these things that reach your heart and your spirit and your soul.

AF: Why do you think that those forms reach your heart and your soul?
SS: I think that because they do have form, they're able then to penetrate your formal areas. And they don't just go every place, whatever. They very distinctly have a place of rest. They come to rest and reside in the areas that are already formal—the body is a very formal place. When we live undisciplined lives, we don't understand just how formal the body is. It's when we begin to discipline ourselves, being vegetarians, eating the proper food, thinking the proper thoughts, that we understand the place form has; not the coldness of form, not the intellect of form, but form, the feeling of form, the form that enters the body and says, "I have a right to reside here, and this is where I belong, in the heart, in the spirit, in the soul." As well as in the intellect, too, but not just there. People who deal with form sometimes want to leave it only there, you see, and I'm saying that it has another place beyond just the intellect.

Interview with Sonia Sanchez

Larvester Gaither / 1996

From the *Gaither Reporter: Chronicling the African American Experience*, vol. 3, no. 5 (June 1996): 41–42, 47, and no. 6 (July 1996): 49, 54–56. Reprinted with permission of the editor.

Sonia Sanchez is the author of thirteen books including *Home Coming, We a BadddDDD People, Love Poems, I've Been a Woman: New and Selected Poems, Sound Investment and Other Stories, Homegirls and Handgrenades, Under a Soprano Sky,* and most recently, *Wounded in the House of a Friend* (Beacon Press, Boston: 1995). In addition to being a contributing editor to *Black Scholar* and the *Journal of African Studies*, she has edited two anthologies: *We Be Word Sorcerers: 25 Stories by Black Americans* and *360 Degrees of Blackness Coming at You.*

She has lectured at over five hundred universities and colleges in the United States and has traveled extensively, reading her poetry in Africa, Cuba, England, the Caribbean, Australia, Nicaragua, the People's Republic of China, Norway, and Canada. She was the first Presidential Fellow at Temple University and currently holds the Laura Carnell Chair in English of Temple University.

In this two-part interview with Larvester Gaither, Sonia Sanchez recounts experiences from her extensive travels, shares with us her thoughts on contemporary issues facing African Americans, and introduces us to her upcoming new book of poetry entitled, *Does Your House Have Lions?* (to be published by Beacon Press).

Larvester Gaither: I've always thought of you as a person who travels a lot, acting as a kind of emissary for Black people in far off places like China, Cuba, and elsewhere. Lately, because of a foot injury, you've had the opportunity to kind of . . . reflect on some things.
Sonia Sanchez: Well, you know, I've never traveled any more—I think—than probably the people of my generation—Haki [Madhubuti] and [Amiri] Baraka, Alice [Walker], Angela [Davis], June Jordan, Audre [Lorde]—all of

the people who were doing what we were doing. I did take chances earlier on. I took a chance and went to China in 1973—you know what I'm saying?—I guess in the same fashion that Baraka had taken a chance and went to Cuba early. I went to China because I was contacted in 1973. John Killens had been invited to go on this cultural tour and he was ill at the time and someone called and asked if I'd do it. Initially, I said "No." And then I thought about it and played with the idea of China. Nixon had just come back from climbing the Great Wall of China and had opened up China to the West. I thought, "Maybe what an apropos time to go into a place and see a people and a country who had, in no uncertain terms, turned into itself in order to allow its people to expand and a country to advance." So I was part of a cultural group. And that group was Alice Childress and Earl Ofari [Hutchinson], and a Black woman who was an actress—I don't remember her name, she wasn't a well-known actress—and also in that group was Candice Bergen. The San Francisco Mime Troupe. A man who had been white-balled in this country by McCarthy—a survivor—was also on that tour. The group was made up mostly of what I would call Leftist-inspired and/or at least those whites of Liberal persuasion. So I went and became a part of that group in order to see this China that had opened herself up again to the West.

What was interesting is that the Chinese people would come up to me in the middle of the street and say to me, "Ah, you African, you African, you African, you African." And I would say, "Yeah, I am but I live in New York City." And they would continue, "No, no, no, no . . . you're African, you're African" because I had worn long dresses, you know, and had my head wrapped et cetera. And I would say, "No, no, no, no . . . Yes, yes, I am African but I'm from the States." And they'd say "No." They couldn't understand because this was not the image that they had of Blacks coming from the States—that was the common folks in the streets.

Larvester Gaither: Did you run into that in other places as well?
Sonia Sanchez: When I went to Cuba for the first time, the woman who had braided my hair—I went to Cuba for the first time in 1977. I think it was for a conference; either that or a Venceremos Brigade—I forget now which— right? And the woman who had braided my hair, by the time I'd got to Cuba, she had done it so tight that my head was aching. So I took the braids out and in taking the braids out, I had all of this hair. And so I went around with this huge, huge, huge natural. And people just looked at me. They came out

into the streets. I mean, they stopped, they looked up. They said, "Oh." Some laughed. Some looked and just wanted to touch it—you know. Some really wanted to know what was that about. There were people who were on the tour also who kind of looked kind of funny because nationalism was, in a sense, passé at that point. People were going back to doing other things to their hair and/or braiding their hair—certainly not wearing naturals.

That was an interesting experience . . . it makes you understand, you know, that how you wear your hair can be a political statement. And people don't really want to necessarily deal with it. Although I don't make it a problem. But certainly it makes you understand that people perceive you in a different way depending on how you have your hair.

Larvester Gaither: The young artists now have children from as far as China, New Zealand, and Nicaragua now exposed to their art. By looking at these young artists today, do you feel that the people, in those same places that you and the others of your generation traveled to, today have an accurate perception of who we are, what we're about?
Sonia Sanchez: You mean like the rap stars?

Larvester Gaither: Yeah. For example, let's look at them.
Sonia Sanchez: I don't think necessarily . . . if they watch MTV and the videos and see these kids up there gyrating on the stages of America. Most of the videos are very sexually oriented, most of the videos aren't necessarily about effecting change, but you know, having fun, dancing in each other's faces in a sense; dancing in each other's booties sometimes, if you understand what I'm saying. I think again that ends up not being the picture of most Africans. So I think that there is a distortion of the image of African Americans, period, all over the world. I think a lot of young people don't understand that they are part of that distortion. They don't understand the power of the image and the power of the medium that they're in. That medium goes, as you say, all over they world. And so when you see a Black woman, you reflect back on what you saw her doing on that stage. And that's probably what you expect for her to do and what you expect for her to be.

One of the things I learned a long time ago is this . . . I was in China going on a bus to the Great Wall. One of the people there said, "Ah, Professor Sanchez, we will now sing a song of your people." And I said "Oh." I thought, "Wow, okay! A Blues? A spiritual? Maybe a little Stevie Wonder?—you know, something." And they said, "Ole Black Joe." And I said, "No. 'Ole Black Joe' has nothing to do about Black folk. It is not about black folks, not written by Black folks, has nothing to do with us." And on that bus a couple of people said, "Ah, Sonia, you're always complaining; you're always causing a problem, you're always . . ." And I just turned around and literally gave them a couple of choice words—right. I'll sing you a Billie Holiday song. I'll sing you a Paul Robeson song. I'll sing you a Blues, I'll do some scatting." You know I was just kidding them with that. But what I'm saying is that this is not about Black folks. I went on, "I will recite you a poem that could be sung"—you see. And the Chinese guide, when I finished, was in tears. She said, "Excuse me, Professor Sanchez, I will never make that mistake again." She said that they were told there that "Ole Black Joe" was a song by and about Black folk.

One of the things I knew from that experience was that I was not walking by myself, that you don't travel alone. When you get on that stage, you're not on that stage alone. When you get on that television, you're not on that television alone. When you're doing an interview, you're not doing an interview that is individual; you're carrying your ancestors with you, you're carrying your people with you. So you can't act a fool on world stages, you see. You can't act a fool on the MTV. You can't say, "Well, someone said if you did this, then you'd be seen by millions of people." You tell them, "Yes. But that violates something that I know about myself. So I can't do that."

You see, the problem I think is that so many of our young people are acting ahistorically. They don't have the information, they don't have the herstory. So they say, "Well, I'll do that for two minutes of time on television or in a movie scene." But we understood that you don't sell out a people for a couple pieces of gold.

Larvester Gaither: Well, for the most part, it appears that our generation certainly doesn't understand that. What do you think caused this? In other words, the generation that comes after the other would always grab hold of a vision even if it was a wrong vision or a distorted vision like the "American Dream." But now, it seems like we're pretty much caught up into this culture of capitalism, this culture of consumption and so forth.
Sonia Sanchez: Well, I think that, as I said, "Some students are ahistorical, some young people are ahistorical." They are not being taught that there's a gap there. When there was a gap that my generation wasn't taught coming up, we went out searching for it. And there were people there who began to

tell us, began to fill in the gap of what was happening in the world. There was Martin and Malcolm and Medgar and Fannie Lou Hamer, Queen Mother Moore.

Some of these students were not told their history and herstory by their parents. They were not told by the schools, they didn't come out to hear what our people were saying. They were told that, indeed, they were free in this country, that they could do what they damned well pleased. And so, therefore, they didn't ever go searching. At least we knew that we weren't free. So we went searching for what was needed and began to move towards our own sanity, our own sense of ourselves. We knew there was a loss. We knew that there was a gap. We knew that there was something missing. We understood that. So we began to make movements to fill those gaps for ourselves and our people. That's what really happened, you see.

I was sent by a writer's organization to go speak to some students. They had purchased seventy-five copies of *Homegirls and Handgrenades*. And the young African American and Latino women had read this book. So, therefore, they had a point of reference and a point of discussion . . . it was a lovely discussion, a lovely talk. And they asked questions and I read things. I also had the manuscript to *Wounded in the House of a Friend* with me, which had not been published yet but was going to be published later on that year. And I read a piece, a very hard piece because there are some hard pieces in that book.

Larvester Gaither: Yeah. There certainly are—
Sonia Sanchez: And they're hard pieces because there are hard times. And someone asked me in an interview, "Why are these pieces so hard?" I said, "Because, my brother, we have moved into some very hard times. And I think it is the role of the poet always to say, Alarm, Alarm, Alarm!" —You see what I'm saying—

Larvester Gaither: Exactly.
Sonia Sanchez: "We're not dealing, we're not dealing." We're not dealing with relationships. We're not dealing to the point where we've seen people killing each other in personal relationships; I mean, literally and also psychologically and emotionally. And we can't afford to let that happen. We've got to sit back and question, you know, "What does it mean to have been with a woman for twenty years and drop her for someone younger?" Do you know

what I'm saying? We've got to look at that and say, "Well, is there something wrong with you as a woman or as a man?" Do you know what I'm saying? It's not a simple thing. There are children who expect continuity, who expect parents to be there for support, you see.

At a certain time in our lives, our family and our people should come before our personal aggrandizement, our personal satisfactions—you know what I'm saying? That's something that people have done forever, and certainly something that our ancestors did—I think. Also too, they understood the need—very much so—to make sure that we continued to grow and then.

So I did a poem that day about this young sister who went down on the brother in the middle of the dance floor out in public. And there was this silence. And I looked up and there were two young sisters crying. And one of the sisters just said, "Hey. That's just like Marie there—ain't it? across the room." And brother I heard it and froze. Because you know why you do pieces sometimes and then you don't know why . . . And then one of the sisters said, "Professor Sanchez, that's not right then—is it?" I said, "Sister, it's not about being right." I said to her, "The sister did that because she didn't carry her ancestors with her, she didn't understand. She was ahistorical." She didn't understand at the turn of the twentieth century Black women were speaking out loud to America, saying, "We are not whores, we're not prostitutes, were raped during slavery." They were saying, "We're church women, we're grandmothers, we are aunts, we are sisters or we're wives—we're good women." Those newspapers were talking about us in a disdainful manner. They were saying that we were these terrible women, just as the Congress today is saying when they're talking about "welfare women." They're suggesting about Black women—

Larvester Gaither: But don't you feel that we do the same thing? Like isn't part of the message which emanates from the Million Man March, in a real sense, scapegoating Black women?
Sonia Sanchez: I just think that we can't go back to a philosophy, again, that the people who are going to cure us are only men. When, in reality, the people who are going to cure us are men, women, and children and our youth. My children, my young sons, went down to that march. I felt that it was a real display of unity as far as men were concerned and by extension for all of us.

And I think that, for cosmetic purposes, it was a very good thing for the world to see . . . a people—men and women because there were some women there as well—gathered together and being very respectful of each other, very loving, not hurting each other, not killing each other. It says in a very real sense, "Look world, look what we can do! This is how we really feel about each other." That's a very important statement.

I think that there are other important statements to be made such as we need to be in our communities organizing. We need to have what I call a ten-year or fifteen-year plan for Black people in this country. We need to probably stop going to a lot of conferences where we just simply talk to each other, you know. We need to sit down and have one huge conference—a working conference, not a talking conference.

I think we need to meet with professors, workers, athletes, business people, students, teachers—that whole cloth of our people need to sit down. The point of the conference is to say that we need a fifteen-year plan for Black folk. The people who are the economists, you know, they can talk about drawing up an economic plan. Those folks in education need to talk about constructing an educational system that functions in our interest. You also must address the issue of identity—how are we going to address the issue of identity going into the twenty-first century?

This plan is one that we must be able to implement all over America; not just New York, not just Philadelphia, not just Dallas, but all others, you know, recognizing that we are interdependent. We need a call to action.

The second part of this interview begins with Sonia Sanchez calling for a major Black Agenda Conference and spells out the need for various committees across the country to respond to the most pressing issues of the day. She also talks about her upcoming book of poetry entitled *Does Your House Have Lions?*

Larvester Gaither: We've always done this [called conferences to plan agenda] historically. Do you think that there is any reason—
Sonia Sanchez: No, we haven't done that, we've talked about it. We simply haven't done it—do you know what I'm saying? We had the conferences, I've attended them, spoken at them. We've done the speeches, we've clapped and said, "Yeah, yeah, yeah." But I'm talking about a call to action where we come in our jeans, in our pants, in our skirts, with our heads

wrapped, you know what I'm saying? And we sit down and for a whole week to one month we really do the kind of work necessary to bring about a fifteen-year plan. No one makes the goddamed speeches. We sit down in these committees, we struggle and we fight, et cetera, et cetera. Then we go on and look at it, and then we tell the people in those committees to continue to meet—do you understand? I'm talking about sacrifice. I'm talking about real sacrifice for our people. I'm talking about sacrifice, you know. . . .

We should form various committees for different issues affecting African people. For instance, whenever Congress makes a statement about African women—when someone makes a statement in the newspapers about Black folks, period—we have what I call a Committee for Image Engineering. This is important because what we are involved in today is image engineering in America. They are engineering the country to come up against us: from O. J. to our youth; from our youth to wherever, they're engineering thoughts against us. They are constructing a way at which you should look at Black people.

Larvester Gaither: I see. What would be the function of these various committees?

Sonia Sanchez: A lot of this committee's job is to always read what's being printed in the papers. And the moment we see something that is contrary to a statement made from the president to the Congress or wherever, we respond with a letter to the Black newspapers. They print it for free. We also send it to the *New York Times*—they'll have you pay for that advertisement. And they say in those letters exactly what needs to be said. It does two things: It lets people see. And it's just called the committee for Black folks. No one is getting the glory. But it's very clear and very concise, very well-written because we got people who can do that. Right? And if people don't want to be seen or whatever, we're just asking for contributions. Always, take the money. Right? But also in the Black newspapers—the community newspaper or whatever—it teaches Black people how to think. How do you think about this? "What do you say about people calling you 'welfare mother.' " What do you say about this? And we then put it in the newspaper and editorial page or whatever.

We're now teaching people how to defend themselves. I go to the supermarket and people say to me, "Professor Sanchez, what do you think about O.J.? What do you think about this," they're asking, "How do I defend myself against unfair employers? How do I think? How do I begin to think critically?" Do you understand what I'm saying?

Larvester Gaither: Yes. And if we don't give them the answers, often times, they give—

Sonia Sanchez: They act to the contrary in the work force, you see. They come up with anything or they get mad, they jump up and cheer, you know, when the O.J. verdict comes across the TV . . . When we anticipated the O.J. verdict, we should have had this committee explaining the following: What the O.J. verdict means to us and how we should act.

This is about anticipating what's going on. This is what we must do. This is how we're going to affect our people. This is so that they're very clear about things, you see. And this is how we also support and protect our people. And this is how we support our leaders also too. When people attack our leaders, then we have a comment to make. And it helps people to understand that this is how you protect him, this is what you say about him. You don't have to invent something. This image engineering is very important. But we need at least ten committees that will speak to the issue of Black folks.

Again, I call upon Black folks wherever they are—not to start a new organization because this is not what this is about—I'm calling on leaders and/or people who consider themselves to be leaders to come together and draw up a fifteen-year plan for Black folks. Just like the Marshall Plan turned Europe from its death and destruction, this is a plan to bring Black folks into the twenty-first century.

Larvester Gaither: You have been writing lately. I guess you're always doing that. What are some issues that you're writing on now?

Sonia Sanchez: Well, last year I put out a book—*Wounded in the House of a Friend*—that we talked about earlier. And some of the pieces in there are impacting on us as African Americans and as people, period, in this country. And I tried to speak to those issues and cause people to look up and begin to think about, perhaps, doing something about it or at least recognizing that you have problems. You know some people don't even want to deal with the idea that you have problems all the way from a woman taking a child into that crack house and leaving her for a fix but the whole issue of crack being in the African American neighborhoods; the idea of a crack house being on a street where we live—you know what I'm saying.

That poem speaks to the fact that crack will make us forget all of our memories of each other. For example, the woman leaves the house, not remembering her daughter's name, forgetting what she looks like because crack has interfered with her knowing who her child was/is, which means forgetting her history, her herstory, and everything that's going on in the world. And that's what crack is supposed to do. It's supposed to kill our memories of each other and as a consequence we can kill each other—you know what I'm saying? And that is the one crisis we speak to in the harshest terms to let people understand that this is what's happening. And we've got to, in a sense, be alarmed by it. We cannot think that if we turn our heads or not even write about it or even mention it, that everything's going to be okay. Because everything's not going to be okay—you know. Those are issues we have to deal with because no one is going to deal with the issues of drugs in our communities but us, ourselves.

I'm writing on a book now about my brother who died of AIDS. It's a long poem to him, which I call a Freedom narrative. Some people call them slave narratives but I like to call them Freedom narratives because he has some of the same characteristics of the move from the South to the North, and this whole idea . . . that he could free himself through an education. And the process of alienation that happens, you know, in terms of education and, you know, with this whole process of understanding what is going on as an African man and as a person here in this country. And the education, joining the organizations and a whole lot of things that he did in order to kind of free himself in a sense.

And so it's a poem in rhyme. It's one long poem and it's called *Does Your House Have Lions*? This is a line that I got when someone told Rahsaan Roland Kirk that he was building a house and Rahsaan said, "Does your house also have lions?" And he said, "Anyone who's building a house needs to also have lions." Which is to the point—is it not? For anyone building a house—your house needs some lions whether that's an alarm system or a community where people watch out for each other. You might have people outside patrolling in your streets—you know. Get your house some lions because that is certainly necessarily needed. I picked that for the title of this book about my brother—the need for us all to have lions, you know, and that kind of protection that will protect us all as we move here on this earth.

Larvester Gaither: Could you share with us a line or two?
Sonia Sanchez: Certainly. I talk about my brother coming North, not for jobs like many Black people did at the turn of this century, but his mother

(my stepmother) had told him that his father had deserted, you know. And so he came with a very angry part of it.

1.

this was a migration unlike
the 1900's of black men and women
coming north for jobs. freedom. life.
This was a migration to begin
to bend a father's heart again
to birth seduction from the past
to repay desertion at last.

2.

imagine him short and black
thin mustache draping thin lips
imagine him country and exact
thin body, underfed hips
watching at this coral of battleships
and bastards. watching for forget
and remember. dancing his pirouette.

3.

and he came my brother at seventeen
recruited by birthright and smell
grabbing the city by the root with clean
metallic teeth. commandant and infidel
pirating his family in their cell
and we waited for the anger to retreat
and we watched him embrace the city and the street.

4.

first he auctioned off his legs. eyes.
heart. In rooms of specific pain.
he specialized in generalize
learned newyorkese and all profane.

enslaved his body to cocaine
denied his father's signature
damned his sister's overture.

5.

and a new geography greeted him.
the atlantic drifted from off shore
to lick his wounds to give him slim
transfusion as he turned changed wore
a new waistcoat of solicitor
antidote to his southern skin
ammunition for a young paladin.

6.

and the bars. the glitter. the light
discharging pain from his bygone anguish
of young black boy scared of the night.
sequestered on this new bank, he surveyed the fish
sweet cargoes crowded with scales feverish
with quick sales full sails of flesh
searing the coastline of his acquiesce.

7.

and the days rummaging his eyes
and the nights flickering through a slit
of narrow bars. hips. thighs.
And his thoughts labeling him misfit
as he prowled, pranced in the starlit
city, coloring his days and nites
with gluttony and praise and unreconciled rites.

8.

father. i despise you for abandoning me
to aunts and mothers and ministers of tissue

tongues, nibbling at my boyish kne.
father. forgive me for i know not what they do
moving me backwards through seams of bamboo
masks, staring eyes campaigning for
my attention. come O lords; my extended metaphor.

Larvester Gaither: You basically write from your experiences?

Sonia Sanchez: Well, some things come from experience. But I'm writing now about my brother's experience—you know what I'm saying? So, I have to imagine and I have to do research. I have to do research for some of the bars that he was in. I have to get the names of some of those bars—you know what I'm saying? My stepbrother ended up becoming a gay person and he died of AIDS—okay? The poem here speaks to that whole sense of alienation from the family. It talks about the sense of anger, because he thinks that his father has abandoned him, and then learning that this was not true—but not for a while. Okay? And as a consequence, not wanting to be like his father and going out into New York, the bars, the glitter and so forth. And really doing what he wants to do and not dealing with school or himself.

There is his voice or the writer's voice talking about him becoming alienated from family, going into the gay lifestyle. But he is not saying that he is gay. But the voice is saying that this is the case. Then I have the voice of the father—because they live together, don't forget—who doesn't see him and the son who doesn't see his father at all. Do know what I'm saying?

Larvester Gaither: Right.

Sonia Sanchez: And the concept that comes down, you know, of the father and the son that you don't see a lot of in the Black community.

Larvester Gaither: Exactly.

Sonia Sanchez: And then, there's my voice that comes in there when he comes down here for a weekend. He's getting drunk, he's getting on drugs, whatever, because he's not dealing with what his life is about. There is also some history in there. I talk about how we shut down the Harlem Hospital because they wouldn't hire Black and Puerto Rican electricians. When they were extending Harlem Hospital—when they finally asked for names—I gave my brother's name. He was upset and I said, "Well, you might do something instead of just, you know, pretending like being in school." Five years later, he became an electrician. It's one of the things that I reorganized in his life.

There's a fight for souls that we go through; for him not to damn his father but to get to know his father because he has the opportunity to do that. So my father and his son get much closer and get together.

Finally, what that's about is that I tell him, "It's okay for you to be who you are. Your parents, they love you. Your family will love you. Your friends will love you. You just don't have to kill yourself in this fashion." Do you know what I'm saying? And it ends where he dies of AIDS. I'm now trying to figure out exactly how it's going to end.

Larvester Gaither: Why do you feel this book is important?
Sonia Sanchez: The book is important, my brother, because it will speak to some of the issues in our community. How we jump up and talk about and laugh at gay people. You even have people who think they can go out and beat up on gays. They're following other people's examples, you know. But we can't do that because we've seen that already in our neighborhoods. We've got to understand that we are not to treat people the way we've been treated in the world.

Larvester Gaither: We even see this anti-gay, homophobic attitude manifesting itself in areas where you'd think there would be more tolerance—
Sonia Sanchez: Yes, that's true. In churches. In schools. In our homes. We who were oppressed and we who were enslaved—and we're still human. They tried to make us not human. Because what they're saying, basically, by doing this to us is that if I'd been enslaved, I would not be a human being, I would not have any thoughts for a people. But in spite of this, you're talking about a people, African Americans, who are human—a human force towards other people. Do you know what I'm saying? That's an amazing thing.

What I try to tell young people is that you think by going out and beating people, hitting people, robbing a store and trying to kill people who don't look like you—that this is how you get back at people? I say that this not about getting back at people, this is about maintaining your humanity and going on and being human. It's amazing. I mean, when you really look at who we are at this point, it's an amazing thing—it really is—

Larvester Gaither: Yes it is. We could just sit here and be amazed when you think about it. It's interesting that you talk about our humanity. Reflecting on our history, we don't have words, I guess, to describe . . . that's why we have the poets like yourself and others. . . .

Sonia Sanchez: What we try to do is move people to say, "You can't forget this because you've got to not let it happen ever again." You've got to remember. So therefore, we'll try to put a line or two in there that we know they will remember, so that you will know. But above all what we do is try to keep us human. The idea that we are human, that we must remain human in the midst of all this madness. And that is not an easy thing to do.

It's not easy because a lot of people just give up and say, "Okay, I don't really have to deal with it this way." They say that "I'm not going to deal with it at all." Or, "I'll just go out there and say anything, hurt anybody, and beat up people" and you say, "No, no, no. For you to act in a human fashion doesn't mean you're wrong." It doesn't mean you're a Tom or that you "ain't got no sense." It means that you have learned what people try to learn via religion and philosophy. We have learned the need to be what I call the forerunners of humanity.

An Interview with Sonia Sanchez

Danielle Alyce Rome / 1997

From *Speaking of the Short Story: Interviews with Contemporary Writers,* edited by Farhat Iftekharuddin, Mary Rohrberger, and Maurice Lee. © 1997. Reprinted with the permission of the author.

Sonia Sanchez, an acclaimed African American writer, has written several books of poetry, numerous plays, children's literature, and short stories. The influences of her literature range from the political, with such figures as Malcolm X, to the musical, with the influences of Billie Holiday and John Coltrane. The subject matters for her writings are those which unify the members of the human community by the commonality of the human experience. Her works include *The Adventures of Fat Head, Small Head, and Square Head* (1973), *Home Coming* (1969), *Homegirls and Handgrenades* (1984), *It's a New Day: Poems for Young Brothas and Sistuhs* (1971), *I've Been a Woman* (1987), *A Sound Investment and Other Stories* (1993), *Under a Soprano Sky* (1987), *Wounded in the House of a Friend* (1995), and *Love Poems* (1973).

Rome: I've read your definition of a poet as a creator of social values, a manipulator of symbols and language images. Does this definition coincide with your perception of a writer and artist of other literary genres as well?

Sanchez: I do believe a poet is indeed a creator of social values and I maintain that it could move on to other genres also. Certainly writers are manipulators of words and language images. Writers can also maintain the status quo or also talk about effecting change. I believe poetry is also, what I call, subconscious conversation. It is as much the work of those who write it as those who listen. So it is not by chance to sometimes hear people say, "Um hum, yeah right." It is that subconscious conversation. We are dealing with those subconscious images already planted in the psyche of people by the society or by people's culture so that they can do a call and response then and say, yes I understand or yes I am moved by that or they will cry out in the night as they sit in bed some place and read your poetry. I get letters from people that will say to me I was reading your book at midnight and I starting crying and that letter comes from India, that letter comes from Italy, that letter comes from France, that letter comes from many places where people say yeah. And what they're saying is what the writer is actually saying, we all have a common experience but my face is blackly black and your face is whitely white or pinkly pink or yellow or brown or whatever. But within that experience, that culture, we all have a common experience and that common experience is one of humanity, one of love, one of disdain, one of respect, and that's the great joy about writing. You give the poem to the world and people look at it and say, yes I understand that experience, yes I've had it. I understand that love poem, I understand that cry of help, I understand it. I've lived it. I've tasted it. And that's why I personally believe poetry is the greatest genre on the planet Earth.

Rome: When you write another genre, say the short story or drama, does your approach to the writing itself differ?
Sanchez: I don't think so, although the manifestation of it might be a different one when I write plays and the short story. When I write plays I am very aware of my characters. I am very much aware of their movements on the stage. I'm very much aware of a story I'm telling in a different fashion and therefore, a different writing comes about. The concentration is certainly on dialogue, the concentration moves the dialogue and moves the people. I'm very much more aware, when I write plays, of lying, that is telling a story. Once, in a play writing class I taught, a student had to bring in a piece, a dialogue. He brought in a dialogue of parents arguing and separating and he had heard this when he was a child. As he read the piece he cried, but as we listened we didn't. And he looked at our dry eyes and he couldn't understand, "Why aren't you upset, why aren't you crying?" The students said, "Well, we weren't involved." He said, "How could you not be involved?" because he was really crying. But the point is those were his parents and he really was there, but the way he wrote it, he didn't involve us with it, so we never cried. And he said, "But it happened just in that fashion." I said, "That's partly the problem, so write it in another fashion and bring your imagination in and lie a little bit and perhaps we will become involved with it."

Rome: Does your emphasis of the transmission of truth shift or become more focused from one form or another?

Sanchez: I think that's what you're hearing about that play and also about the short story. Sometimes because I start a piece off with the "I" then people assume it's personal, but it is the collective "I" I'm talking about. The collective "I" of many women, or the collective "I" of a certain culture, or the collective "I" of all men, or whomever. It has nothing to do with me personally but I use the "I" to bring you into the story and the immediacy of bringing you into the story saying, "Come in and taste this immediately." And, yes, quite often I realize when I write a piece, even when I do poetry, I write it and say, this is how it happened. But as I write I realize that how it happened is not necessarily interesting. So I have to, in a sense, come back and embellish and invent or bring the imagination in to bear on the piece. And the imagination is not necessarily involved in whether this is true or not.

Rome: Do you constantly maintain the same level of truth to yourself in your writing? Regardless of the genre, do you strive to relay the African American female perspective in your writing?

Sanchez: I do that in many ways but it's not always necessarily one in which the person is always the "shero." I mean, when we're talking about truth, people have to look good always or you have to be a "shero" as opposed to a hero. Therefore, the truth might be where I show a damaging aspect of the African American experience. My new book is called *Wounded in the House of a Friend.* In it I have a poem about a young African American woman, this young black woman who takes her nine-year-old daughter to a crack house for a fix. That's a horrible truth that's there, but if I ignore that truth and say, now I'm gonna do this story about this woman who takes her nine-year-old daughter to the zoo; there are women who take their daughters to the zoo, parents who take their daughters to the zoo, but there are also women now where crack has wiped out the whole concept of history, of family, of motherhood, of peoplehood, of whatever. And I read that piece to a group of homeless women who were now staying in this little house in Philadelphia and when I read one of the women said, "That's right, you can't do that any-more." And that cracked my skull. She didn't say, wow, isn't that something, listen to that story, and isn't that interesting, she said, "I can't do that any-more." My skull cracked and I sat there crying because I knew that what

I hit on, what I wrote about was very real. You can't deal with something as addictive as crack and expect to stay human or to have human ideas. The whole point of allowing people to become addicted in that fashion means that you break the pattern of motherhood, and you break the pattern of being human.

Rome: I've often read that critics consider you to be a radical. Do you consider yourself to be a radical or are you a realist?

Sanchez: I don't know what it means to be a radical. In this country people will call you a radical to demean you, but they will turn around and call a Latin writer or another writer from another country a radical writer and it'll be okay. I think I am a writer who attempts to deal with what it means to stay human, with what it means to be a human being and sometimes I do it in a rough fashion. Sometimes I do it in a lyrical fashion. Sometimes I sock you in the eye and say, "Look up, look up. You must not walk this walk." You can say radical if you want to. You can say lyrical if you want to. You can say committed if you want to. You can say whatever, the point is that I write because I must write. I write because I must bring attention to what is happening in the world. A new piece that I have just begun talks about bodies floating down the river Rwanda. And at the same time, I juxtapose next to that bodies floating the river of 125th Street going for drugs. They're different deaths, but the same death.

Rome: In your writing you portray things that are very real cross-culturally. Does it matter in which community or just the human community itself?

Sanchez: The human community, right.

Rome: In your writing, does your approach to the short story differ from your approach to the poetry or any other genre that you write?

Sanchez: I used to tell my students that if you can write poetry, you can write a short story, then you can write a novel or you can write a play. That you should call yourself a writer, not just a poet, not just a short story writer, not just a novelist. I do believe that we can really do that. It probably depends upon where you want to concentrate. I came into writing a story because I was writing a long poem, I realized that I wanted to say more about it and that's how I moved into the genre of short fiction. Sometimes I call my short fiction prose poems because it takes up six pages and I do it poetically.

And I take a slice out of someone's life at some point and put it on paper. So I do make use of the short fiction or the short story when it suits my purpose and I have something else to say and I need to say it in that fashion and I gravitate towards it. I don't always know why I do but I do.

Rome: Do you find that one genre versus the other lends itself more to a manifestation of power? In poetry you have more immediacy and you can say what you want more effectively quickly. Do you find that the short story deters from the power of writing?

Sanchez: No, I don't. I never have any problems, any discussions, or any arguments about which is easier, which is better, which is more powerful. I've read some powerful short stories that have made my flesh crawl. And then at the same time, I've read some powerful poems, understanding that each line is a paragraph sometimes that has turned my body inside out. I love literature and as a consequence we should teach our students and ourselves that there is not one better than the other. Sometimes we fixate ourselves at one genre because we get used to it, you get fixed at it, you get truncated there and you assume that's where you belong. But we're all probably Renaissance women and men, which means we can move in and out of various genres with ease and joy.

Rome: In the creation of a new piece of literature, what is foremost in your mind in regards to any specific piece? Is there one message that you set out to permeate your piece?

Sanchez: I'm finishing up two books. A long poem to my brother, which is almost like a short story. It has all the trappings of a short story because when you have a poem that is book length you're telling a story. It's a ballad, this is rhyme royal. You're telling the story and you have to grab people's attention the way a short story has got to with the same few lines. And in order to do this I felt myself dividing it up as I would do if I were writing a short story sometimes in terms of movement into the piece. This story is about my brother who died of AIDS, and I found myself doing it chapterlike, of short-story-like. This is a section, this is a section there, this is the climax, this is a confrontation, this is the denouement, this is how I'm ending it. All of that came into play in this long poem and I found it was interesting how I had to construct this piece. It was a very difficult piece to write because I think there was a transcrossing. All the knowledge you have about literature comes into play, although with the rhyme royal I had to fixate myself with rhyme because it requires that it has a certain form of rhyme that you have to deal with. But at the same time, I'm aware of telling the story within the rhyme. There's always the fighting to tell the story and coming to the poetry form for the rhyme to happen. There's a real struggle that goes on sometimes that's fascinating. I'm very grateful to the various forms they move you to write, they move you to see overlapping. The greatest novels or short stories that I have read have been very poetic, very lyrical, the ones that have made me sore. And the ones that have dealt with a lot of imagery and those short stories that have made me think and didn't tell me we're at this point now, we should be thinking this or now you know you're at the climax here, now you're ready to experience this. The ones that let me wander in and out in a stream of consciousness. Those are the ones that I've enjoyed.

Rome: Once a piece of yours goes through its preliminary phases, what does your revision process entail?
Sanchez: That is always the hard work. The easiest work sometimes is getting it down and then the revision and sometimes discarding lines that you like. Or putting in another book for another piece because you know it doesn't work but you like it so much that you decide to keep it. Revision is a mother. I teach my students by bringing in one of my poems. The first regurgitation then the finished product. Then I have on xeroxed paper the second revision, third, fourth, fifth, sixth, seventh, and eighth revisions where I've written why didn't I stay with the first revision of the poem because you are depressed by then. You've pulled all the juices out. But it's at that eighth or ninth revision that something happens and the juices begin to pour back in at some point. They pour back in and there's the final product. And there is a difference between the first regurgitation and the last and there are similarities also. They need to see that and know that it is the going through all of those revisions that you finally come back full circle to what you need to keep and what you need to discard and how you get the juices to flow. The same thing happened with a short story I wrote called "After Saturday Night Comes Sunday." I had started that piece with a different voice, a male voice, and halfway through it I realized it was the wrong voice and that it had to be the female voice. I had had the male voice telling the story of his descent into drugs and how it affected the children,

and it was the wrong voice. I had to go back and change it, and I made it the female voice telling the story although it was the man's story. Sometimes, in writing the short story, it's the wrong voice, it's not the first person but the third person and then, all of a sudden, it works when you do that. That only happens sometimes when you've finished the whole thing and nothing gels, nothing works. And then, all of a sudden, with a change in the voice, it works.

Rome: I've noticed one of the things you use in your writing is Black English. How do you feel about that form? Do you feel it lends more realistically to what you're trying to say?

Sanchez: Sometimes it does; I can weave it in and out. Sometimes when characters speak, they speak Black English and what are you going to do, whiten it? Change it or lighten it? Educate them? And also, in doing that you would deny that people speak in that fashion, you say that it's not worthy of a place in literature. *Their Eyes Were Watching God*, there's Black English in there and it's a great book. And it's when you understand that that you're writing literature, that people who speak in Black English have great thoughts also and they're worthy to be drawn as characters in novels, and short stories and poems also. You put them in there and you say, "Look at this, this is how I speak and contrary to what you think I'm human with these human ideas, these human thoughts. Here I am and listen to it, it's a viable way of talking and speaking."

Rome: There is a pressing need for people to align themselves with certain theoretical camps nowadays, it's sort of the "in" thing to do. Do you align yourself specifically with any of these camps?

Sanchez: What theoretical camps are you referring to?

Rome: Postmodernism, multiculturalism, ethnicity, etc.?

Sanchez: You don't have to align yourself because people will pull you to their camp and you go and you tell them what you think. I think the following about this. I think that we're so willing to put tags. When I teach something, I don't put a name on it quite often until the end of the semester. The whole idea that the students think they can't figure out a story or a poem, so we read a poem and I ask them, "What do you think about this?" and we have a long conversation. Then I say go read what Jane Schmoe said about it, and they come back and say she said the same thing I said about it. Yeah right, you can think, you can figure out a poem, you can say the same thing. And then we assume, when we give a poem or a section in literature, we say read that and see what Jane and Joe Schmoe say about it 'cause we assume the student can't figure it out and I don't. I make no assumptions, I know my students are just unpublished critics, and I know they can think because they've had to live eighteen years. When I get an eighteen-year-old and a twenty-year-old and a twenty-two-year-old in my class, they have maneuvered Philadelphia, or California, L.A., New York City, and they've had to think about that. They didn't do it easily; it is not easy living in modern-day society. So they have had to figure out ways to deal with mothers, fathers or no mothers, no fathers, which means they had to think critically before the point of sitting in my classroom. So, I expect them to think when I give them something, and we come back and discuss it. I say casually, this certain person said the same thing and I read. They look at themselves and say, "Ha, ha, I figured that out myself," and this is the joy about teaching as far as I'm concerned. It's that nothing you say in this classroom will be considered stupid, will be considered dumb, will be considered too far out. I've had some students who have taken criticism far out. Their analysis of some things has been so far out everybody stopped and looked, but it's possible. And because it is possible, because all criticism is your idea of what the text is all about, I say this is possible and this is viable. Then you allow them to understand and consider what other people have said, and to consider this critic who is the critic par excellence on this person. And what do you think about his ideas? And then because you've released the whole idea they say, "Well, it's okay but it's not as good as mine." And I love that because that's the way it should be, they should know about what other critics say, but they should not demean their own sense of what that text was all about. That's what learning is all about.

Sonia Sanchez: Telling What We Must Hear

Juanita Johnson-Bailey / 1998

From *Ms. Magazine*, August 1998, 52–53; rpt. *Flat-Footed Truths: Telling Black Women's Lives*, edited by Patricia Bell-Scott and Juanita Johnson-Bailey. © 1998. Reprinted with the permission of Juanita Johnson-Bailey.

With the unblinking and critical poet's eye, Sonia Sanchez has been setting her readers straight, telling the "terrible beauty," and reflecting images in ways that simultaneously solicit tears and laughter. For over thirty years this revolutionary poet has been undeterred from a path that began in the sixties when Black militancy was the vogue. Still, she has not given up the struggle to let her poetry be what she refers to as a "call to arms" for her people. But her people have not always responded with reciprocal dignity and purity of heart. So her way has at times been solitary, weary, joyful, and painful.

She has won numerous awards, including the prestigious PEN Writing Award, a National Endowment for the Arts fellowship, the Lucretia Mott Award, an American Book Award, and an honorary doctorate in fine arts. Her latest book, *Wounded in the House of a Friend* (1996), follows a long, consistent line of such outstanding works as *Under a Soprano Sky* (1987), *Homegirls and Handgrenades* (1984), *A Blues Book for Blue Black Magical Women* (1978), *We a BadddDDD People* (1970), and *Home Coming* (1969). Her work also includes plays, children's books, short stories, and essays.

In this conversation she moves between discussing her poems and artistry with a ready laugh and a fast staccato speech. Her words are audible in personal moments of active resistance, her mettle is evident in the stance of contemporary courageous Black women writers, and her truth ever echoes in her work—always militant, always radical, always challenging.

The Poetic Beginnings

I really think my first exposure to poetry was from my grandmother, who spoke in what we call Black dialect. My earliest remembrance is when I was around four-ish. She would say things in a certain way, and I would repeat it. And she'd look up at me. I would kind of do it again, smile, go off in a corner someplace, and go on saying it. Some people felt that I was mocking her. I was not. It was just that something in my ear told me it was a brilliant way of saying it. So I would repeat it.

Grandmother knew books were important to me, and naturally we had a lot. I would always pick up a book, open it, and try to figure out what was being said. Either my grandmother or cousin Louise taught me how to read at four.

What I remember most is the love and respect my grandmother had for me. She knew that I was different. I already had figured out that I was odd; children figure that out at an early age. She said, "Just let the girl be. She be all right. She gonna stumble on her gentleness one of these days." Grandmother passed on the whole idea that I could do what I wanted to do. Women like her kept hopes and dreams alive in us. Once when I jumped out of a second-story window all she said to me is, "You okay?" And I said, "Yes." And she said, "Well, go on and play." She didn't grab me, even though I did have some bruises. She would shoo me out to do this world. And that's what I've been trying to do—this world.

My mother died giving birth to twins when I was one year old, and my grandmother died when I was six. The response to my grandmother's death made me tongue-tied, and after that I stuttered. This meant that people left me alone. So I started writing little things that everyone said were poems because they rhymed. I wrote because I stuttered and no one ever wanted to take the time to listen. I used to pass little notes; it was the way that I spoke.

One of the first little poems I did was to Walter, who was a terrible little boy, but I liked him and he liked me. I also wrote a poem about George Washington crossing the Delaware, which my sister found and read to the family. Everybody fell out laughing. After this I began keeping journals, which I couldn't hide in the bedroom that I shared with my sister. There is no privacy with a sister. Since it was my job to clean the bathroom every Saturday, it was no problem hiding my journals there. I stuck everything

I was reading and writing underneath the tub, the kind with the raised legs. I would be sitting in there at three o'clock in the morning, writing.

I believe that I was born a poet. A lot of people are poetic but never really learn or nurture the craft. Therefore they'll write a poem once or twice a year. A college poetry teacher, Louise Bogan, told me two important things. First, she told me that a lot of people have talent, but they do nothing with it. The other thing she said is that you have to write on cue because if you wait for this muse to drop down on your shoulders, it might drop once a year. Therefore she made us write a poem a week. That's when I first got disciplined.

I ran across certain people growing up in New York City who helped me along the way. One of these people was Jean Blackwell Hutson, the curator at the Schomburg Library. I had finished school and needed a job. I read the ads in the *New York Times* for writers and sent samples. I got a telegram—that's what they used to do, send telegrams—that said, "You are hired." I jumped up and down and celebrated with some of my friends. Then I went to work. I had on my blue suit, my blue pumps, my blue bag, my white gloves, and my blue hat to let them [Whites] know that I knew how to go to work. In my purse I had money to eat lunch, money to get back home, and the telegram. They said report at nine o'clock. I got down there at eight-thirty. I handed the telegram to the woman secretary—and she said, in a soft voice, "All right, okay, have a seat." So I sat down with a magazine, and someone came and peeped around the corner, looked at me, and went back. Then another face came. Finally a man came and said, "We're sorry, but the job is taken." And I said, "I have a job here." And he said, "Well, the job is taken," like, "Well, what's your damn problem?" I said, "But no one else has come in here except me. How could . . . ?" I was amazed. It was just that fast. The secretary was sitting there with her eyes downcast. And I said to his retreating back, "I am going to report you to the Urban League!"

I left so angry that I got on the train and, instead of getting off where I was supposed to, I ended up at 135th Street and Lenox Avenue. And all of a sudden here's this place. I am hot. I am sweaty. It said "Library" and I said, "Let me go in, pick up some books, and read." A guard outside made me sign in. I asked, "What kind of library is this?" and he said, "The Schomburg." And I said, "The Schomburg. What's the Schomburg? Is it special?" He said, "Well, why don't you ask the lady inside." Inside to the right was this glass area where Jean Hutson, the curator at the time, sat. I went over, gestured to her, and she came out. I asked, "What kind of library is this?" And she said, "This library contains all books by and about Black folks." And I said in my sharp, acerbic fashion, "Must not be many books in here, then."

She told me to sit down and she'd bring me some books. As I inched myself into a long table with all men sitting around it, they looked up at me. I was the only female there. She brought me *Their Eyes Were Watching God*, *Souls of Black Folk*, and *Up from Slavery*. I picked *Their Eyes Were Watching God* and started reading. Softly I said, "Oh, my God. Oh, my God. Look at this." The language was so beautiful. I read maybe a third of it. I went to Ms. Hutson and said, "This is a beautiful book." She said, "Yes, dear. Go read now." When I finished the book I stood up again and said, "Oooh, what a beautiful book." One of the men said, "Miss Hutson, will you please tell this young woman to stay still or leave." For an entire week I hung out at the Schomburg when I was supposed to be looking for a job. And Ms. Hutson fed me books. She asked, "Is there anything you like to read?" When I said gently, "Poetry," she sent me all the poets she knew. On the last day I said to her, "I have to go and look for a job. But one day my books will be in here." Years later, when I was a professor at Amherst College and I brought classes to the Schomburg, she would tell that story much more beautifully than I do, with a very funny smile on her face.

The Sister Circle

I used to have trouble sometimes when I read my poetry. I took a lot of abuse. The first time I read in New York City, people just sat and looked at me. Some people booed 'cause I said, "I'm a Black woman poet." I'll never forget it. I wrote poems that were obviously womanist before we even started talking about it. Men would get up and go on about their business because they said I was reading only for women. So one day I said out loud, "My poetry is just as important as your poetry." It was at a huge conference. And I was not invited back to a major conference for three years.

In my head my audience has always been Black folks, Black women. I am not a revisionist. I don't say that I have always understood sisterhood. Most women are socialized not to believe a whole lot of loving things about women. My generation began to forge a new way of looking at the world. We began to say to each other, "I don't take your husband. You don't take my husband." We began to work in women's groups. So now I greet all women as sister. Some Black women get upset about that because they say, "White women are not your sisters." And I'll say, "Yeah, and a lot of Black women are not my sisters, either." The point is to understand that until we organize women in this country the way we should be organized, we are in a lot of trouble.

The premise that we are sisters brought me full circle, back to the church where my grandmother and the women called each other sister. My grandmother was the head deaconess in the church. So on Saturdays her sisters came to do the cooking and the talking. I would come in and slide behind the couch that sat away from the wall so they would not put me to work. The women would be in there snapping beans, peeling potatoes, and fixing up the ham. In the midst of their work they would start talking about people—about somebody beating up somebody. And they would say, "Well, we don't let that happen." I knew Mama (my grandmother) wanted me to hear this because I would snicker and she would shoot her eyes behind the couch. Her eyes said "If you want to hear this, you keep quiet."

I used to hear her say, "Well, that ain't right of Sister Smith to do that." And someone would say, "You know, she really ain't nice." Although they called her sister, they knew some of those sisters weren't sisters. So I'm not inventing anything new. I'm just picking up on the ideology of my grand-mother that says simply, "Yes, I will call you sister, but you gotta make yourself sister."

The things we heard in the conversations among the women taught us something. I learned to curse by listening to Miss Dixon, a friend of my stepmother. When Miss Dixon came to our house, my father would leave. He couldn't stand her because she drank and cursed. But I loved when Miss Dixon came. I knew I would learn another curse word. She would come in loudly and say, "Sonia, bring me some beer." I would open the beer, taste the foam, bring it to her, and listen to her tell stories.

Miss Dixon was a huge woman, a big woman, who had been in show business. And she was the one who taught me how to watch people. She would say, "Girl, you cannot get along on this earth without knowing who people are. You gotta listen to people. Hear what's coming out of their mouths and hear what's coming out of their bodies, and know what odors they have."

The first poem that I wrote to Miss (Mama) Dixon was in *Under a Soprano Sky*. It was about being downtown at City Hall when this man pulled his car up on the sidewalk and pulled his penis out and said, "Do you want some of this?" I'd been talking to African women from all over the world, and this man could only see me as a whore on Market Street. I called on my old friend Miss Dixon, and she said, "What you gonna say to this man? You better tell him what needs to be said, Sonia." And I did. Afterward I wrote the poem "style no. 1," which mentions her by name.

When I finished cutting him up with my mouth he turned red and drove off real fast. I laughed out loud on Market Street. And Miss Dixon said, "I bet you he will think twice about coming up to somebody else."

Extending the Circle

Teaching a course on the Black woman taught me what it was to say "sister" to people. It was a very hard time for me; I had separated from my husband, Ethridge Knight, a poet, who was on drugs. The female students were driving me insane, always coming in for conferences. They needed help being Black women on a White campus. Jokingly I said, "We need a course called 'The Black Woman.' " And they said, "Teach it!" So I designed this course. But I had not put into that syllabus what happened after we were in there maybe the third or fourth week. This young woman stood up and said, "I hate all Black men." And she started to talk about incest. I hugged her, and we all collectively caught our tears. I instinctively began to talk to her and that weekend read every damn thing I could find on incest. And it became part of what we talked about forever.

I tried to write to those young sisters about what it was to love themselves. I wrote *We a BaddDDD People* that year. Ethridge tore up the finished manuscript for this book because he was not writing. When I found myself on the floor, trying to piece together this book, I knew it was time to leave. At that moment I understood why those sisters gathered in my grandmother's house every Saturday. Ostensibly it was to cook the meals to sell on Sunday to raise money for the church. But it was really where they passed on information to each other, where they helped each other, and where they passed on information to some little terrible kid sitting behind the couch. They were telling me how you don't let someone hit you twice.

One night I got a frantic call that a former student was climbing the walls. Some of the sisters and I went to her house. She had taken something because this man that she had married had come home and she smelled his former lovemaking as she was making love to him. She flipped. We pumped her full of coffee and walked her back to sanity. It was for her I wrote,

> *he poured me on*
> *the bed and slid*
> *into me like glass.*
> *and there was*
> *the sound of splinters.*

You can't put splinters back together, but that's what we did as sisters. Sisterhood is very important. That hood is a covering. Sisters make everything possible on this earth.

Calling Up the Ancestors

Because of women like Miss Dixon and Mama (my grandmother) I've always been in touch with our female ancestors. In that sense my work is spiritual. And most of the work has a history to it. I am always researching and then creating from that research. I carry the mamas, I carry the sisters, the women who were on the block being sold. I carry those first Africans who came to this country and must have screamed out at the gods.

But in spite of our oppression we have maintained our humanity. We might be in danger of losing it with this younger generation, so our work is very important. We must work hard to make them understand the history/herstory that we have in the world—the humanity and the love that we have. I say to young people, I did not fight all these years to pull these sisters out of history, to put African women back on the world stage, to write about them and teach about them to have you get on stage and act like a fool or to become sex objects on MTV. It is a constant fight at the university and all over the earth to bring African women on center stage again, out of people's homes where they have relegated us—always somebody's mammy—public or private.

When I started to read literature I realized we'd been taken off the world stage. I say to young people, I didn't write "Improvisation," which is about the middle passage and those sisters screaming when they are being sold on these American planks, for you to get on MTV in a state of undress, rub your crotch, or make believe you are making love to the microphone. When you know your history, it means you don't allow someone to come up and record your derriere while you shake it back and forth. You don't go across the floor, lapping up toward a man.

It hurt me to see a woman on television announce that a young Black woman had performed a sexual act in the middle of a dance floor and that later the guy turned her over to his posse. I wrote a poem based on this incident and read it at the Bronx Community College to young African American and Latino women. They were returning students, and many of them had a child or two. I pulled out the proofs of *Wounded in the House of a Friend* and read the poem "Like." It begins:

L I K E

All i did was
go down on him
in the middle of
the dance floor
cuz he is a movie
star he is a blk/
man "live" rt off
the screen fulfilling
my wildest dreams.

They said, "That's just like Tenisha." Then somebody said, "Yeah." And someone said, "Ms. Sanchez, that's not right, is it?" And I said, "Sister, that has nothing to do with right. She went down on the young brother because she was ahistorical. When you have history, you don't ever embarrass yourself or your people on the planet Earth." I told them how at the turn of the century Black women started clubs because White women would not let them into their clubs. We were called whores and prostitutes because of our enslavement. We couldn't help it. It wasn't prostitution. They raped us. These Black women went to newspapers and said, "We're not whores, we're not prostitutes, we are church women, we are good women. You cannot denigrate us in the newspapers the way you have done." And now, I said, "You willingly denigrate yourself on TV." They cried and they said no one had ever told them that before.

Memories That Heal and Preserve

One of the things I'm trying to pull on is our residual memory as women. Somebody has said something somewhere along the way to help us. We have just blocked it out. Education has blocked it out. You forget that you see. What I try to do with these young girls is to tell things we were told when they straightened our hair in the kitchen on Saturday nights.

We are in danger, great danger, of losing the memory that connects us, that keeps us alive. The thing that has sustained us as African people was that we had memories. The woman on the dance floor should have known what she was saying very distinctly, that "we [Black women] are immoral, promiscuous, and unreliable." But she was ahistorical.

Once, when I read that poem, a very middle-class woman said, "You know, I love your poetry, but you really shouldn't read a poem like that out loud. White people think we are all like that." And I said, "Yes, I should. They know we don't all take crack. But these incidents are reported in the news."

I took another idea from the newspaper—about a sister leaving her child at a crack house. I put it up on the bulletin board in my bedroom. Every morning I read it and cried. Later I wrote, "Memories. What happens with memories? Crack kills memories." And the second thing I wrote was, "Child. This will silence the child." Then I wrote, "Will silence the people also. That's why crack is here, to silence the people and to silence our memories."

Crack wounds. And that's what I said in *Wounded in the House of a Friend*. The title of that book is from Zechariah, and the whole section is about prophecy. "And what of these wounds, naked in our back? . . . For we have been wounded in the house of our friends." That's not just a personal house that we are wounded in. It is the house of America that has allowed this to happen. But as Africans we are also wounded in our private houses, our bodies. When you bring crack into Black neighborhoods, it makes you forget all memories of yourself. So in "Poem for Some Women," about the young woman selling her daughter for crack, she couldn't even remember her daughter's name or what she looked like. Crack will kill memories so you *can* sell a daughter, give her up as a virgin. People dealing crack might not take it, but they also lose their memories and their history.

The first line of "Poem for Some Women" is "Huh?" And I started off on that level because it had to be a question mark. There was nothing that was final there. The woman's voice had to be first. It was not going to be my voice.

In telling, I try to give Black people strength, power, and a sense of themselves—who they are—who they must be—and what they must do during the short period they're on this earth. I try to make my people laugh, at the same time to teach and inform, to make us know and feel our beauty.

And another goal of my writing has been to reconcile us with ourselves and to reclaim our history/herstory. We must understand that before we can move on. Although we think we do it without them, some ancestor is pushing us. The title *Wounded in the House of a Friend* came at three o'clock in the morning while I was asleep. I woke up and wrote down the title. You see, our ancestors will wake us up in the middle of the night if we are not on time.

Poetry has kept me connected to this long line of African people who stayed alive just to tell their stories. I understand why I keep doing this work. It is part of a long tradition. It is what I am supposed to do. Writing poetry has kept me alive. It kept me breathing. It kept me human. It kept me a woman. It kept me from killing people. It kept me from killing myself.

"As Poets, As Activists": An Interview with Sonia Sanchez

David Reich / 1999

From *World*, May/June 1999. http://www.uuworld.org/1999/archives1999. html. Reprinted with the permission of the author.

One day, back in the 1960s, when the Beacon Press poet Sonia Sanchez was running the world's first black studies program, at San Francisco State College in California, she noticed a stranger in her classroom, furiously taking notes on her lecture. When she got home that day, some FBI agents were there to meet her, with her landlord in tow. They told the landlord to evict her because she was teaching "all that radical stuff."

Recalls Sanchez: "I asked them, 'What do you mean?' and they said with utter disdain, 'W. E. B. Du Bois and Paul Robeson and Marcus Garvey and Pablo Neruda. . . .'"

"I thought all that was literature, and America thought it was seditious," she adds with a laugh that holds equal parts disgust and saving irony.

Judging from her subsequent work as a teacher, an activist, and a very political woman of letters, the G-men's intimidation tactics didn't do much to muzzle Sanchez. Since the 1960s, she's taught at schools like Amherst, Rutgers, the University of Pennsylvania, and Temple University, where she is currently Laura Carnell Professor of English and Women's Studies. She has also published hundreds of poems and prose pieces and nineteen books, the last four of them with Beacon, and spoken or read from innumerable platforms, often for progressive and women's causes.

In the process she has run afoul not only of the FBI but of patriarchal establishments from the Nation of Islam (for teaching Muslim women about birth control) to the editors of a journal called *Negro World*, who asked her to review the Black Panther leader Eldridge Cleaver's memoir *Soul on Ice*. "Cleaver had just gotten out of jail," says Sanchez, "and he was very much the darling of the Left. I thought he was problematic from the beginning. Any man who would write a book that talked about practicing rape on black women in order to rape white women was problematic. I started the review, 'Eldridge Cleaver is not a revolutionary; he's a hustler. I come from New York, and I've seen quite enough of hustlers in my time.'" As Sanchez tells it, her review was never printed, and the book was reassigned to a male reviewer.

The *World* talked with Sonia Sanchez on a cold, gray afternoon in February in a conference room at the Schomburg Center for Research in Black Culture in New York City's Harlem, a neighborhood the poet moved to as a girl, after spending her first nine years in Alabama. Under five feet tall with tiny bones, Sanchez responded to our questions in a clear, strong voice, sometimes closing her eyes to recall past events or conjure up a fitting answer.

World: I read somewhere that you did your first poetry reading at a bar here in Harlem. Did people come to the bar to hear you, or did you just show up and read for whoever happened to be there?
SS: We—this is Amiri Baraka and Askia Muhammad Touré and a bunch of other poets from the Black Arts Movement—wanted to get our work to where the people were. And one of us said, "The people are in the bars." [Laughs.] So we targeted this bar on Seventh or Lenox—I don't remember why this particular bar—and went in and asked the owner if we could come in and read some poetry. And the guy laughed and said, "Okay, but I'm not going to stop selling my beer and drinks." We said, "No, no, you don't have to do that. We just want to read for a little while and engage people in this whole conversation." And he said, "If you want to do that, lady, mister, if you want to do that. . . ." What he really meant was "If you want to take that chance, you're more than welcome." [Laughs.]

World: What kind of a bar was it?
SS: It was a neighborhood bar, nothing fancy, with people drinking at the bar on stools and at little tables. And so we came back that night to read. Someone—I don't know who—pulled the plug on the jukebox, and that got everybody's attention. We said, "We want to read some poems," and before the people in the bar could moan because the music's gone, we started to go "pshom t-t-t-t", staccato-style, "d-d-d-d"—you know, like machine guns. And of course we used a couple curse words because we knew that would gather

them. People stopped when they heard the curse words. After we got them, we didn't use any more curse words, but they were listening now. It must have taken all of fifteen minutes, and when we finished, they clapped and said, "Good, good, good." But we weren't going to overstay our time.

I remember walking down Lenox a couple days later, and some guy across the street says, "Hey, ain't you the lady that came into—" And I said, "Uhhuh." He said, "That was good! I went home and told my lady. And she cursed me out because I didn't have her there. You gonna come back?" And I said, "Yep, we gonna come back."

We didn't go back to that particular bar that I remember, but afterwards a lot of us went out to San Francisco and Oakland, where on Sunday mornings we'd go out with musicians and dancers and gather the people into the square to listen to poetry.

World: In several poems and prose pieces you talk about your shyness and stuttering as a child and how you took up writing as a better way to get your thoughts across. . . .
SS: I think writers are born, like mathematicians and scientists. What stuttering made me do is write earlier.

I think I started stuttering because of the great loss of my grandmother, who died when I was six. She was a pivotal person in my life, a woman who came to my father's house and picked me and my sister up and said she would take care of us because my mother had died trying to give birth to twins. They all died—she died, and they died in her. My grandmother was the typical grandmother who spoiled you outrageously, and I was what they used to call a tomboy. . . .

World: Oh, yes, I read that at age four you jumped out a second-story window. Is that true?
SS: Yes, yes, yes. One of us kids had decided the hardest thing you could do was jumping out this window. But when people got there and looked down and saw it was a distance, everyone said, "Uh-oh!" And I looked down, too, but my whole point of looking was to figure out how to do it. Because the idea of being leader with these boys I used to play with was really intriguing. And there was this thick kind of tree-bush, this huge thing right there. I thought if I just leap far enough, I can hit the tree and slide down.

And I got ready to do that, not thinking that I might miss the tree. And of course as I got ready, the other kids ran to get everybody because they recognized the danger here. And I went boom—hit it!—sure enough, and slid down. And sliding down, I hit the ground harder than I expected and skinned my knees, and my aunts, who were just always appalled at all I did, went clucking their tongues. But Mama, as I called my grandmother, came out and said, "You okay?" I said, "Mmm-hmm." She said, "Well, okay. Go on and play." She protected me against the people who really didn't want me to go outside and play—because I played hard and came back all beat up, dresses torn, braids out, all that stuff.

World: They wanted you to play with dolls.
SS: Well, yes. Because my sister went out and she came back with nothing— no dirt, no hair undone. And my sister was a beautiful little girl. I remember once, while the church sisters were visiting my grandmother one Saturday, my sister and I were playing with cutout dolls, dressing them and stuff. I didn't like this, but it was all I could do that day for some reason. And one of the sisters said, "Oh Pat, oh Pat, oh Pat is so beautiful. She is so beautiful, just like her mother." And Pat raised her head to this chorus of words that sanctioned her and told her who she was. And they all smiled, and she went back to playing.

And then someone said, "And Sonia." So I raised my head for this sanction of praise words, and there was silence. Then my grandmother said, "Well, she looks just like her daddy. But she's smart."

It's amazing how your family will tell you at a young age what you will do in life. You pick up on it and do it. And so I spent the rest of my life being smart, whatever that means. And I guess my sister spent the rest of her life being beautiful.

World: You've already hinted that your work has a lot of political content, and I wanted to follow the subject further. Shelley once wrote that "poets are the unacknowledged legislators of the world." Is that an appropriate role for a poet?
SS: Yes. All poets, all writers are political. They either maintain the status quo, or they say, "Something's wrong, let's change it for the better." That's what my life has really been about.

Someone once asked me in an interview, "If you had been born white, would you have the passion for justice?" I had to think for a moment, but then I said, "I would have had the same heart, the same liver, the same lungs, and the same brain. And I would have had the same eyes, too. And I think at some point, I would have looked out at the world and seen something wrong with it, and I would have talked about change."

I said, "Of course, being born black, it was much more immediate for me. When I moved to New York City, I still remembered Alabama." I still remembered the time an aunt took me on a bus—she was taking me to work with her. The bus was half and half, with whites up front and blacks in the back. When more whites got on, the blacks had to move back; and when even more whites got on, the blacks then stood up; and when more whites still came on, the driver stopped the bus and told the blacks to get off.

And this aunt, I remember, didn't get off. She began to inch forward with me. The bus driver stopped the bus and said, "Get off." She said, "I'm not getting off. I have about three more stops to go." And he said, "I said, 'Get off!'" People stopped and listened, and I remember holding onto her hand, knowing, feeling the tension in her hand. And he said, "I will put you off," and he stood up to do it. And she spat on him. And I remember looking at that man and looking at my aunt Pauline, who was a loving woman. He literally pulled her and pushed her off the bus, and then he called the police on her.

We were taken downtown, and the family was contacted. My father was a schoolteacher. My family knew its place in the South. But Pauline had stepped out of her place. There was a meeting that night, and that same night, Pauline was on the bus out of Birmingham. Because she was not going to be allowed to disrupt the place. And since she was leaving, no one would bother the family because they had gotten rid of the offender.

Of course, a lot of my writings at the very beginning did not identify me as black, did not even involve anything political. But at the same time I was going to the library every day and bringing home books, probably all novels and all smut, one day when I was eleven or twelve, the woman there looked at me and said, "Here, I want you to read this." And she gave me an anthology of what at that time was called Negro poetry. She also gave me the Russian poet Pushkin, so I know this woman was probably someplace left of center. I'll never forget this black woman.

I read this anthology of Negro poetry and came across Sterling Brown, Gwendolyn Brooks, Countee Cullen, and Phillis Wheatley—and I came back and gave her that book and—I really wanted to keep the book, right?— I asked, "Could I take it out again?" And she said something I will never forget. She said, "I thought you wrote poetry." And I jumped because nobody knew I wrote poetry. I don't know what she had seen in me, but she said, "You can keep it out as long as you want to."

Around then I was writing these little poems. We were asked to do an assignment at school about George Washington, so I did this poem about Washington crossing the Delaware, and my sister got ahold of it and came into the kitchen, and read this poem aloud—it was in rhyme, of course. And of course the laughter was not cruel laughter, but from then on I hid my poetry. I hid it under the tub, one of those antique tubs that you pay a lot of money for now?

I cleaned that bathroom every Saturday, so I could hide my stuff under there. When I got up in the middle of the night to go to the bathroom ostensibly, I was really in there writing.

World: You said just before that poets are either a force for change or a force for maintaining the status quo. How do poets today divide up in those terms?
SS: The message writers get is, "If you write something acceptable, I will reward you." I don't blame writers for how they respond to that. There's no part of me that says, "You see? She got that or he got that because. . . ." Not at all. I say, "Very good. I'm glad you got it. You're a poet, and you should get it because I know that process of writing, I know what you do."

But there's another group of poets who say, "I want to write about what is happening to people. I want to challenge the idea that everything's okay in the world." And when you do that, the country says, "No, no, no, no, no."

You know, the first time I got up on stage and talked about the Vietnam War, some people booed me. Now, I could have reacted like a little flower and said, "Oh gosh, isn't this terrible. How could you do this to me?" But I said, "That is a discussion we need to have."

So you push people to come to a level where they should be. Because finally, my brother, we have to begin acting like human beings. We have all the accouterments of being human. But we do things like wars, enslavement, murder, keeping information away from people, not teaching. And some of us have said, "If you do that, you're not really moving like a human being. You need to understand that we are put on this earth to act in humane ways towards each other."

When I started writing, I was sometimes sharp, acerbic. You slap people, and they go, "Wow, I got slapped by you." You say, "Right, and now that I've got your attention, let me tell you. . . ." But you can't keep doing it that way.

At some point you say, "There's another way to do it." Maybe you say something beautiful or something coming from a point of love, and you grab people that way.

World: You've just alluded to something I wanted to get at—the difference between your early and more recent work. Has your work gotten deeper, less didactic, less hard-edged, more generous since your first published poems?
SS: My books have always had a balance. I've always had one poem that went "bang!" But I always had soft ones in the same book. Of course, a lot of critics were thrown by my work. They had never been told, America had never been told, at least in my time, that it was racist. . . .

World: The country had never been told it was racist?
SS: When I began to teach, and I started coming to the Schomburg, then I recognized that Du Bois and all these others had done it. But at the time, we're young poets, we think we're inventing this stuff ourselves.

And most people jumped. They said, "How dare you say that! That's not the case." And then someone would say, "Then you're not a good Negro." And you'd say, "You're right, we're certainly not." In my pieces about Vietnam, in my pieces about being black, in my pieces about drugs in the black community, in pieces about "let us organize and unite," critics were concerned about that content, and they could say simply, "Well, it's not poetic."

But at the same time, there were other poets, beat poets, writing the same way, and no one accused them of being didactic. The beat poets said, "You're a racist, and you're sexist, and you're everything else." Well, they didn't say "sexist," not the beat poets.

Anyway, I've always written love poems, but I thought there were other things that needed to be said out loud—like the poems about what it was to have a father who comes north and is not allowed to teach in the North because they said he was not educated properly and who had these grand ideas about an invention or a product or something and went to the bank with the idea, and the bank wouldn't lend him money—and two years, one year later, I saw his invention out on the market.

What they were saying to a man like my father was, "You cannot be involved with these grand ideas, but you can be involved with women." So I wrote a poem to my father that says if you're a black man in this country, you can be a man via a Cadillac or via women, lots of women, but not via ideas.

World: Isn't that the poem that the poet and critic Haki Madhubuti calls "cold and unforgiving"?
SS: Yeah, but all men would say that. [Laughs].

World: So you don't see any evolution in your work—especially in tone?
SS: I see evolution, but. . . . Let me just take the poem to my father—and many men, when I read this poem, including many who knew my father, have gotten pissed at me. It says,

> how sad it must be
> to love so many women
> to need so many black
> perfumed bodies weeping
> underneath you.
> when i remember all those
> nights
> i filled my mind with
> long wars between short
> sighted trojans & greeks
> while you slapped some
> wide hips about in
> your pvt dungeon,
> when i remember your
> deformity i want to
> do something about your
> makeshift manhood.
> i guess
>   that is why
> on meeting your sixth
> wife, I cross myself
> with her confessionals.

Some men look at that poem and only take the words and not the subtext, or what's between the lines. Between the lines, when I say, "You slapped some wide hips about in your private dungeon," et cetera, it means there's something missing for black men when they're relegated in this country to being only lovers, to being men who only have dicks, not brains. And to say "I cross myself with her confessionals" means simply that I'm also implicated because whatever man I choose might also still be involved with that.

But then, in a later book-length poem called *Does Your House Have Lions?*, I go all the way into my father. The father here is trying to reconcile with his son and, by reconciling with his son, will reconcile with his daughter also. In writing that piece I went back to that earlier poem about my father and thought there was something else happening, so I had to reexamine him and his movement with women, and also his movement with his children.

World: What made you want to reexamine him?
SS: I went back to that earlier poem and saw that I'd written what I wanted to write at that time but saw its limitations, too. And so in the new piece about my father I assumed his voice, and in assuming his voice, I learned who my father was. It's the only way you really do learn who people are—by assuming their voices.

In the poem my father tells us,

> i was a southern Negro man playing music
> married to a high yellow woman who loved my
> unheard
> face, who slept with me in nordic
> beauty, i prisoner since my birth to fear
> i unfashioned buried in a open grave
> of mornings unclapped with constant sight
> of masters fattened decked with my diminished
> light.

Now, my father never talked about my mother in all the years we were growing up. And when I was writing this piece, I asked him why. He said, "Because I lost the only woman I ever loved." And then I understood the progression of women after that. I wrote:

> this love. this first wife of mine, died in
> childbirth
> this face of complex lace exiled her breath
> into another design, and i died became
> wanderlust

demanded recompense from friends for my
heartbreak
cursed the land for this new heartache
put her away with a youthful pause
never called her name again, wrapped my heart in gauze.

And he did. And only then did I understand why he was Romeo-bound.
Because I said, "You became a Romeo of sorts," and he said, "Yeah." So I
wrote,

became romeo bound, applauded women
as I squeezed their syrup, drank their
stenciled
face, passed between their legs, placed my
swollen
shank to the world, became man distilled
early twentieth-century black man fossilled
fulfilled by women things, foreclosing on my
life.
mother where do I go before I arrive?

And if that seems more sympathetic, well, it is, on the level that I'm older, my
father's older.

World: One of the first pieces in *Shake Loose My Skin*, your book of new
and selected poems, is a poem about Malcolm X that you wrote in the
1970s. What did Malcolm mean for you and the other poets you were
working with?
SS: Malcolm articulated all that we thought. For many of us, Baraka and the
rest, he gave us his voice. That's why many of our poems became so angry at
that time—because we picked up on his voice. We said in our poetry what he
was saying from stages or from 125th Street and Lenox Avenue. Or in the
mosque, or at a university, speaking to students, who cheered him—and
those were mostly white students.

Malcolm cut through a lot of crap in this country and put out in the open
what many young people were thinking and didn't know how to articulate.

He became our articulator—and that's for blacks and whites. Because, seeing Malcolm, I for the first time recognized that truth would cut through class and color and gender. Many of the poets who followed him around learned that.

We also learned how to use humor in talking, to lessen the impact, and in our poetry. You know, as an aside, I always wonder what this country would be like if it had allowed Martin, Malcolm, and the Kennedys to live. You do know it would be a different country—and that was why they were all killed. Because there were people who had another vision for this country that wasn't one that spoke to equality.

World: Is what happened to the Kennedys, King, and Malcolm analogous to what happened just recently with the impeachment?
SS: It gets a little muddy here because Clinton is not a liberal. When he says he's a centrist, that's indeed what he is.

World: But he's gone over the line in certain ways.
SS: Well, a centrist can go left or right. And when Clinton did that health plan—probably with influence from his wife and other people—people on the far right went crazy.

But the attack on the president is, I think, a class attack. They could kill the Kennedys, but they would never put the Kennedys' business out in the street the way they're doing now. Because those people loved the idea that the Kennedys were aristocratic, that Roosevelt was aristocratic, that they came from money. But a poor white man, with a single mother, they can trash him in any kind of way.

So it is a class thing. We in this country never want to deal with class. And there's the color thing, too, because he does all the things they think black men do—from playing a musical instrument to liking women to hanging out.

And you and I understand the irony of all those men down there talking about Monica. But they figured if they could keep talking about her, they could change the country's attitude. And this brings me back—I'm coming full circle—to the point that as poets, as activists, we've succeeded on some levels at making people more sophisticated. And there's a core of people, who have come out of the sixties, who remember the antiwar movement, who remember how Reagan, eight years of Reagan, made us go backwards on many levels, from the budget to what's going on with people of color—and even the middle class.

I heard someone on NPR say, "Oh, the people, the people—two years from now, we can make them forget that this ever happened." But when I talk about the impeachment to my classes, they say, "Isn't that a shame?" It's been ingrained in their psyches that maybe Clinton is this and that, but you don't do that to a president.

So I said, "Two years from now, are you gonna vote? Because I teach my classes not for us to be elitist but to apply what we learn to this real world out here. And one way you do that is to vote." I told them, "Toni Morrison, when asked by Charlie Rose, 'Do you vote?' said, 'Oh yes, I do. When I vote, it's like a small prayer by the road because I remember Rosa. I remember Fannie Lou. I remember all those people who were hosed down in order to get the vote.' She said, 'I know I'm voting for limited people, but you don't wipe out the system that you fought for.'"

World: I want to go back one last time to the question of art and politics and ask if you draw a line between the two in your own work, and if so, where you draw it. I'm thinking in particular of the poem "July 4, 1994," from your first Beacon book, *Wounded in the House of a Friend*. The first two sections of the poem are very dense and lyrical, and then in the third part you break into something more prosy and overtly political.

SS: I think you can mix the two kinds of writing. In that part at the end, when I say that we have got to finally stop killing each other, I wanted to say it in just that fashion, in clear words. I read that poem to high school students, and I get a loud reaction when I get to that last part. They listen to the lyricism, but when you get to that last part, you're hitting home with them. And they'll say, "Yeah" or "Why peace, then?" I say, "Because I don't want you to learn geography in Korea or Vietnam, and be buried there."

World: That poem ends with the lines, "It will get better, it will get better"— a hopeful refrain that you use there and in one other poem. And yet you have plenty of other poems that are anything but hopeful, with many depicting wholesale violence, racism, abuse against women, and so on. I'm wondering whether these very different kinds of passages reflect two of your contradictory moods, or whether the different poems just use different personae, or whether you have a belief, a conviction that things really will get better?

SS: I do believe things will get better, but only if you work for it.

World: Is that belief based on evidence or on faith?

SS: It's based on a number of things. Once you begin the movement forward, that dialectic cannot be stopped. You can impede it, you can bring people to power who will stop it for a while, but once the motion begins, history will not go back. It will not be stopped.

World: So it's evidence and faith both?

SS: There's a faith that people are basically good; they're not basically evil, as some philosophers say. And if you can show people the goodness in themselves, they will always rise to the occasion.

For instance, when I first got to Temple University, I would walk into a comp class and there were all whites there. Mostly males. And they went, "Ahh!" I mean literally, like "a black woman's going to come teach me!" So I wrote my name on the board and said, using humor again, "You can sit right by the door, and if you want to leave after a week, I'll sign you out." Well, they stayed. Because what they saw in the classroom is that you were fair, that you treated them as human beings, that you were like every other professor they'd had, and maybe a little more human than others.

We got to know each other, and they opened up. They would write about their parents, who were racists, and I would say, "Well, then go home and beat them up. Teach them. And if you can't teach them, know that you have moved to another level. That you are, on that level, better than they. But it's a conscious effort on your part, to be better than they."

My point is that you can teach. You can teach people to be better than they are. Because we teach racism in this country. This country could wipe out racism tomorrow if it wanted to—you could pay people, give them benefits for not being racist. You could run an ad campaign and eradicate it in a year. Probably less than that. But nobody does it because racism pays.

World: In terms of how our economic system is structured?

SS: Exactly.

World: What about faith in the sense of "religion"? I know you used to go to the AME church with your grandmother and that some of the poems you're writing now invoke African nature deities like Oya and Shango. Do these or any other religious traditions figure into your religious practice or spiritual life today?

SS: I don't consider myself religious in the conventional sense. I think my religion is my work, and my god is the love I express towards people and the country. When I acknowledge in my writing a Jesus or a creator or an Oya or whatever, I'm acknowledging things I know exist out there and are probably one and the same, or they have equal weight for people. But I think you become holy, my brother, when you recognize that you're holy and that this work is the work of holy people—holy men and women who are trying to make every space they enter a holy place where people take responsibility for their actions, where people attempt to learn how to walk upright as human beings.

We all carry the god within ourselves. That was a hard lesson to come to. It was a hard thing to learn.

World: How did you learn it?
SS: I learned it through work, through activism. And through teaching. And understanding finally that there's no one truth out there.

Traveling Conversation: India Dennis-Mahmood Interviews Sonia Sanchez

India Dennis-Mahmood / 1999

From *Feminist Teacher*, vol. 12, no. 3 (July 1999): 198. Reprinted with the permission of Gail E. Cohee, coeditor.

In March 1997, Sonia Sanchez visited Emporia State University in Emporia, Kansas, as part of our activities recognizing Women's History Month. Sanchez, one of the most studied and admired poets of the 1960s Black Arts Movement, is known for her activism as well as her more recent scholarship and numerous volumes of poetry. She is now the Director of the Women's Studies Program at Temple University and the Laura Carnell Professor of English and Women's Studies at Temple. Her involvement with feminism and the social issues revolving around the lives of people of color, together with her experience in academic environments, made her the perfect educator to honor as our guest. In the name of shaking up a few souls, and of providing students with a startlingly honest art experience, Sanchez was also the perfect person to invite into our community in order to remind us all of our connections to a larger world. No one at Emporia State knew Sanchez personally when the invitation for her visit was extended. Students active in the feminist student group on campus, the Women's Programming Board, simply made the invitation and then sponsored Sanchez's visit.

When students are called on to sponsor campus events, they are presented with opportunities for significant campus activism. Because students often extend their educations through their participation in these extracurricular events, particularly by questioning or adding to the new knowledge presented to them in college classes, faculty play an important role in precipitating student interest. Like it or not, as faculty who have decided the specifics about what students will study in their classes, we are also responsible in some sense for the choices they make about their extracurricular studies.

In the particular case of Sanchez's visit, one of the students involved in the Women's Programming Board had been introduced to Sanchez through an African American literature course I had taught. This one student's interest in a feminism that explicitly included women of color, combined with her interest in African American poetry and her introduction to Sanchez in particular, is, in fact, what led to Sanchez's visit.

As a white scholar of African American literature, there are many instances when I feel called to bridge some gap between white and black. Sanchez's visit to our campus was no exception. As is no doubt the case at many midwestern universities, all of the student groups on our campus, unless specifically serving students of color, are predominantly white. Because this is also true of our feminist student group, race is not always a lens through which feminism is addressed. Consequently, an important part of faculty activism is bringing to students the history of feminism, the history of coalition building, and some clear talk about what's at risk when we're not inclusive. If necessary, and I think it almost always is necessary, we must remind our white feminist students to think about race as well as about gender, class, and sexual orientation, even as we let them both falter and triumph as they plan and organize for themselves.

As trusted advisors, we can do a great deal to make sure that visiting feminist speakers are not always white, of course, and we can also push students to form coalitions even when they are not always comfortable doing so. In addition, however, it is important to realize that visits such as Sanchez's to our campus also provide special learning experiences for students of color, which we need to understand and help facilitate. As feminist faculty, we must recognize the unmet needs of our students as we participate in learning environments that are overwhelmingly white. In my own close work and study with black students, particularly black women, the need for the modeling of life by other, older women of color has often been palpable. By recognizing and respecting that need, white feminist faculty members can create opportunities for our students of color to talk with visiting scholars and artists of color in order to gain important perspectives on both their educations and their lives. As home faculty, we can then weave the knowledge these opportunities bring into the larger tapestry of our students' ongoing educational experiences. Just a few such opportunities, in my experience, can make all the difference to individual students.

In educational settings such as that found at Emporia State, with very small numbers of students of color, faculty committed to social justice education have a particular responsibility to those students—not simply because they are the minority, or "super minority" as stated here—but because, as minority, they play an inevitable but often painful role in their classmates' education. We do, of course, have a responsibility to educate the larger student population about issues of race and racism and to allow all of our students opportunities to negotiate the color line and to come to terms with their own ignorance. In doing so, however, we often create awkward and difficult situations for students of color in our classrooms. As a consequence, in many ways, of course, we pay close attention to these students and provide additional support and time to talk. I would also suggest, however, that providing or facilitating special educational opportunities for these peer educators of color is an excellent way to give back, emotionally, to these students what so many day-to-day experiences on our college campuses take away. In other words, providing such opportunities does not constitute preferential treatment; it's simply payback.

The following interview was conducted by India Dennis-Mahmood on the morning following Sanchez's poetry performance. Sanchez's visit, like that of many speakers, was constrained by the limited time she could take from her other responsibilities. Emporia, however, is situated such that the most convenient airport is in Kansas City, a full two hours drive away. At my encouragement and through arrangements made with members of the Women's Programming Board, Natasha Russell, also a black student, drove Sanchez and Dennis-Mahmood to the Kansas City airport while Dennis-Mahmood and Sanchez conducted this interview. The following dialogue, then, took place on Interstate 35 between Emporia, Kansas, and Kansas City, Missouri, on the morning of March 7, 1997, as Sanchez was returning to the airport and a flight back to Philadelphia.

Dennis-Mahmood: Me and Natasha were talking about how on the college level we have some African American students who are trying to try to find their place in society—we were talking about the ones who try to be diplomatic with their ideas and then we were talking about the ones who will be more militant and take on a more defiant role rather than be passive. I was thinking that at my university I don't know which one prevails. Sometimes it seems like we're all just trying to get by—you know that ebonics— "I'm trying to get paid, I'm trying to get mine." I don't know what we should be getting out of our college experience in a small town being the minority, the super minority.

Sanchez: Well, I think you come to a place and you get out of it what you need. If you have one set role that you play it's probably wrong—"wrong" in the sense that like anything else you change often depending on the situation. You don't always respond in the same fashion because then people can always anticipate what you're going to do, what you are and who you are, and that's not the wisest thing, to let people know exactly who you are and how you will respond to any given situation.

Dennis-Mahmood: I was wondering, too, since some of us are ignorant of what goes on around us, how do we try to stay in tune besides the media with what goes on so we'll know what kind of role to play?

Sanchez: The media's not really going to give you all the information: the media is only going to give you the information when it's obliged to do so. I think that you just always have to make sure that you get papers delivered that at some point will try to speak to some issues that exist, to get magazines like the *Nation* that will analyze things that are going on in the world. I think that we become responsible for knowing what goes on in the world and we can't rely on people, even newspapers and magazines, to let us know. I think it's important to tell students that they should always be aware of what goes on. They're not in isolation although they might feel as through they're in isolation in a midwestern or western plains environment and sometimes feeling isolated and/or alienated. I think if you know you're coming someplace for an education and you're going to be here four years, five years, six years, you do it And you organize people around you in such a fashion that you can live here those four, five, six years you're here. And so therefore it doesn't end up being a negative experience. But I think that's what we have to do wherever we are these days: make a home. Wherever you are, wherever you reside you have to make that an area and a place where you survive in the best fashion. And not just say, "Well, I'm here for four years and I don't have to do anything to help me survive." So, I think any place you are you make it the best situation that you're in at this particular point.

Dennis-Mahmood: What about a black consciousness? Are we going to be neutral in the decisions we make or are we going to be conscious of our blackness when we make decisions . . .

Sanchez: Here on this campus, you mean?

Dennis-Mahmood: Yes. What's going to happen to some of us on the campus? Like I said, some of us go into the world willing to sell our souls, but I feel like some of us will develop a consciousness. I don't know if it should be black first and then American or what.

Sanchez: Well, I think that most people don't move out of a vacuum, most people move out of a sense of their heritage. I don't think that any Jews would ever allow you, at school or where you live, to deny that there was a Holocaust or to deny their history. Why? Because they understand when they say "Never Again" what that means. I fully understand what they mean by that Never again on this earth will we allow anyone to make us forget our history, our herstory, our pride, and try to wipe us out. And we always have to move, I think, in the same fashion, remembering our enslavement period. I don't think that's being chauvinistic in any fashion. I just think what it says to people and what it would say to African Americans on the campus and outside of the campus is important. It's like when you "make it" in a sense, you know you have to give back to people who don't make it. And that's what you do because you have so many blacks who do not make it. So therefore, for example, you adopt a school—I've adopted a school in North Philadelphia. You go into the high schools and junior high schools and you make a point to be there. But at the same time I'll go into a friend's school where kids pay lots of money, and do the same kind of thing. I mean you are responsible to everyone to give information about themselves and how to move on this earth in a peaceful fashion, to speak to racial, sexual justice on this earth. But there's nothing wrong with knowing from whence you come. And we African Americans have such a mix of where we've come from.

Dennis-Mahmood: In most of the works you read last night and in your books, I noticed that you are always aware of that history. Should your history come out in your art? Is it very important that your history comes out in your art?

Sanchez: Well, I think our histories come out in how we walk, how we talk, how we look, you know? I mean people look at us and they know who we are before we open our mouths. I think our herstories and histories come out in how we paint, how we write, and the music that we play, if we choose to do it in that fashion. I mean, some people might decide to write a symphony; African Americans have written symphonies. But within the mix there's something that speaks to a history or herstory. We're obliged to do what it is that we think that we need to do. Some people do abstract art and in that abstractness you would think, "Well there's no African American or there's nothing African," but if you look at art that comes from the continent of Africa and you look at abstract pieces you understand that yes, indeed, that is part of your history, because certainly, when you look at some of the sculpture from Africa, it's about as abstract as you can get. So, all that I am saying is that where you're from is nothing that is going to bind you. I am not talking about something that binds you or restricts you or keeps you from exploring the world. All that I am talking about is that if you have a sense of yourself, it allows you to go any place in the world. Do you know what I'm saying? It releases you. You don't mind people knowing that's who you are, that's your herstory or history. You can go and leap mountains if you want to, you know. And you are not going to be limited as to what it is that you do.

Dennis-Mahmood: That's absolutely true. What about if you feel like you have to suppress your history or if you haven't come to terms with your history, does that have an impact on what is considered authentic art, African American art?

Sanchez: Well, I don't think so. I mean, there are artists who have decided that the whole ideal of life is not important in their art. I don't think that it denies the art that they do. I don't think that will deny the fact that you are a black artist, you know. It just means you have chosen, the person has chosen, to do art that does not say to the world that this is my heritage, you see, but I think it is possible to do art that says I am this black woman who paints, draws, sculpts in this fashion. And I think that always your sensibility, your sensitivity comes into it whether there is a specific look about it, that says indeed that represents me. Do you know what I am saying? I mean, someone might decide I will paint only landscapes. You can't say to the person, "Well you can't do that," you know? "Where is the black person on the landscape?" But the point is we know that you are a black woman, a black man, painting landscapes. You have the right to paint landscapes if that's all that you see beautiful in the world. And if you do that, that doesn't deny your blackness, you see. You can't be rigid about that and say, "Well, because he didn't paint an old couple sitting on a chair someplace in the middle of Kansas that it's not black art" Sure, it's your art. You're a black person. That is your art. The point is that you can be very well identified with who you are and go out somewhere and paint what you want to paint, you see. I think that it always comes down to what you feel about yourself.

Dennis-Mahmood: Let me ask you something about the black aesthetic. Can you define what you feel the black aesthetic is?

Sanchez: What many of us attempted to do in the late 1960s was to answer the question because the question was posed. It wasn't even a question, it was a given that there was no such thing as a black aesthetic, that there was only one aesthetic that existed in the world, right? We said, however, "Look at this. I know for a fact that this is a black poem that I've done. It is black because it came from a history or herstory, a sensibility that in some way via the rhythm, via the cadence, via the way that I composed, constructed the words, this actually came out being this black poem." You know what I am saying? And we understood that. And especially if we began to view a portrait or picture in a poem of my grandmother who was this black woman that no one in the world had ever written a poem about, even thought that she had any worth, any reason for being. So if I put her on that paper and put her in a book, I said not only does she have a worth but she is beautiful and the very fact that we said she was beautiful changed the whole idea of this aesthetic. It is part of the definition of aesthetic that something too big is not beautiful, so therefore, if you had a big nose like many of us have a big nose, you couldn't very well be beautiful. Plock in the middle of your face, you see. I mean, what I'm saying simply is that we did something that I think is important to do when you are a so-called minority. And I hate that word, "minority." We are African people in the Americas. We subverted the whole idea that black was terrible. We turned it around and said no, black is beautiful. We weren't saying that because we thought everybody was beautiful. I know I am not "physically beautiful." But what we were saying with the concept of black is beautiful is that we all have some beauty about us, you see, and no longer can we be looked down upon—when people would call you black, you thought, "Oh, my God. We're going to fight." Because it was a dirty name. No longer will we allow the idea that the only thing that is beautiful in this world is white. By the very fact that we said that black is beautiful, it was a given that that meant Asian, Puerto Rican, Native American. All of that became beautiful for the very fact that we said it. What we did is we released people to look up at themselves. That is what all those women writing today are talking about. What they're saying is, "I've been released now to talk about 'I think I am beautiful.'" Because those same feelings we had about ourselves, thinking we were not beautiful, thinking as Maya said years ago in her autobiography, the dreams that people have about wanting to have blue eyes and blond hair have been released. I would wake up one day and lo and behold I would be blond and blue-eyed and beautiful and not this black little girl. Because everyone looked at black children and thought we were not important, not beautiful. And that infiltrated our being as such and made us perform and be less than ourselves and we're saying simply at this particular time the joy of having been on this earth is to subvert the whole idea of the aesthetic to make people who are people of color look at themselves and say, "Look at this, I, too, am beautiful." And that's what I meant about putting the African, period, and the African American back on the world stage. That says, simply, I'm not on the world stage to kick you off the world stage. I am on the world stage as an equal. And let us deal with the world in an equal fashion because before it was in an unequal fashion that we were dealing with it. And that's important for children and young people to see. That you can be on equal footing with anyone on the planet Earth.

Dennis-Mahmood: But you had to really progress and work hard at that because like you said, just being a human being with all our human nature, it's hard to be parallel having come from so far, to stand side-by-side, sharing that stage. Correct?

Sanchez: Well, I think that what you have to do is that you have to have vision at some point and you have to have the vision that it can happen and it will happen. And work at doing that. I mean people don't want to share a stage, don't want to share power. I mean that's what this is all about in this country today. No one wants to share power. And most certainly not to give it to a people who were enslaved once in this country. The idea of saying you were enslaved once, you want to end up being, sharing the power that I have, that I have assumed for all these generations, for all these centuries? And we say yeah, *uh huh.* Because if you look at it, we built the South.

We were indeed carpenters. We were indeed engineers. We built those buildings that people resided in, we built the White House. That was black labor that built that White House. We know how to build, and most certainly we were not helped coming out of our slavery period. No one said okay, now we're going to educate all of you all, because you came out. I mean, we literally, many of us, had to end up building our own schools and educating ourselves to catch up. And look how we did it against great odds. Granted we still have not in courts caught up, but we certainly produced some great minds, some great artists, some great human beings on this earth. Now that's amazing considering that we were never given real help and, if you look at the public schools today, in many cases certainly no help is given at all. Certainly there is an attempt to waste the minds of young people today. And that's what that Tupac poem is all about. On many levels, I read that poem for young people and they respond. What's interesting is whether they're black, white, green, purple, blue. They respond. I consciously did that piece just for the youth, youth meaning people younger than eighteen, nineteen. His appeal cut across genders and color. It's that very distinct young kind of culture. There's a young culture out there that does not even filter down to us sometimes. Unless we consciously reach for it. And when you reach for it, and listen to what they're saying—one of the many things Tupac was saying is that they're killing us. We're not going to survive this. They're not helping us in schools, not helping us stay alive. They're killing us. Look at us, blood. Look at us. Now he had contradictions, he talked in a negative way about women, etc., other times he talks very nasty about his mama, who has survived to raise him. All I'm saying is that we have got to be very much aware also of a youth culture that has surfaced in this country. And that youth culture sometimes is very anti-older people because they're saying, "You are responsible for this stuff, you are responsible for the wars, you are responsible for us not having good schooling, not having all the things that we really need. You're even responsible for us not having housing, for the homelessness that goes on here." And it's very clear. It takes no prisoners. So, it reminds me of myself when I was younger. When we did those early books for Broadside Press we took no prisoners. *Home Coming*; *We a BaddDDD People*; *It's a New Day*. We went whoah, we got you. And we understood that. The reason I was so upset about Tupac dying, his assassination in that sense, is that he was not allowed to grow. If you really understand talent and genius, people really grow. They evolve. And they wouldn't allow him to evolve

because, first of all, to have had such a large audience and to have cut
through different agendas and different colors, different races, means at
some point you're at risk. Bob Marley, same thing. He could cut through
everybody. He was at risk, you see. That's really what happens a lot.

Dennis-Mahmood: This is switching from generations to gender, again.
I know I'm very ignorant when it comes to feminist issues. I was telling
Natasha that on this campus I always feel that there is a separation of race
and gender, but I always say if I had a choice or if I had a choice of actions
to take I would take action first for my race and then my gender because
I always felt that gender would evolve and reach the top of the hierarchy
naturally, but I guess I'm wrong about that?
Sanchez: I don't think it's a point of being wrong about anything. I think
that one of the things that we, that black women, have to understand is that
they've been involved in womanist issues all their lives. Have you seen the
new book edited by Beverly Guy-Sheftall called *Words of Fire: An Anthology
of African-American Feminist Thought?* It shows us how, from the very
beginning, black women have been feminists in America, have been
womanists in America forever. So I don't think that it is anything we have
to really respond to because I think by the very nature of our slavery, by the
very nature of our struggle here, black women struggled always on two levels
from the very beginning. And they were on equal levels: as a woman and as a
person of color. Okay?

Dennis-Mahmood: Okay.
Sanchez: And the problem sometimes with white feminists is that they
exclude the idea of color. And so what you have to do, as a Chair of Women's
Studies one of the things I'm trying to do, is make that understood. That you
can go into a class and you never hear the word color, you never hear the
word—it's like when they talk about women all the time, you know they talk
about white women. And there's a conscious effort there to just bring in
some little thing about black women or women of color, you see. Because of
our herstory here in this country we have always moved in this womanist,
socially conscious, woman-of-color fashion, always with values that spoke to
us surviving in this country, keeping the family together and moving towards
some kind of freedom. It was not moving only as a woman to get some
power or to get part of the action here. We are always moving with a history

behind us that kept pushing us to prevail, to excel, and the herstory was what had happened to us in this country. How we had been perceived in this country. I mean, we have the herstory of the turn of the century when white women were organizing in their different clubs, that they excluded black women. Because we had the history of slavery in our bones, and they knew and understood that that herstory involved rape. And the men had said we had enjoyed that rape, you know, the white men had said that. So a lot of it had to do with those women who were very angry at us because a number of black women on those plantations, part of that herstory in the South, those men really loved, you know, quiet as it was kept, and you read Linda Brent, you read *Jubilee*, you can read any of that literature that speaks to those early years. You understand that white women were just upset with black women on those plantations. They really were very angry at us, so therefore it was a way of paying us back in a sense, by not, those Southern women organizing with the Northern women, by not letting us come in, and they did it under the guise that we were prostitutes, we were whores, we were women of ill repute, you see. In the same fashion white men continued to kill black men under the guise that we were always raping white women, you know. And Ida Wells-Barnett in her classic book, *A Red Record*, said simply that the reason why these men were hanging and killing these black men was usually because they wanted something from them. They wanted the land, they wanted their business, whatever. And it had nothing to do with race, at all. If black men wanted to rape white women so consistently during the Civil War when all those men had left those plantations, going off to war, it would have been a very apropos time to do that, to have done that. And we know that didn't happen. So, what I'm saying is at some point our sensibilities, our sensitivity, our herstory made us approach the whole idea of what it was to be a black woman in a different fashion, in a different sense. And that's why I think Alice talks about being a womanist, as opposed to a feminist.

Dennis-Mahmood: Can I ask you something about equity? In this struggle, what does the black man have to do with it?

Sanchez: I don't think that we separate people in this struggle with each other. I don't see it as a separation although some people probably do. I think that the emotions and your movements have been always to remind, have been always to try to educate people as to what it really means for women to do the work that they needed to have done in order to elevate themselves.

At the same time when they elevated themselves they automatically, I think, elevated everybody else around them. I mean, this is a funny kind of thing, in that you can't mess with the universe without messing with other people. You can't say there is a women's movement, and then not understand that the women's movement doesn't stop other people from progressing, it just makes other things happen at the same time, and it causes people to begin to look at themselves in a more human fashion. Of course you get reactions from some people who say well, those women, those women, those women, but you know they would have said that whether there was a women's movement or not, you see. I don't ever see this as a separate thing, saying what can a man do for this and what can a woman do for this. I think that you choose your battles and you move accordingly. I think you—if you say out loud, I am a womanist or I want to go into women's studies and/or I want to go to a university to learn something and I'm a history major or political science major, the very fact that you are a black woman coming into those departments will change some of the stuff that goes on in there, by the very fact that you are there. Even though you think, I'm not going to say anything, I'm not going to cause any ripples, the very fact that you are placed into that arena causes change. The very fact that you are there. The very fact that you have come into a place, the place, the status quo, the silence, behavior patterns, because you are there people will have to react differently. Am I making sense? It's not always easy to understand. The very fact that when we moved into the university as black professors, it changed the whole climate of the university. No one wanted to admit it. That's why people were so unhappy about it, because they knew that people could no longer in a meeting speak in a negative way about people. People knew because you were on a campus, in classrooms, that a different kind of teaching would come in or would begin. You had invaded an arena that has been for all practical purposes all whiteness before, except for some few black students. And what you did is you changed the cosmos, which is an amazing thing to think about. When people jumped up and said a simple thing like black is beautiful, then the music industry changed. James Brown got up and said, "I'm black and I'm proud." Some singer says, "I'm a winner," "We're moving on up." People began to sing about Vietnam. When we took stands on the Vietnam War and then Marvin Gaye did that classic album still classic today, talking about Vietnam. It is amazing, about war, "mother, mother," talking about war.

People hadn't done albums. Maybe Bob Dylan had gotten up and sung but black folks who are some of the most conservative folk on the planet Earth had not, that's why people got so angry with us because we got up on stage and took a position on the war. If you take a position on what it means to be black in this country and what it means to be human then the natural progression for many of us was to speak out about the war. Because there were more black men going to fight in Vietnam than our population warranted.

Dennis-Mahmood: Is that saying something about us now that we're not as sincere or conservative or that our principles aren't exactly intact like they use to be?

Sanchez: I don't know about that. What I know is that some people will look up and decide that the best way to navigate the terrain that they are in is to be quiet. That is a very dangerous thing to do. Because what we have learned as a people is that being quiet will not save you. And what we should have learned from other people, other cultures, is that being quiet does not save you, or ignoring what goes on does not save you. You certainly have that in modern times so it helps us a great deal. But I think quite often people just assume, well, the best place to navigate any of this is to just go ahead and get my degree, go ahead and be quiet. And I will go ahead and get what I need and get out of town. But I think you have to carry an aura of dignity wherever you are. And to defend yourself doesn't mean you have to scream, jump up and down, and be violent. To defend yourself means you just have to have the information of your herstory or history and then when people try to exploit you or try to deny your humanity that you have to speak to it, that's all. Everyone has to defend him/herself at some particular point in life. And the most important thing that you have to have is information then as to how to do that. How to speak to our humanity in the midst of other people. How do I bring myself into a group of people and they always know that I come in, in a dignified fashion, in a humane fashion, that I bring my herstory with me not to damn them but because it is part of my herstory. Just as when people walk into a meeting with you, they bring their history or herstory with them, too. And you recognize it automatically, but it is not to mess with you, it's just because that's who they are. We have to learn how to make our herstory ordinary. Just everyday. And that comes, I think, with study, that comes with working at it, that comes with feeling

comfortable wherever you are wherever you go. And it also comes with
feeling as if you are an equal. Many people don't feel as if they are equal.

Dennis-Mahmood: I find that although I feel educated in the background,
I feel defensive when I am offended. I sat through class a couple of
times and I have had some feelings that just ate me up and they came
out of nowhere. I never anticipated I would get upset. I said I would
stay cool and calm, but it's like either way you go, you feel some type of
rebellion.

Sanchez: I don't think it's rebellion. It's just that people say things in the
classroom that are incorrect or insensitive. I think that there is a way that we
can say it without jumping up saying, "How dare you say what you just said."
I mean unless it is out-and-out racist then you sometimes have to say that,
too. But when people say things that is opinion that riles you, that upsets
you, you can say, "I'm really offended by that statement and let me tell you
why I am. Suppose if I was to say the following about—blup, blup, blup." It is
some way to bring it back home. And then you bring it to people's attention.
Just to say, "I'll tell you why I am offended because in my culture and this and
that, whatever." You give the information. Some people say it on purpose,
some want to see how you would respond, if you respond or if you don't
respond, what they can get away with. Or maybe this is what people have
been saying for years and years and no one ever complained before so why
should you complain? Well, you complain because you are a human being
and you must, I think, keep it on a human level. You try to keep it on a
human level.

Dennis-Mahmood: Here I'm in a fine arts class. I notice that white students
never want to give us credit for anything in arts or throughout history,
period. I notice how receptive they are to any other section of diversity
whether Native American or Jewish. But believe it or not when we hit the
African American topics they have this primitive attitude. Sometimes I don't
really know how to respond.

Sanchez: I think the only way you can get around that is to always have,
wherever you are in your arena, that history with you. I have African art
up in my office. They say that looks familiar, and you say yeah, that's whatever it is. And then right away you don't say another word because it hits
them. That every bit of modern art that has come down to this time has

come from that kind of herstory/history. It's amazing. And they look
and see it, and they are startled because they don't know about it. They
haven't seen it in all its stark beauty. On many levels, it is so much easier to
relegate our art to what we call primitive art. Or it's so much easier to
relegate our form to being always oral form. It's not anything that you
really want to read, that you want to hear someone recite. I learned how to
read my poetry well because Louise Bogan, a white woman who taught at
NYU and read her poetry well, said in order for people to truly understand
your work you must learn how to be a good reader of poetry. And you must
read poetry aloud, yours, other people's, aloud. That was real, that was not
make believe. So I've done that, I've learned how to read it well. But that
doesn't make me an "oral" poet. They want to relegate you. When Allen
Ginsberg reads his poetry aloud, and he has learned how to read it well from
listening to Baraka and other people who have read their poetry well, when
he chants, whatever, in his poetry no one says, "Well, he's an oral poet."
I experiment a great deal, I mean one of the great joys about thinking you
write well is that you, I, experiment and so the last poem I did on stage
was an experimental poem. I knew it was. I know it is. I know it's hard.
But I tell my students in class, you can experiment with any thing you want
to do if you know your form. So I decided to experiment with a poem
that would use few words and sounds. I mean, just like Coltrane took
"My Favorite Thing" in a melody and went out with it. I mean, you have a
right if you think you're good to do what you damn well please. And that's
what I try to do.

Dennis-Mahmood: I was thinking about the ancestors that you were
speaking of. You build that persona and make it such distinguished dialogue
and are good at it because you are wonderful.
Sanchez: But that's because you learn.

Dennis-Mahmood: Yeah, and some people can't see that.
Sanchez: They don't want to see it, they always want to limit you to where
you are, and I say that's fine but I always let them understand that once they
do that they limit themselves, you see? And the joy about art is that I turn
around and say, well you'll be left behind because I don't limit myself. I go on
to do what I have got to do. And it's tragic that some whites and blacks in this
country still limit themselves.

Dennis-Mahmood: The last poem you did was of a slave woman?
Sanchez: That was the Middle Passage, right. That's called "Middle Passage."
It's very obvious what I was trying to say. From the very beginning the
person speaking is trying to make people understand the psychic costs of
that containment, you know? It's very obvious some of the economic costs,
but a lot of people went crazy during that period. And then went crazy and
became sane, produced sane children, produced sane people, you know
what I'm saying?

Dennis-Mahmood: No choice.
Sanchez: Yeah, right. People never think about that part—they didn't even
give us the credit to even go crazy. Ultimately the portrayal of the black
woman in slavery is that she enjoyed all that happened to her and that she
was a nice mammy, that she was a willing contributor to her own demise or
her own exploitation. And the whole point of that piece is to—you know
that there's something wrong whether she's saying it was the travel that was
bad, it was the journey that was bad, it was the oh no, it was the crossing
that was, oh no, no, no, no, it was the raping that was bad, it was—and in
trying to place where it was she gives a litany and you understand that it's all
of that. It was a combination of all of that, you see. And that's what that is
about, not just one thing, it was not just the raping, not just the crossing, not
just this but all of that and then I wanted people to get into her mind. In the
midst of her even saying things one, two, three, it was madness behind it.
You know, and then at the same time it's a strange kind of sanity because she
survived. In the midst of that. And that's how close madness is to sanity, I
mean there's not much difference sometimes between the two. And it is that
reality that was there that I wanted people to hear, because on the one hand,
you know, things seemed okay but that little thing could just break her and
make her not be okay. So it's all of that, that was there. I mean, for a woman
to give birth to twenty-one children like a machine and then at the age of
twenty-nine want to die . . . at the age of twenty-eight, twenty-nine, thirty,
just want to be taken off the planet earth because the body is tired, the body
is hemorrhaging, the body is saying I cannot do this anymore. I wanted all
that, you know, to say every nine months, every nine months, every nine
months and just repeat it. Sometimes repetition can be a pleasant thing, but
repetition can be an unpleasant thing also. And so it's all of that—the way I
place the words on the page is the way that I said it, it was the way that I try

to read sanity/insanity together. The first time I read that piece I sobbed on stage. I had not realized—I had written it, and I had talked it through as I wrote it, and all of that, right? And then I performed it for the first time. I sobbed, I broke down because I could hear the voices, forever. And depending on how I am I never read it the same, any time I do it. And there is this weaving back and forth and I can hear the gathering sob sometimes and sometimes I get through it, but then sometimes, depending on the conditions of the world, you just hear them crying, or hear her crying and it just surfaces and you know it's really more than you bear. Like the poem to Cosby. I read it about a month ago at the time that Ennis had been killed and I broke down. I literally broke down because it just seemed so ironic that I was doing that thing about violence. Trying to tell people not to be violent and Ennis was dead from violence.

Dennis-Mahmood: I really like "Just Don't Never Give Up on Love."
Sanchez: I like that piece, too. That woman, I really met her. Literally recorded in my head some of the things that she said. She had been married fives times. But it didn't work for me to put five times in the piece. But the first husband was a man who drove her crazy because he was so pretty. That's what she said. And the second man was her true love, she said. But he was killed when he was outside working. And the third man died of high blood pressure. The fourth died of a heart attack. And she was married to this guy, this man who was ninety-six years of age, but who didn't like to come outside in the park the way she did, he liked to stay home and watch all the programs on TV. So I said to her, I am going to write about you because I find this stuff an amazing story. She said. "Um-hmmm. Okay." She didn't believe it you know.

Dennis-Mahmood: I should give you some peace now, shouldn't I?
Sanchez: Okay, I appreciate that.

Sonia Sanchez Speaks

Cheo Tyehimba / 2000

From whatchusay.com. <http://www.whatchusay.com/archives/2005/01/
sonia_sanchez_s_1.html>. Originally published Dec. 3, 2000, for The Black
World Today.com. Reprinted with the permission of the author.

Sonia Sanchez, one of our nation's most under-appreciated poets, decodes
race and presidential politics, uncovers pieces of socialism in our capitalism,
and champions change for self and country.

From the metaphor makers of the Black Arts Movement to the lyricists
of today's Slam Nation, generations of poets have been influenced by the
deeply passionate and political word iconography of Sonia Sanchez. She
has been awarded numerous prizes for her work, such as the 1985 American
Book Award for Poetry for her book, *Homegirls and Handgrenades*. She is
currently a tenured professor of English and women's studies at Temple
University and her work is currently being cataloged by the Schomburg
Center for Research of Black Culture in New York. At sixty-five, she is
busier than ever, teaching, lecturing, and completing various manuscripts.

Q. Do you remember the very first poem you wrote?
A. I was a little girl. I wrote a poem to a terrible little boy named Walter who
cut off one of my braids. I really began writing a lot of poetry after my
grandmother died; when I was about six. I loved "Mama" and so therefore
this death completely threw me a great deal and so I started writing. One of
my first poems that was published was to her. To this grandmother who
loved me very much and protected me and in a very real sense. She raised me
until I was six.

Q. When was the first time you knew your poetry had the power to change
lives, that it was indeed political?
A. There are a couple of periods. When I was in New York working with
CORE (Congress of Racial Equality), the four little girls were murdered in

that Birmingham (Alabama) church, I went to the church with a poem.
I don't have that poem to this day because I just put it up on the bulletin
board for people to read and somebody picked it up and left with it. But
I realized then how communal our poetry is. The other thing is the poetry
that I began to write after the killing of Malcolm X. We took up his mantle
because [Amiri] Baraka sent letters to all the writers, artists, and musicians
in the city to come join with him to begin the Black Arts Repertory Theater
in New York City.

Q. What party are you registered with?
A. I used to be independent but I registered democrat here in Philadelphia
because of the politics of the city and being able to vote in the primaries.

Q. If the current election fiasco is a barometer of things to come, we've got
serious work to do as we continue to navigate what many perceive as a white
supremacist capitalist patriarchy (to borrow bell hooks's well-worn phrase)
that predetermines not only elections but seemingly our very fates.
A. Within capitalism there is some socialism. No one calls it that. And
what you do is try to work toward a system that will respond more to the
needs of the people. And you push it through any system that you happen
to be involved in. But you're not going to get people to change, like 1-2-3,
especially if you put names on it and give it tags. I teach a lot of stuff,
I never give it names. If someone asks me, I might say oh yeah, I guess you
could call it that, but I don't. I call it the best method for people to live
and survive.

Q. Despite the fact that Gore has been an elected official since 1976
and is probably better qualified to be president than Bush (who wasn't
elected to his first office until 1994), Bush may very well be our
forty-third president. Which candidate do you think is more prepared
to lead?
A. Gore, only because he is going to put people on the Supreme Court.
People are coming off the bench, they're dying. And the reason we've
had such a turn around of laws is because they put Clarence Thomas
on the court. I was one of the people who stood up publicly against
Clarence Thomas. Gore, in my head, if we make him accountable,
might help.

Q. Your thoughts on America's democratic process and its inherent contradictions?

A. On many levels, it really doesn't [matter] who is president because it is almost like the Queen of England, it's a ceremonial position. I think the last president who really had any power was Roosevelt and the ones who think they do have power get assassinated in this country. For instance Toni Morrison was once asked "Do you vote?" and she said yes, because I remember all those brothers and sisters, all those men and women who fought to get the vote. She said, "When I vote it's like a small prayer out by the road." Unfortunately, it's a shame by the time you get the bloody thing [the vote] the process has really become corrupted. But the point is what you take within you about the idea of what is good about voting. Democracy is not here; we must bring it into existence. So you carry the idea, you carry this prayer with you into a booth that some day we will make this process work. I used to say in the sixties that if we didn't write love poems, if we did ever get free we wouldn't know how to love. You got to practice it anyway. So we have to practice voting until at some point we're practicing at the highest level.

Q. At a debate at the Apollo Theater during the presidential primaries, Al Gore and Bill Bradley seemed to do a kind of political minstrel show. It was a "Am I Black Enough For You" contest where sound-bites and campaign promises were pitched to placate black fears. The serio-comic tone of the debate, the lore and sensibility of its very location, somehow just felt wrong. What's wrong with campaign politics?

A. There are several people who involve themselves in the whole democratic process who I call political "socialites." You promise me something, I promise you something back; you give me a job, fine, I'll vote for you. They really aren't carrying the message of the people to the platform. This is about personal aggrandizement. Sometimes it's about "let us now have fun so the people cannot be annoyed." I think we have to be very honest about the issues. We have to challenge any candidate to say specifically what they mean. But better than that you have to have your own national program. You don't come to people asking for promises, you come saying, "This is what we demand."

Q. In a recent CBS/*New York Times* national poll, 33 percent of Americans agreed with the statement, "It makes no real difference who is elected president, things will go on as they did before. "The same poll was conducted twenty years ago and only 19 percent agreed with this statement. Is activism in this country dying a slow death in America?

A. No, it is not. It's just not being publicized. It is being downplayed and being replaced with hostility and anger and cynicism. They will write about the cynics of the world but not necessarily about the activists of the world. They will give you programs that make progressives' ideas the butt of humor. They will use the word "revolution" to sell cat food and toilet-stuff. It disempowers by co-opting, co-optation of everything that speaks to humanity. We need to teach and empower people at the same time.

Q. These are the greatest times in the history of the American economy and there is still debate over what to do with the so-called budget surplus. What would you use the money for?

A. I would certainly use it for education but I would not just throw it at the states. I would support someone like Congressman Chaka Fattah (D-PA), who has put in the same legislation than [Adam] Clayton Powell used to put in, trying to make sure that the schools in different states get the same amount of funding . . . For example a school in a [suburban] city here in Pennsylvania is getting about $14,000 while a school here in Philadelphia is getting only $7,000. That kind of disparity is wrong . . . There's no problem with Social Security. We all pay money into it and it gains interest over the years. If y'all would just stop taking that money and fighting secret wars, people would have money to retire on.

Q. Many believe that race is declining in significance in this country; that it's a political/social construct that is finally taking a backseat to class issues. Will America ever be a race-neutral society?

A. I don't know if America will ever be a race-neutral society. But I certainly think that if we keep talking and having a dialogue that we can make people understand that the issues of race, class, and gender are equal issues that should be addressed and that none take precedence over the other. They are all interconnected to each other but sometimes what this country does is it will take class or gender over race or it will say to a whole generation that there is no race problem at all. We have to learn how to talk about these things in a very passionate and dispassionate way, an intellectual way and an emotional way.

Q. America's racial sea changes continues to baffle and bamboozle. African American culture has been reduced to a single, race-neutral, marketing term: "urban" which is really license to exploit African American culture. But of course, this is nothing new.

A. Anytime we've had anything going on for us, especially in music and the arts you've always had the co-optation of it. The Beatles did it. Elvis did it. But they could bring you [only] the surface pain of the blues, you know? We make them icons and they make a lot of money and yet they can't feel the real pain of these people who have been living the blues forever in this place called America.

Q. "I been keeping company with the lay away man each time he come by we do it on the installment plan." This blues riff is a line from your collection of poems, *Wounded in the House of a Friend*. Today, a new play on an old riff is what I call the "Little Kim Generation," a kind of ultra-consumerist, hip hop-derived, sex-based "feminism" where some women use their bodies or material possessions for empowerment in the same way men have. Things have shifted a bit in what is socially acceptable, but how much has really changed?

A. I don't think that it is possible to use your body to empower the soul. We might use the body to get the material stuff that we want and we think that will make us empowered. But that's nothing new. I've seen it in universities, young [women] say, "Well since I was treated this way, I'm going to be just like men and go through men the way they go through women." The premise is trying to get back at people for being treated a certain way. But it's not a human response to people. It's difficult as it is just being human on this earth, the world, the country conspires to make us less than human. The way to go is not to try to hurt or bad-mouth people. You can't get empowered that way and you'll just have a very tired body by the time you get any money. True empowerment happens when you learn how to navigate and organize within yourself and within this world.

Q. As an educator, what is your philosophy or process?

A. I've been teaching for thirty years. I first started teaching at San Francisco State in the English department. One day two FBI agents came to my house and told my landlord that they should put me out. One of the FBI men put his hand in my face and said I was one of those radicals up on the campus and that the landlord should put me out. He said, "You're teaching 'Du Bois'" (pronounces it the French way). I stopped in my tracks at the door. Yes, I was teaching Du Bois, Robeson, The Chairman, and Garvey. But I was teaching literature. So I responded, "But I'm just teaching literature." And it hit me. I was teaching sociology, economics, the culture of a people. See, they understood that better than I did. That I was teaching a history and herstory of a people, of a movement, of what was going on in the world. They understood the books I'd chosen. This country had conspired to keep Du Bois dead in this country. No one studied Du Bois. No one studied Garvey. No one studied Robeson. Those people were all white-balled in this country and by resurrecting these people, they looked at you as a problem. But I didn't understand that until they came to my house. It changed my whole way of teaching literature. I approached it with the history, the sociology, the economics, and the politics of it. And I thank those two FBI agents for showing me how.

Q. What have you learned about successfully navigating through change?
A. I think constantly being honest with yourself and constantly remaining on a quest to learn. I've changed myself, and I know if I can change, anyone can. I am not a revisionist. The first time I heard Malcolm I ducked. I had to learn then what he was saying and listen to him. When people talked about gay people years ago, I laughed like everybody else, right? And then I looked up, and my brother was gay, and I grabbed his hand and loved him. My students were gay, I grabbed their hands and loved them and respected them, OK. Hear what I'm saying? I know change is possible and I know the country can change but I think we need consistent work to do that. But some of us get tired and beat up. If they know you're honest, this country will beat you up, starve you out, and tire you out. Then they say, oh, what happened to her? Or what happened to him? So I think at some point we need places for people to rest, to renew, to regroup, to come out to continue the battle. Someone once said I was an eternal optimist, and I said I am a scientist in that I know that once you initiate change it cannot be stopped. The law of physics tells you that when something starts in motion it will never stop. We have started the motion towards change in this country and it can never be stopped. Dr. King said that the earth is tilted towards justice and it is. It is.

Poetics and Politics: A Special Encounter with Sonia Sanchez

Claude Julien, Cécile Coquet, and Arlette Frund / 2001

From *BMa: The Sonia Sanchez Literary Review*, vol. 9, no. 2 (Spring 2004): i–9. Reprinted with the permission of Frenzella E. DeLancey, editor.

In June 2001, the group of African American scholars at the University of Tours in collaboration with the CEAA (Cercle d'Études Afro-Américaines whose president is Michel Fabre) invited and welcomed Sonia Sanchez for a one-day symposium: "Poetry and politics: Sonia Sanchez's works." The event took place in the aftermath of an international conference that was organized by Professor Claudine Raynaud and held in Tours on "(Re) Writing History: Incidence(s) of the Event: African American History and Culture in the Aftermath of the Civil Rights Movement." To address the question of the place of the event in her works and her action in the events of the time, Sonia had been invited but, unfortunately, was not available at the date of the meeting. Her presence in Tours, a few months later, gave that project a notable development and produced a creative and intellectual space within which the relationships between historical records and instants of personal life-times were researched and talked about.

By combining the roles of political activist, scholar, and witness, from her participation in the Civil Rights and Black Power movements to her involvement in the political and cultural domains, Sonia Sanchez expresses the continuities and discontinuities of history and liberates an experience which is activated through connections and relations of knowledge and desire across borders and boundaries. As Paul Ricoeur defines the event as what is given evidence of and is emblematic of past occurrences, then Sonia Sanchez's words and works speak, in the forcefulness of their often omitted testimonies, to the singular modes of being in the world as well as to the communal aspects and links upon which is based the history of political societies. By testifying to the particular and the collective, she creates a language that opens up a new sphere with its emotions, understandings, and imagery, the possibility of a historical event with its own temporality enunciated in unpredictable places and times, to be discovered in the violent, disjunctive, or metaphorical outbursts of reality. During the question-answer session, Sonia Sanchez insisted on giving students a detailed and personal account of historical or sociological facts to show their intensity and impact in the construction of history. Then the reading of her poems illustrated and enlightened life forms that existed in and for themselves as well as in the greater design of cultural and political reality and desired infinity.

The relationship to oneself and the other is a common feature of all the articles presented in Tours in honor to Sonia Sanchez. Given her involvement in the events of the 1960s, the topic of the conference had been defined with the purpose of drawing links and connections between art and politics in order to analyze the place and the role of the artist in the public sphere and the critical space of poetics in politics. At times of major and global transformations in modern societies, it is highly relevant to question the authority of literary forms and the future of their practices in the negotiation and translation of a political aesthetics. In an interview to the magazine *Terrain* in June of 2003, Edouard Glissant, asked to define the relationship between poetry and politics, suggests that poetry is not political, that is to say the two elements of the relationship cannot be engaged in mutual conditions of dependency or freedom since they constitute an inclusive and intimate wholeness. ". . . il n'y avait pas de poésie qui ne soit politique et qu'il n' existe pas de poésie politique en soi." He considers that the noblest referent in poetry is the world figured in the varieties of its temporality, and as a place of encounters, conflicts, and transformations: ". . . l'objet le plus haut de la poésie était le monde: le monde en devenir, le monde tel qu'il nous bouscule, le monde tel que nous voulons y entrer." The definition of poetics as the understanding and creation of human beings in their relationships to themselves and others provides a valuable and critical starting point to qualify the work of Sonia Sanchez as it was expressed by herself and researched by the authors of the essays in this number. Participants speak from multiple perspectives when analyzing Sanchez's poetry (Paola Boi, Françoise Clary, Ugo Rubeo, and Arlette Frund) or theater (Geneviève Fabre). Their collaborative visions oversee the production of a space dedicated to the celebration of life in the poetical writings of Sonia Sanchez.

Claude Julien, professor of American studies at the University of Tours, reminds Sonia Sanchez of their meeting at a poetry conference in Martinique, and welcomes her in Tours. He introduces the main theme of the conference: "Poetry and politics," and gives the floor to Cécile Coquet, assistant professor at Tours, for the first question.

Cécile Coquet: Sonia, thank you for coming to Tours to be with us. I wanted you to know that some of my students who are here today are very moved and almost ecstatic to see a figure of the Civil Rights Movement and the Black Arts Movement in "flesh and bone" as we say. We have heard this morning that you once described your artistic project in terms of black rhetoric, which is to be understood in its revolutionary meaning. I would like to know if you would say that such poems as for instance "there are blk/puritans" have a revolutionary connection with the rhetoric of the Black Panthers? Perhaps you might want to read that poem . . . (Sonia Sanchez reads the poem) Thanks.

Sonia Sanchez: I think that we always have to look and see what happens in America at the same time and how some of the groups came about in the USA. I think ideas of some of us as we talked were ideas that had been discussed in groups, actually in such organizations as CORE as to what position we will take on America, on the economics of America, on the participation of whites in the organization, on the participation of Malcolm in the Civil Rights organization. There were all kinds of things happening. So many of the poems we wrote were not necessarily reactions to the Black Panthers. The interesting thing is that the organization and even some of the critics we came in contact with took what we were saying and used it. The interesting thing is that you don't copyright ideas, at least I don't think you should copyright. It is a good thing you can't copyright ideas or lines or titles. What really happened at some point is that you saw many of the discussions that we had become manifestos in organizations. Many of the ideas we talked about were actually put into practice by organizations such as the Black Panthers, the Nation of Islam. But I had begun that discussion in the sixties about not only our place in America, not only our place in the economic sphere of America but also how we were going to see ourselves as we moved and what was the role of the people that we knew in that particular movement. So many of us sent poems to the Panthers' papers and we did not only demonstrations but we did readings with the Black Panther Party in San Francisco until Eldridge

Cleaver came on the scene and took position on the poets and the artists, that is to say he said we were "cultural nationalist."

As a teacher, I came across some of the young women who were being malused by the Black Panther Party: they were like used as whores under the guise of revolution, and I did a long poem about that. Some middle-class blacks in San Francisco, who did not identify with any of the things that were going on out at San Francisco State or the times, actually invited me "to a discussion." Their children were there, and the women were certainly concerned about them. These middle-class mothers wanted to know if I would allow my children to join the Black Panther Party, and I said probably at that time if my sons were older I probably might not be able to keep them from joining the Black Panther Party because on paper it looked good. However, I said if I had had a daughter right here at that time at that age, I would do everything to keep her from being in a Black Panther Party because they have no understanding of what women are about. I went on record saying that. I was talking in an interview not long ago and I said how crazy we were at some point you know, or how fearless we were. Three Panther men came to see me over at San Francisco State about what I had said and I got up in their face and I said yes I did. However we were not allowed to participate anymore, and Emory who had done the first cover on my book *Home Coming* was not allowed officially to do the cover of the second book. He was not allowed because I had taken a position "against the party" whereas I had taken a position against some of the party's practices; it is important to differentiate between one or the other. That is not what this movement was about. I took a very unpopular position, but it was a fascinating time with all kinds of contradictions. That poem mirrors in a sense and anticipates some of the ideas of many of the people who are alive. I want to say also that it was the beginning part of the party, but when you had people like Shakur and other people later on in New York, the New York Tens when they were up for trial, you found that they had an understanding of activists and writers, and many of us gathered together to make sure that Angela was free, make sure that the Panthers were free, and also we began to write about what was happening here. No one had a real clue how the government had decided to destroy these organizations, that is why with the young hip hop people today, when they had this whole thing that resolved in probably the death of Pac and Biggie, we were saying aloud to them this was a repeat of the Panther, the discussion between the East Coast Panther and the West Coast Panther is the same dialogue that went on in a sense. That is a very long answer to your question. But since you are students, I'm trying to give you a history. Sometimes people come with strange answers with no herstory or no history to it. And to me it does not make sense.

Arlette Frund: I have a question from James Emanuel who couldn't be here today. I'll read the question: "Could you pretend that I am in your audience on my birthday and that I raise my hand and ask: 'Professor Sanchez, could you tell us whether you think there is an African American blacklist functioning?' If you cannot do this comfortably, do not try."

Sonia Sanchez: Oh! James. There are two questions there in the sense who is doing this: is there an African American "blacklist" that means they don't include certain blacks or is there a black list against African Americans in America, I am not sure which one, so I'll answer both. I don't know if there is a black list as much as there is a white list. There has always been a way of boycotting ideas, we saw it happen with Du Bois and Robeson in concrete terms, and we did not recognize that fact until we began to resurrect them in the curriculum, in universities and you saw how solid people had become. For my first book *Home Coming*, a woman was cleaning in the Library where they had a meeting as to what books they should buy for the library in New York City, and they gave a list of books and they said we cannot have *Home Coming*: it is too graphic, it is cursing and this and that. She literally came up, called somebody who called somebody, and I picked up the phone and said: "Hi!" They said they had a message from this person, that person. I called the library and asked to the person in charge of acquisition if it was true that they had decided not to buy a book by Sonia Sanchez. I said I got that information from a reliable source, and they turned around and bought the book. You have to go ahead. Gwendolyn Brooks tells the story of how they banned "We Real Cool." Maya talks about that, Toni Morrison talks about that. You have to ask the question why they would ban the following books whereas it has been proved that these people are writing classics. Yes, there have been lists from the very beginning but you need to confront these people, you need to speak on these issues.

People get into the studies program I teach, and they say: "We cannot come to your class because you teach women writers who constantly attack black men and gay and lesbians," all that kind of stuff, and when they walk into the class they were told not to take, I welcome them and tell them they are going to see some real human beings. This country has done that but we have had people who picked it, who picked the American system all the way back. If you understand truly, in the eighteenth century what they were saying is that there is a small group already running things, and it is not freedom for all of us they are talking about. We understand too that, from the very beginning, the so-called riots or disturbances that they had in America came with black and white folks, and had to do about work and oppression, whatever, and this country controls people. The whole idea of color entered America in a very interesting, strange fashion because people can be poor but they have that white skin. Really? Half America is passing, so you might not be too secure in that, and you're still poor. I would tell James, well, he knows, that many writers who had been talking about change have been on that very subtle list where you are not invited places because we don't want to hear that voice, that voice they say is disruptive and I say if you are so bloody secure in who you are, so what? Then listen to the disruption and see. But the great thing about teaching students is that energy that comes out of the university and outside of the university and it has kept me alive and propelled me to understand that you must constantly talk about that which many people don't want to talk about and will not discuss.

Question: Could you tell us more about your idea of survival, a major theme in your works?

Sonia Sanchez: My idea of survival, as I said earlier this morning, when you have not been told about your history or herstory the first time you come out to that race, is simply you've got blinders on; I've just been told we had been enslaved, I didn't know it, so you don't look this way. Let me tell now what it means to be black, let me tell you now what this has meant to us, let me tell you now how we must survive, let me tell you some history, some herstory, and that was what it was about. The first, second, third, and fourth books were all directed toward that, because you had to say to people, who did not believe it, that they were human. Contrary to what America says, in the midst of directing some of this poetry in that way, there were other poems that went other places too, there was always an audience to welcome Baraka, Larry, Miss Brooks, Sterling Brown, all of us we all had, Langston before, we all had an audience that was white. People never want to come up and say that, and there were always students who came and said OK. Contrary to what people want to believe, Malcolm's audience in the universities was all white, there were few blacks in the universities, and those white kids sat there because they knew he was saying something that people had buried forever and ever, and he was disrupting and unhearsing some certain truth. When I saw that happen, I sat back and looked and my head cracked, and they are saying fashion. Once a student said: "Your poetry saved my life," and this is a white female and I looked and I said: "I know, it saved mine too." You understand the connection that went on, so all the specific things about survival, by extension it was survival of other people too. They had to understand that. When I read other poets, when I read Yeats, I know what he is talking about, it speaks to me, but I am not Irish and I don't have to be Irish. You've got to hear that, that is why poetry is such a great genre because it cuts through class, color, gender. If you open your ears, you'll know and learn how to live, you'll see beauty, sometimes it will be horrific but, at the same time, it will be this beauty. So, at some point, you can't keep writing about the same things, I tried to tell it to my students. How are you responsible for your life now? How are you living? I am not saying that someone will not disrupt your life, I will allow that piece to say this is disruption, but this is not a class where you are going to be a victim forever. I don't allow victims so what are you going to do about it? How are you going to say in a different way? How are you going to look up at people and say simply. I said this morning, when I went searching for myself, I found others. I found Japanese Americans in concentration camps, it was homicide. I went looking for myself and I found Jews in concentration camps. You cannot let anyone be wiped out and feel you are safe, none of us is safe when someone does that. Then I turned around and saw Puerto Ricans who were not being taught Spanish because their parents wanted them to be good Americans. You have to speak about that. I saw Chinese building railroads in the Midwest. These are world issues you talked about on stage, you integrate in your poetry, you widen and, still, I am black woman talking about the world issues, and I intend to be included in those world issues; you are talking about peace that's my peace. Poets and some of the black poets talked about the Vietnam War; in my book *Home Coming* I have a piece about there were more black men fighting in Vietnam than our population warranted. In the midst of reading that poem once, a black doctor stood up and thanked me for that poem: because the black men were the point men, which meant they got killed first, he said to his lieutenant if he continues to make black men point men, he'll make sure that anyone who comes with a wound dies. That is a hard line. Just in the same way people got turned off by Toni Morrison's character who says: "I will kill that child to keep this child from being enslaved." But if you go back to primary sources, you learn that, on some plantations, when black women were giving birth, they bought doctors because those women were taking the babies up and crashing their skulls: "You will not be a slave," so Toni's novel was not contrary to what people did.

In *A Blues Book for Blue Black Magical Women*, I was refuting the whole idea of death and I was trying to bring life. I was saying simply that life is that metaphor and life should be a metaphor for all people, not death. If we begin to make life a metaphor, then we understand that for human beings, at some point, we will move the world ahead towards life as opposed to death. I kept refuting it, bringing memory in, and saying, using *The Book of the Dead*, "this is life" using Black English at the beginning, and then consciously moving on using visionary things, things I saw at some point, and, always, this idea of success, not death, life, promise, and finally womankind, mankind, personkind. There is a possibility that humans can populate the earth in a real sense, in a very important sense. My work changed, in *I've Been a Woman*, you could see the change. In *Homegirls and Handgrenades* I celebrate Norma, I talk about South Africa at the same time I talk about Atlanta and the murders, let me show the connections here, let me talk about Nicaragua at the same time I talked about Cuba and you have to make those connections. One went from there to *Wounded in the House of a Friend*, this is from the Bible. In that piece, I talked about personal wounds, private wounds, wounds that come from a country, from a people. We realize we are coming into a century where we are wounded in the house of our friends, our families, our tribes, our nations, we are killing each other and this is a very dangerous time. I maintain that poets always start jumping out there first. You got to alert people and say you can't let happen, you must be aware. We are the voices of peace, we are the brave fearless voices that say you cannot do that; it is so much easier to fight than sit in a room for months and figure out peace. It is important for teachers to know that, when you walk into a room and give assignments, there are other assignments that you give at the same time. Assignment that will make students better human beings at the same time that they are writing sonnets and villanelles and blank verse at the same time. Assignment that teaches how to untwist the tongues of hatred in the world. That is what I am talking about here and that is a hard assignment, because I found earlier in my life easier to talk about people. The bottom line is that we always look for something wrong, no, we should look for what is good in people, we know that everyone has contradictions but people can be pulled to move beyond contradictions.

Question: There is a strong dominant force in the United States to say that there is no relationship of art to politics. I try to explain the relationship to my students. How do you explain it to your students?

Sonia Sanchez: You can't explain to them because they come almost with a stand that says: "I want to learn everything, but don't talk politics to me," because their parents have told them not to get shot when they go to that university, but to get educated and get out, not to take those black courses, those radical courses. So, what you have to do, I think, is that I don't try to teach politics, I might like to include political poetry or what they call radical poetry or whatever. What I try to teach is what it means to be human, and in the classroom at the end of each session, I make students join hands because some place in that discussion of poetry and writing, someone has said something that has hurt someone. So I make them touch whatever and say anything they want. So the people who have been silent will say something, and then they saw what happened in that classroom, how you give each person the space, how you don't allow cruelty in here, it is possible to discuss poetry without being cruel. It is possible to talk about literature without dissecting and killing people. Sometimes literally killing people. So, as a consequence, I try to come in and bring examples and talk about things, and I also try on purpose to use my life as an example of how incorrect I was once, because I am old enough to do that, but they know that you are political, they might not say anything in classrooms but they write it for you in essays and papers. They make the connections, and one thing I try to do in the classrooms, is not only teach by examples but also try to teach people that all art is political: either you maintain the status quo or you talk about change, that's the bottom line. If then you want to maintain the status quo, I can tell you not to do that because quite often it pays, it will pay, but on the other hand you and I know that motion does mean life and being alive, motion is history and herstory, and, at some point, you can't stay static, you have to take a political position (particularly in the sixties you had to), and, when you do, you take the weight for it, but you have to be strong enough to do it, so all artists are political. I let people understand that, if they take the position, it is because of the communal spirit, that community of so-called slaves, it is because of seculars, it is because of that progressive way and that, because of that non-progressive way, the dialectic of freedom beckons, the dialectic of movement happens, we move because of that. So I have written what I call political poetry but the personal poetry that I write, as some brothers and sisters showed today, is political. For you to say simply: "father, do not send me out among strangers," you've got to understand that, at some point, you are say-ing: "you've got to teach me about my history, herstory before I can go out in the world, before I can hold a job." You cannot expect to send your children to this arena and be saved. But if you really read me a lot, you hear the humor, and I use humor in a political fashion, the humor in the blues, the humor in the seculars, the humor in our literature, that says that, in spite of, we will survive.

I want to tell about beliefs, about people who look at you and really believe that, about black humor, because we have always understood, at some point, the need to put another spin on that thing, it gets to be so much, bat-tles whatever, that you've got to diffuse the battle at some point and take it to another level. I want to tell you about the humor that black folks have used to maintain, not only sometimes, their integrity but also their lives, the humor of a man playing jazz turning his back on the audience, that's humor, that's survival, that's also understanding what goes on at some point, and that's also highly political if you understand it.

"This Thing Called Playwrighting": An Interview with Sonia Sanchez on the Art of Her Drama

Jacqueline Wood / 2001

From *African American Review*, vol. 39, nos. 1–2 (Spring/Summer 2005). Reprinted with the permission of the author.

Critical and popular emphasis on the poetry of Sonia Sanchez, while clearly merited, has often overshadowed her work in drama and her role in the development of an African American female dramatic voice in America. Yet, as this interview illustrates, Sanchez has always acknowledged and continues to recognize the potency of drama. She uses it as a venue of the artistic expression of social protest and the condemnation of injustice, as well as to explore personal anguish and spiritual transcendence. This brief discussion of some of Sanchez's plays introduces the dramatic work discussed in the interview that follows.

To date, Sanchez has created five plays that have been produced and published: *The Bronx Is Next* (1968); *Sister Son/ji* (1969); *Dirty Hearts* (1971); *Malcolm Man/Don't Live Here No Mo'* (1972); and *Uh Huh: But How Do It Free Us* (1974). Sanchez's latest completed play, *I'm Black When I'm Singing, I'm Blue When I Ain't,* was produced over twenty years ago in 1982, by Jomandi Productions in Atlanta, Georgia, and again in a much abbreviated form as a thesis project by Karen Turner Ward at Virginia Commonwealth University in 1985. The play is currently being prepared for publication. While she still feels the need to write plays, Sanchez has observed that her poetry has taken precedence over her drama for a number of years. Since March 2003, her dramatic writing has included a play concerning mature black women's retrospective looks at the 1960s' militant movement, which is as yet unfinished.

Each of the plays she has written, however, has impacted the genre in its own way, particularly in terms of race and feminist politics. Large and loud in its celebration of life, her drama reflects themes also evident in her poetry: anger against racism and bigotry, as expressed in poems like "Malcolm" (*I've Been a Woman*, 1978) and "Morning Song and Evening Walk" (*Shake Loose My Skin*, 1999), Sanchez particularly recognizes the complexities of African American women's struggles against sexism, as in "Song No. 2" (*Under a Soprano Sky*, 1987). She has written plays about black militant revolution, plays that explore the role of ritual and form in African American drama, plays that engage questions about the dual oppression of African American women. As a result, rather than remaining exclusively recognized for her contributions to African American poetry, Sanchez also merits acclaim as an important influence on black drama, a politically courageous, and artistically innovative playwright.

Sanchez's fiery dramatic voice, which both glorified and chastised the black militant movement, first burst forth in the 1960s. During the Black Power Movement, African American drama developed an aesthetic of black consciousness through Black Revolutionary Theater. This theater's main premise, according to its most famous proponent Leroi Jones/Amiri Baraka, was to exist as "a theatre that actually functions to liberate Black people . . . that will commit Black people . . . instruct them about what they should do . . . [and] involve them emotionally" (Coleman 84).* These strategies were developed through strong language and volatile situations, ritual structure, and stereotypical or symbolic characters that addressed, and at times encouraged, often-violent confrontation between black and white cultures. Some of the best-known names of this militant period in African American theatre were Leroi Jones/Amiri Baraka, Ed Bullins, Larry Neal, Loften Mitchell, and Ben Caldwell. Few women are even mentioned as militant playwrights of the period, except for Sonia Sanchez. Already known as a feisty, irreverent gadfly figure of a poet, Sanchez, as she points out in this interview, was actually invited to join in the development of black consciousness theatre. She became one of the few consistently visible female playwrights active in the development of black revolutionary dramatic aesthetic, although it is evident that she was not recognized at the level she deserved, primarily because she

*Mike Coleman, "What Is Black Theatre," in *Conversations with Amiri Baraka*, ed. Charles Reilly, University Press of Mississippi, 1994.

was a female in a male-dominated movement. Ironically, her insistency on a self-conscious critique of the Black Power Movement raised numerous issues concerning the black militant community, particularly black sexism, issues never seriously addressed by those men who welcomed her participation in the development of black revolutionary literary aesthetics.

Sanchez's first play, *The Bronx Is Next*, a provoking commentary on interracial racism and interracial sexism, was commissioned by Ed Bullins for the 1969 edition of *New Plays from the Black Theatre*; it had premiered in the *Drama Review* in 1968. In this play, Charles, Roland, and Jimmy are three Black Revolutionaries forcing tenants into the streets as part of their organization's protest plan to burn out the horrible tenements of Harlem. The play typifies Sanchez's bold spirit as it illustrates her early capacity to celebrate the Black Power Movement and, at the same time, to critique it. The play's emphasis on the role of black neighborhood organizations and grassroots activists with their openness to violent revolution (even to the point of completely burning down several New York boroughs) shocked many and emboldened the militant community. This young black female playwright's emphasis on the merits and difficulties of black activism in the face of racism in the *The Bronx Is Next* characterized for many African Americans the rallying impact of revolution upon the varied facets of the black community. Yet, at the same time the play presents male characters who dominate scenes by disrespecting both young and old female members of the community. The black male characters, for example, in a frightening decision to avoid a delay in their political program, manipulate a weak old black woman back into a building that they know will be burned. This action and their belligerent treatment of a young black mother demonstrate a callous and dominating paternalism found in many of the militant plays of the Black Arts period. These violent characters reflect the actuality of sexual politics as Sanchez witnessed them in the movement itself. The patriarchal oppression of women within the Black Power Movement is thus central to the play's impact both in the sixties and now.

In addition to *The Bronx Is Next*, two of Sanchez's other published and produced plays should also be considered as part of the black militant genre, *Sister Son/ji* (first published in *New Plays from the Black Theatre*, 1969) and *Uh Huh: But How Do It Free Us* (first published in *The New Lafayette Theatre Presents*, 1974). Both plays continue Sanchez's unflinching examination of paradoxical notions of liberation in the Black Power Movement. *Sister Son/ji*, in part, explores the vital role in the movement of college students whose personal interactions often mimicked confrontational, unhealthy male/female relationships derived from sexist behavior within the larger black (militant) community. The only character in the play, Son/ji describes through a series of dream/memory monologues the pain, frustration, joys, and wisdom she experiences as an African American woman maturing in an environment of black aggression. Descriptions of social and personal divisions among characters in the play emphasize Sanchez's criticisms of black paternalism within the movement.

Uh Huh: But How Do It Free Us is by far the boldest of Sanchez's early plays in both language and critical stance. The play hauntingly exposes the deleterious effects of drug use and hedonism upon some movement members. In a series of three groupings that challenge traditional linear plot structures, Sanchez engages three major issues facing the black (militant) community. In Group I, Sanchez looks at polygamy (an influence from Black Muslim thought) through the fraught relationships of a male character and his two wives. Destructive competition occurs between the wives as each attempts to monopolize her—their—husband's admiration and affection, while he in turn makes new love conquests. The characters' actions assert Sanchez's recognition of polygamy as a diversion that supplants rather than enhances black power and encourages the maltreatment of women.

In Group II, Sanchez again looks at the power dynamics within male-female relationships. Four black male characters (Brother Man, First Brother, Second Brother, Third Brother), a White Dude, and a Black Sister and a White Sister confront each other and their own addictions to sexual pleasure and illicit drugs. Although these characters insist that they have dedicated their lives to the Black Power Movement, in reality they demonstrate no redeeming qualities and certainly no productive allegiance to the militant cause.

The characters in Group III are identified as Brother, Sister, and White Woman, and represent the dynamics of romance, politics, and race-crossing that Sanchez implies were other behaviors that obstructed the militant movement. In this instance a black male revolutionary uses his black activist girlfriend to establish a politically correct identity while playing his rich white girlfriend for financial and social support. Brother's arrogance, promiscuity, cruelty, and material selfishness indicate Sanchez's highly critical view of many (militant) black males. And Sister's ready submission to Brother's abuse at the same time reveals Sanchez's anguished awareness of the weaknesses and strengths of African American women of this period as they struggled to salvage personal lives. The playwright thus raises vital questions about the health and rigor of the black militant community while asserting a distinct black female consciousness at a time when women's issues were scarcely being raised in male-dominated (militant) discourse.

Dirty Hearts universalizes issues of oppression. The allegorical characters are presented in a series of conversations and sequences of poetic litanies as a Dirty Hearts card game unfolds. On the one hand, the white male characters First Man, Second Man, and Poet have a presence so well established within the social and political structure (the game) that they need no names to identify their power. Their whiteness creates for them an undeniable self-hood, as do the good hands they deal themselves. On the other hand, political and social identities for the black man Carl and the Hiroshima maiden, Shigeko, are significantly marginal. In this case, disempowered identity in *Dirty Hearts* is codified ironically by naming a lack. The oppression these characters must face is indicated by Carl's consistent receipt of the Dirty Queen of Hearts. Juxtaposition of the disempowered Carl and Shigeko against unnamed white male figures of domination and the play's indeterminate ending allows Sanchez to interrogate struggles with which her contemporaries contended and the challenges that continue to confront oppressed peoples across American society.

As these brief descriptions of her important published plays suggest, Sanchez emerges as an insightful codebreaker, courageously striking a path in her early drama that has contributed to a literary legacy for today's young, successful African American female playwrights. She has interrogated gender boundaries and opened frontiers in language and structure, while producing themes both divisive and threatening to the dynamics of patriarchal black militant discourse. She formulated in her early plays ritualistic action and shocking language to shatter the complacency of Eurocentric as well as African American audiences. Sanchez forms a major presence in the development of an African American women's dramatic aesthetic, and her theory and practice concerning African American drama need to be more fully acknowledged and examined.

My telephone conversation with Sanchez took place on April 9, 2001. A small woman in stature, Ms. Sanchez's presence still seemed quite large to me, even over the phone. She spoke with a strong, gracious, and emphatic tenor about her relationship to her writing. As her comments in this interview indicate, Ms. Sanchez's perceptions about drama in particular and writing in general have matured over the past thirty years, and generate insight into the dynamics of racial history, personal growth, and the African American female presence in African American literature and life.

JW: We can start with your general work ethic. One thing I have found interesting is that there seems to be a hiatus between the plays that you published in the 1960s and the '70s and the ones that you are working on now. Is that the case? Did you ever really stop writing plays?

SS: Well, I didn't stop writing plays. It's that you always want to see them published and on stage, and sometimes they're not. So it's not the same kind of emergency, perhaps, as the poetry. I take my time with the plays because I know it might take a minute before they're performed, before they're produced. It's not the same kind of urgency as my poetry. Still, I am working on a play now, and I feel an urgency to finish it because I promised it to a couple of well-known people, and I want to make sure that they get it and read it.

JW: When you were working on your early plays, did they come to you simultaneously? Or did they derive from one another in terms of theme or idea? How did that work?

SS: One came out of the other. Some came because I was asked, "Are you a playwright?" And I said, "Yes, I am," although at that time, I had not written a play. Well, I had written a children's play, actually, called *A Trip to a Backwoods Farm*. It was not an adult play. So of course, you know, I said, "Yeah, I write plays." I'm a poet; why not say that? And I was asked then to give a play. So, I had a play available for the anthology *Black Fire*. I did send it to Larry Neal and Baraka, but it got misplaced. That play was *The Bronx Is Next*. When I went to San Francisco State to help establish the first Black Studies Program, I was asked by Ed Bullins, "You have a play?" He was doing an anthology called *New Plays for the Black Theatre*. And I said, "Oh sure, I have a new play." He had put *The Bronx Is Next* in the *Tulane Drama Review*, the *TDR*, and so I told him, "Oh yeah. I'm just finishing one." Well, I sat right down that night wrote *Sister Son/ji*, actually. It was an all-nighter . . . and my children cooperated. They were these little babies who slept through the night, and I was so pleased that they did.

JW: You wrote *Sister Son/ji* in one night?!

SS: Yes, I mean, it was all night. Because, you know with the babies you don't get a lot of time. And they were sleeping straight through; so luckily enough they decided to do that . . . they helped out a great deal.

JW: You said that some plays came out of the others, so the next play would have been . . . ?

SS: The next play would have been one that I did in Pittsburgh. That was called *Malcolm Man/Don't Live Here No Mo'* [a children's play], and also the play *Uh Huh: But How Do It Free Us?* That play came next because some of the young men were almost equating their lifestyles with the whole idea of changing the world. Or freedom. And so you saw things like, people would get up and announce that they were getting with polygamy. So I asked, "Uh huh, but how does that free us?" How does that lifestyle free us? I can't see any connection here at all. I meant that to be a very mean play, and it is a mean play because of the theme of the drugs and relationships. Some of the men were having two relationships, you know, one with a black woman— and one with a white woman, and doing a disservice to both women by causing antagonisms between the women. This reminded me a great deal, my sister, of what happened during our enslavement when the men came down to the cabins. The white male would go and navigate between the black woman in the slave quarters and his wife in the big house. And during the militant period, you had the reversal—black men, not all, but some black men, moving between a well-to-do white woman and a black woman. Isn't that interesting? And what you see each time is that the men were reaping all the fruits here. The women were antagonistic towards each other, and it was all about a man. So after all that was happening, I thought about it. I said I really have to do a play that talks about how this happened, that the men really reaped great personal harvests. And it wasn't about liberation.

JW: With the idea of relationships in mind, *Sister Son/ji* also deals with the role of women and the struggle of black women. There seems to be a consistent concern in your plays about the issues of black women in the community.

SS: Well, during that period you saw some really destructive things as far as black women were concerned. In the midst of all of this great flourish and expanse of self-determination, there was still the problem of, I'll put that in quotes, the "problem" of women, you know. Who's taking care of these women? How are these women going to survive with these children? What are these women doing as far as these so-called love relationships are concerned? I mean, how are these women really going to survive? In the midst of all this stuff that's happening, all this talk that's going on about what a new time this was, my play is talking about . . . what seems like the same old times as it relates to black women. The same kind of problems that surfaced with our mothers and fathers were surfacing here even though people had new language, a new way of looking. A new ideology, right? You had the same core; at the base was the same problem.

JW: Do you think that yours should still be labeled as a black militant voice? Some still seem to talk about you that way.
SS: No. That's because they don't continue to read. When they read about you, what's been published about you in the past, that's how people label us. That's how they try to cripple us, that's what frightened people off. Then people wouldn't read you, wouldn't deal with you, and then people wouldn't get the message you were bringing. A clever way of doing it.

JW: And since growth is such an important part of being an effective artist . . .
SS: Oh yes, I think that the reason why art stays alive is that the artist grows. I mean the body doesn't stay the same; the brain doesn't stay the same. Your art can't stay the same. This is 2001; I can't be writing what I wrote in 1969. I don't look the same; my ideas aren't the same either.

JW: You're from Birmingham, Alabama. Do you consider yourself to be a voice of the South?
SS: Oh, I think so. I'm a voice from the South and from urban cities. I think it's a combination. Since I have come out of the South, I have memories that inform my work a great deal: memories of my grandmother, memories that form me as a human being. So all those memories I use as I write.

JW: This brings to mind your trilogy, the trilogy with *The Bronx Is Next* as the first part. You've talked about these plays as a reversal of the black migration to the North. There would be a shift from urban setting back to the South. Could you talk a little now about what the issues might be? Do you see these two settings as conflicting with each other?

SS: I think what happens, you know and I don't want to talk about it too much because I am still working on it—but just in general, you would now have what I call urban people who might have wrenched a lot of the South out of their loins trying to resettle on northern ground, with the difficulties that happened when southern people tried to settle on northern ground. How difficult it was dealing with all that concrete. If you live in concrete a long time, there are possible difficulties with people who are urban, people who are accustomed to speaking their minds, saying what they want to say, doing what they want to do, going back to a South that is moving towards a certain way of looking at itself and its inhabitants. But I would say still—watching what recently was going on in Mississippi with the Confederate flag, in Atlanta and the problem there with its flag, and in South Carolina—there are still vestiges of that. And I think that black people who have lived in the North for a long time might have to watch what it is that they're doing.

JW: So, place is essential to your work, then?

SS: Yes, but I'll talk about it later when I am finished.

JW: Okay. You have so many poetry anthologies that are accessible. Did you find it difficult to publish and produce your plays? Your early drama?

SS: Oh, yes. Because the early drama—oh, that's interesting now—the early drama actually got produced a lot in New York City, in the Village, at Joe Papp's, you know. They did a production, Gloria Foster's *Sister Son/ji* at his theatre, which was very well done. Novella Nelson directed Gloria Foster, so it was very well done. Papp did four one-acts plays; mine was one of them. There were a lot of theatre houses in the Village. *The Bronx Is Next* and *Sister Son/ji* got done in those places. And also in the universities. *Uh Huh: But How Do It Free Us* was done in places like Michigan, California, at the universities. A lot of that very strong activity towards the black theatre was taking place. I would show up at a place, up in Buffalo, maybe, and someone would be doing *Sister Son/ji*. It just was very beautiful. I have gotten letters from people who say, "I got a scholarship to a university because I performed a section of your play *Sister Son/ji*, and they knew that I could act because it was a very hard play to act." And I felt very good about it.

JW: I know that one play, *I'm Black When I'm Singing', I'm Blue When I Ain't*, was produced relatively recently in Atlanta.

SS: Jomandi Productions. Also, before then, it was produced at the University of Virginia as a thesis. One of the students [Karen Turner Ward] called me, and in getting her MA had to direct a play, and she asked me if I had a new play. I sent it to her, and she directed it and starred in it. And it was a magnificent performance. But that's a very creative play.

JW: You mentioned influence of early black women playwrights of the Harlem Renaissance on your work. I wondered who particularly affected you?

SS: I didn't realize that they had written because you don't see them in those major anthologies. I had to stumble upon black women playwrights like Angelina Weld Grimké. You may see them only as poets, and usually, as poets only in a plaintive, romantic kind of voice. And I came across some of these plays about lynching, about miscegenation, about aborting—in the sense of deciding not to have children [as in Grimké's Rachel]—because you don't want your child to be raised in a racist country. And I was stricken, and I kept saying what I'm doing is not outside the milieu of black literature. It's within that same tradition that's gone on before me. And that's what was so wonderful to understand, that actually you're part of a tradition. But no one ever published them, so you think that you are coming maybe with something new.

JW: And they were concerned with women's issues, too. So you see later writers like you as actually continuing to carry the torch?

SS: Oh yes.

JW: You seem really open to experimentation particularly in terms of form in your plays. Can you talk about how this developed?

SS: Well, I think what happened is that I just began to look at this thing called playwrighting, and because I thought if I'm going to bring something that is different—I mean that's different from just what we were seeing at that time in the American theatre—that I should experiment with not only the language, but experiment with the form. When I did *Sister Son/ji*. I had nothing to go on. I just decided, when I thought it out and wrote out what I wanted to do; I kept saying I don't want a lot of scenery or props on that stage. I wanted it bare because this is a bare woman talking about her life. And she's been stripped down only to the necessities. You know? Should I bring a curtain down for her changes? And I said no, let that all happen on stage. Let her go from the old woman to a young woman in college via a rack with clothes and the wigs and so on: the natural wig and something to wrap around her, bracelet and a long chain, big earrings that would show that she's now young. And there she is within that time, the use of music and the use of [costume]. Then the audience participates in her birth, going back in time. And without hesitation. That's why it's a hard play because the actress never has a chance to take a breath off-stage.

JW: Speaking of your experimentation with form, can you talk about the role that ritual plays in black drama?
SS: We saw that happening a lot with Ed Bullins and with Barbara Ann Teer and the National Black Theatre in New York. I used to go and see so many actors and actresses on the stage and the whole idea of bringing the community and the audience into our ideas in a very formal way of looking at the world and the earth and problems and issues and people. And so it's within this ritual of life, this ritual of living, or the ritual of interrupted living.

JW: But when you use the term *ritual*, how do you define it? What does it really describe in black drama to you?
SS: Barbara Ann Teer does a long article on this. And I think some of these ideas are also expressed in *Kuntu Drama* and *The Drama of Nommo*.

JW: By Paul Carter Harrison?
SS: Right. Teer was one of the first people I saw who began to deal with ritual and how the National Black Theatre saw it. Then we as playwrights chose either to use it or not use it.

JW: So you as a playwright pulled from this communal version of ritual what you found valuable to your own drama?
SS: Yes.

JW: Are there any contemporary playwrights who catch your attention?
SS: Well, of course, August Wilson. He is indeed doing a lot, most especially for males right now in drama. Bringing that cycle, bringing men out of the

First World War up through the twentieth century. And we're seeing them progress. We're seeing what it meant to come from the South and to form relationships in places like Pittsburgh, and the interaction between men and women. The plays are very much male-oriented, very much looking at the way black males have survived some of these urban cities, how they have come through. And it certainly needs to be said. It's done very well. And I'm glad that it's being said.

JW: In addition to issues specifically relevant to women or men, what would you say are the most important issues that need to be addressed in black drama? Or black literature in general?

SS: I don't think there is a way to see only one issue. As black dramatists, we need to deal with all issues that face us, all the way from AIDS—as I did with *Does Your House Have Lions?*—to male-female relationships, to environmental issues. Even the idea of how we are going to stay alive on this earth. I think there are many issues that are facing us. To get specific, there's a young woman in our workshop who is doing a play on Broadway with Ruby Dee, and one of the issues is abortion. She shows how one of the old women in the community did abortions in the past, before women started going to hospitals for them. That has always been a part of the culture of women. Whether you were black or white, Latina, or Asian, or Native American, women have always known how to do that because there have been times in their lives when they could not deal with another child, or they were ill and they had to. I mean, those issues have always been issues. . . . We really need to have a play, a very well written play on something that coldly takes just one side, saying, "I'm just for the family," you see? I mean every woman I know who ever had an abortion was not anti-family, was not anti-child, was not anti-husband, was not anti-baby. What they were at the time that it happened, they were trying to save themselves. It wasn't just some casual, "Let me just go and abort this child, this fetus." And they never forget it. It's something they'll always remember that they had to do at a time in their lives, that their lives were so convoluted, that their lives were just so . . . they were so sick. But they always remember the child that they almost had. And I think that when we put it in the hands of people who have an ulterior motive, or program, we never see the humanity of the woman, the husband, the doctor. We only see people so easily spouting slogans. So it's not the time . . . we're past the whole idea of spouting slogans. We need to look very carefully at the issues that surround women at the time when they have to decide, "I can't do this. I can't have another child, or I'll go crazy." And so it's not by chance that in my childhood I heard the whisperings when some woman died. The whispers had something to do with something she had done; she had gone someplace and gotten sick, trying to do this. If abortions had been safe, there would not have been the whispering. So we lost women, who had to go places that were dirty, dirty.

JW: Yes, *They That Sit in Darkness* addresses this issue of too many children as early as the Harlem Renaissance period.
SS: Oh yes, it's a beautiful play.

JW: Speaking of beautiful plays, your *Dirty Hearts* has ritualistic language that is particularly fascinating, almost lyrical. Can you talk about it a little?
SS: I love *Dirty Hearts*. It's a play that looks at how men and women deal with each other in the midst of destructive attitudes towards them. The character Shigeko is a Hiroshima maiden . . . I had met a Hiroshima "maiden." A number of them had come to America, and some people brought them to my house. I had a little reception for them, and one wore a heavy veil, to veil the scars. Some of them didn't. I wrote something about her afterwards. Of course, there's the character Carl, who wanted to be included always with whites because he saw himself always in relation to whites. That part is about him thinking, "I'm here, I've arrived," and then he gets slapped down again.

JW: The white characters have no names.
SS: Yes, the Poet and the Man. I did that because there are so many of them, and so few of the Carls and Shigekos that they stand out when they come in the midst of so many. When their name is called—when they are either rescued or wiped out—they need to be remembered. The Poet and the Business Man, we know them; they have substance already, identity already. They're not concerned about their names per se because they know who they are. They exist; they're part of the society; they have order. Carl and Shigeko, however, have only been identified through tragedy—through slavery or through a bomb. So they need a name to hold onto, to, in a sense, help them see themselves as identified. And they also need a name, too, so

that when they are wiped out or thrown out or kicked out or paternalized, they will be noted.

JW: Yes, this idea of being noted or remembered prompts me to ask you more about *I'm Black When I'm Singing.*
SS: The play opens in an insane asylum. The chorus consists of attendants in the hospital. And there's a woman sitting on a toilet. She is very obviously, you know, on the toilet . . . . on a sparse stage. You see the attendants on the side, the three of them, dressed in white. She looks at the audience and says something to the effect of, "Yeah, that's right, I'm who you think I am." She's a famous singer. And she finishes and gets up and collects the feces and begins to eat it. And the audience gasps, of course. And they realize they are brought into her insanity. Or is it really an insanity? Has she just decided to take leave from the world for a while? The doctor comes in, and the chorus becomes a refrain talking about what is going to happen next or what has happened, depending upon how dramatic it is, and it's all in poetry. She's not a friendly patient, and the doctor says, "I just want to know . . ." She's a multiple personality; there are three people "in" her. And that's how we get the different blues singers. And she says something like, "Yeah, yeah, you want to know about . . ." say, Bessie. "She's okay. She thinks she can sing. But she'll get her come-uppance. They're gonna find her on a road someplace, and they're not gonna take her to that hospital, and she'll die." And then "Miss Bessie" comes out, let's say, and I had to write lyrics for the first time. And people composed the music for them.

JW: And did you find that writing lyrics and creating multiple personalities was a different kind of challenge?
SS: Oh, it was. Oh, that's massive right there. I mean just the whole idea of assuming a Bessie Smith–type persona. . . . The person speaking is maybe a Nina Simone type, a strong woman and, sometimes, off kilter for a minute. And there's a Bessie type and a Billie Holiday type. And there's the one who is going to replace Nina, a Diane Reeves kind of persona or Abbey Lincoln type, who is much more settled. And so the battle is set. The doctor comes back and forth, and she releases these characters. The one that she doesn't ever want to release is this Diane Reeves type, the type that she knows will consume her. It's a very involved, hard play with a lot of characters. They did a fine production in Jomandi. And the woman in Virginia [Karen Turner

Ward], the chairperson at Hampton, and the Hampton Players. They have a
history. They mounted a big production when she got there because she had
done it for her master's thesis. They ran it for Black History Month, and
I went down for the opening. And I'm telling you it was an amazing
production. She wrote me that they ran it for one month on the campus,
and every night it was packed.

JW: In closing, I wanted to talk a little about *The Bronx Is Next*. It's clearly a
black militant play, coming out of that period. How much of it is yours, and
how much of it was the Movement's?
SS: I think it's a play like back in the 1920s or '30s, rather, when they were
coming out with plays that were considered militant and left. And it's on the
level of the Harlem Renaissance, where you're doing plays that speak to
issues that need to be spoken to. That whole idea of recapturing the spirit
of black people who were broken down by urban experiences. Rescuing
them . . . but I also wanted to show the contradictions. On the one hand, you
have these men—on purpose you see only the men doing the work—that
was on purpose, okay? People don't understand that. They just think, "Well,
why didn't you include some women?" Well, yeah, the women were the
people in the community. But the reason why the men could take that old
woman back inside the house and give her something to sleep and then
burn her is that the men were the ones involved. The men took that woman
back inside and left her there. That was a very male way of dealing with that
old woman. I don't think women—I know—most women would not have
dealt with her that way. And that's what I'm saying. I had only males in
charge of that neighborhood, only males in charge of staying in there for
a year, organizing the blocks, you know, each one in a block. And then at
the given time, when they got the order to burn down Harlem, they had
organized people in such a way that they were then going to be literally
trekking on home. I mean they were not going to be in cars; and that walk
South is the beginning of the second play of the trilogy. You have the
trucks; you have all of the things that they would need. But the point is
what has happened to these people. There's a long walk home similar
to the Native Americans' trek. Except they will not be lost along the way.
They will make this trek during the summer, with protection, with food,
places set up along the way where they can sleep. But it will be a trek
back south.

JW: But what fascinated me is that *The Bronx Is Next* is clearly a militant play. It's your first play published, right? In 1968? And yet, at the same time that you are supporting the militant platform, you had the courage in the sixties in this play, to criticize the movement from within.
SS: Yes, that's the difference. I think that's how you grow. I mean, you have got to be able to look critically at what is going on, what went on as you lived it. As we lived some of this, I saw exactly what was wrong. And it's incumbent upon you as a human being to talk about that, to express it, to write about it. You know, to start a dialogue about it.

JW: But there were male authors then who were writing militant plays but did not address divisive issues within the movement.
SS: Well, you know, because I think that people just thought it was not necessary. But the point is that it was necessary to do it. You won't grow if you don't.

JW: But even beyond those who felt self-evaluation was "not necessary," weren't they [male militants, in particular] actually against anything they saw as internal division, for example, the women's movement?
SS: But you see, women began to talk about everything: the sexism, the problems with children. There was no help at home quite often. Men were too busy with the movement. Women who were doing work for the movement also had to figure out a way to get these things done, too. There were a lot of issues that women began to raise. Certainly, sexism was a big one. But also the idea, sometimes, of men leaving the women, women who were highly political, just as bright as the men. But sometimes the men would leave them for a younger woman, a woman who didn't know anything, so they were going to have to teach that new woman, instead of keeping the wives that they had who also understood what was going on in the country and the world. What I'm saying is that many women began to leave behind the issues of the movement and began to include everything—life—children, love, desertion.

JW: In *Uh Huh: But How Do It Free Us?* These same questions about male-female relationships are raised. I find this play so interesting. It deals with these themes through ritual.
SS: That's why I have the dancers. They observe everything. And comment on it. As a kind of mouthpiece for the people in the audience.

JW: There's a real openness about sexual perversion, about drugs, and sexuality in *Uh Huh: But How Do It Free Us*? I'm referring to the middle piece with its emphasis on horse [heroin] and prostitutes.

SS: Well, that was about . . . some of what happened then. Be you black, white, green, purple, or blue, when you're involved in that drug culture, the women that you might have in there with you are not going to be house-wives. We had people who were thinking that they were still part of the movement, yet they were even anti-woman. In the midst of all of this, you've got these men, you know, and they really looked down on these women. The section where the white male is walking with the black woman, he felt free enough to crush her right in the midst of the black men. But all the men, white and black, were together on how they treated this black woman, on how they treat women. That was important to say. Of course, you get a little flack for saying it.

JW: Yes, what about the response you got at the time that *Uh Huh* was produced in the early seventies?

SS: You got some silences. But the point is, you had to say it. And I wanted those plays to be looked at by younger women, for them to understand what was going on because there was silence about the personal relationships, sometimes.

JW: Didn't you work toward a certain dignity in the whole characters in this play?

SS: Definitely. Oh, I certainly hope that came through. The same with the Black Bitch character in *The Bronx Is Next*. She says something like, "Look I'm just trying to take care of my kids, here. This white guy comes in here once a week, and I'm not the first person who's done this, right? Or the last." I've had white women tell me, "That could be me or my mother if circum-stances were different." The point is that she was saying, "I am who I am. Do you know who you are? The way you treat me? Who are you? In the long run, after you do all this liberation stuff, you're still gonna treat me one kind of way, and it's not gonna be well."

Sonia Sanchez:
The Joy of Writing Poetry

Kadija Sesay / 2002

From *Sable: The Lit Magazine for Writers*, Winter 2002, 7–15. Reprinted with the permission of the author.

During the several weeks that this interview took place, Sonia Sanchez traveled back and forth from her home in Philadelphia, her second home—her father's apartment—in Harlem, and Howard University, where she accepted the pressures of teaching a class of thirty-nine students (with at least another thirty-nine, disappointed, praying that she would teach another the following semester—she couldn't). There was little visibility of her slowing pace in participating or attending activist events despite the fact that she had a broken foot. Through it all, Sonia Sanchez continued to pour poetry through readings, conversations, and discussions on panels.

There were days, when, after teaching, then dinner at her favorite Chinese restaurant in Du Pont Circle, a place she loves as they serve tofu'd noodles that complement her microbiotic diet, she insisted that myself and her son Morani, take the food home, lest it waste, before we went to her hotel, to do the next part of the interview where she was happy to talk until she became visibly tired. Foot elevated, bottle of water at her side, Sister Sonia begins our conversation in a rhythmic prosaic conversation that later becomes punctuated with chants and stories in rhythm and rhyme.

Discovering Lansgton et al.

SS: Some of the writers who originally influenced me were Langston Hughes, Gwendolyn Brooks—I read them all in the anthology that a librarian had given me when I was in high school. So I had a chance to read all of those Harlem Renaissance poets that were in this great anthology. I used to go to the library almost every day and read books like, "her heart was beating; she melted into his arms"—I used to read all those books, right? She looked at

me and she said, "I have something for you," and she gave me an anthology
of Negro poetry. I wondered how she knew that I liked poetry because I had
not told her or anyone that I was still writing poetry. Margaret Burrows,
Countee Cullen, those are the early ones, Margaret Walker, Sterling Brown.
And I began an investigation of some other poets from Pablo Neruda to
Nicolás Guillén. I discovered Guillén via Langston Hughes, because he translated Guillén; that's how I found some of the French Caribbean poets also,
via Langston. Langston also translated them, so it was that whole kind of
interesting mix then, of poets who were writing, and of course when I started
to write I read Baraka because Baraka's writing was coming out of the Village,
and others who were coming out of the Black Arts Movement who were
writing.

All of these poets on the scene helped inform my idea of poetry, and it
included a lot of African American poets; it included, very much, Latin
American poets, Caribbean poets; it included these people who were trying
to look at the world and say there was something wrong with it and that one
day, that we in some way had to effect some kind of change.

KS: What is your favorite Langston Hughes poem?
SS: Everyone would say, "I've Known Rivers," you know, which is a favorite
because it's his signature poem, and there's a serious poem. "Let the Rain
Kiss You," I use that poem for students. It's a wonderful, wonderful poem.
But scrap all that; it's "Ask Your Mama: 12 Moods of Jazz." And a lot of
the work out of *Good Morning, Revolution* is a very underrated collection
that he did which is what I call "revolutionary poetry" and the poetry that
he did on the blues. I have a title I used for Langston Hughes celebration,
"You Tell Me Your Blues and I'll Tell You Langston," because Langston has
this most fantastic "blues" and what folks call the blues poems that he does
that populates Harlem, but also the real blues as it's seen in *The Weary Blues*,
the blues poem he did. He gave us these images of black men and women in
a place called Harlem, surviving and not surviving; loving, sometimes, and
not loving well.

We would say something like, you know, if you want to know me, look at
my feet. This is a classic example of black folks here because the feet had a
very important thing to do with our system in all the urban cities. If your feet
were 8½ you cut the sides out of a size 8, so that your bunions would not be
constricted. So when Moms Mabley used to come out on stage and say, look

at my feet, the audience laughed and said, "yeah," because our feet have taken us to wars all over the world and then when we came back, and we had to use them, it was those same feet that took us to run from the lynch mobs, the feet that ran through Harlem during the riots. So when you look at our feet, we know exactly how we have fared in this country and how we have not fared in this country.

So Langston tells it in simple words in poetry, Moms Mabley, or Richard Pryor in the culture of comedy. Richard Pryor knows how to navigate the urban brawl; the beauty of it and the horror of it requires that we cry at the same time as we laugh. One of the most important things for us today is to have the comedic talents of Richard Pryor.

So naturally for Sanchez, she delves backwards and sideways into African American social history, discussing it in the traditions of art through politics.

SS: Langston was a very important man to us all. His poetry enthused with the Harlem beat, he enthused black folks' pain, black folks' voice, black folks' tap dancing through Harlem and throughout the world. But I like Langston also because he was a political man. I had a picture of Langston with Nicolás Guillén and Ernest Hemingway in Spain when they had all gone to fight that war. (Hughes reported on it for the newspaper, the *Afro-American* based in Baltimore). I went to Cuba in the late seventies or early eighties and I met Guillén, at a national conference of writers. After I had done this talk they gave me a standing ovation, they said what can we do for you and I said I'd like to meet Nicolás Guillén, they looked at me and said he's actually here. Two hours later, I was sitting with some of the people from the conference and they took me to Guillén's office. He had a huge office, he was standing in the middle of the floor and his circulation must have been bad in his legs as he couldn't move well. I walked in and he said, "Sonia, Sonia Sanchez como Langston," and as I walked across the room, and I embraced him, his arms had developed so, because he had little power in his legs. He embraced me in such a strong fashion, I couldn't breathe and I thought, "Oh my God, I've come all the way to Cuba to die—in the arms of a poet!" I looked up into his face and he was beaming. And now, this is significant—I realized that I could relax and leaned into his breath and we began to breathe at the same pace, at the same rate and it was okay. I had no problem then on. People need to learn to lean into each other's breath, and realize that it's okay to breathe each other's breath, this African breath or this Cuban breath. If people could learn to do that, it would be much more healthy and we would maintain this climate the way it needs to be maintained.

The Joy of Writing Poetry

KS: Do you have a favorite time of day and a favorite place to work?

SS: Well, I thought I did, I thought that I would at some point be able to just write anytime. I've written sixteen books, most of my writing is done at night, and I've got to get out of it, because it tires you out, you know. But traditionally I wrote during the summer and late at night, from about 12:30 AM until about 3:30 AM after the children had gone to bed; after I had graded papers and then I would get up at about 7:30 AM and go to school. There was never any space or time to do it otherwise, that's what I was conditioned to do, that's why I come alive at about eleven o'clock. I feel the lull about nine–ten o'clock and really should go to bed then. Now I'm attempting to write whenever I want to, whenever I have the time. I'm going to redirect myself to writing in the morning, writing in the afternoon, writing in the night. It's nice to be able to do that when you're not working, so I need to get back to my memoir that I am writing at this point.

KS: How much of your creative process is your life and how much of it is work?

SS: Well, I think that most of the creative process has got to do with the people I've seen, the lives of women I've seen, so although I use "I," I mean the communal "I." It's the "I" that separates out many women's lives and that's what that's about. So, people always want to say that, "This is about you." Of course your life does inform some of your poems, but if they know a little bit about your life, they assume that all the rest is all about your life, too, all the private joys and all the private unjoys and the enjoys, but it is not something that I let envelop me. If that occurs then I give it meaning to other lives, and other times I let it fly to other places, the place of that private pain or private joy—to allow other things to happen.

KS: Do you write in the emotion?

SS: Oh no, I always let it pass—because if you are too involved with it, it doesn't come out right. If you let it just sail past for a minute and then let it re-enter your psyche, months, a year later, then you review it in a different fashion, and it's a much more objective process.

When I received a call from Shirley Graham Du Bois's lawyer in New York, I was talking on the phone with sister Gwen. She'd been having a few problems with her heart and I was calling her to advise her on the kinds of foods she should eat. I remember the phone clicking over and someone said, Shirley Graham Du Bois died in China and I didn't say, "Thank you"—or "I'll call you back," I just hung up the phone; I literally backed away from it and it was not until, maybe a couple of days later, after I put the children to bed, turned up the television for the news and I just broke down crying. It was a good year later actually, before I sat down at my dining room table and I started writing a poem for her. Shirley Graham Du Bois (wife of W. B. Du Bois) was my mentor. She helped shape some of my early ideas and thoughts. Before that, it was too present, too immediate.

KS: Do you ever get bored with writing poetry?
SS: How can anyone get bored with writing poetry? It is the greatest genre on earth and the most reliable one. If you are away, for instance, from a novel, for any length of time—I've been writing a novel for a while—the characters get rebellious and as I like to call it, they don't have any manners. They say, "Hey, where you been?" I say something like my father's been ill, etc., but they say, "I don't care about that," and they change and you can't reign them in, you have to change them and you change also, but you don't always recognize that at the time. You can't just go back and change it and pick up that part where you left it.

But you can discover a poem unfinished much later, when you're clearing out a desk and the poem might say, "Hey, where you been?" but then say, "Hey Sonia, here I am, I love you, finish me." That's what a poem will do and there's no recrimination, no anger in between even if you've left it for ten years. How wonderful that is! And that's why I love writing poetry.

I have a number of poems in my journals, that I go back to. Some will probably never be finished because they are not strong enough, but it's okay to go back and read them now and then. Sometimes I go back, and take a line and use it in another poem. I write everyday, even if it's a summation of the day, a thought I had or something I've read because it is important for me to keep connected with writing.

KS: How often do you revisit your work?

SS: You have to revisit a number of times. It's rewriting that requires hard work. You've got to navigate just a bit better than you're doing. It's the ear and eye combined that help you do this and that's a hard task.

Sometimes I go through the first revision, the second revision, the third revision, the fourth revision, the fifth revision, the sixth revision and then go, "Hold it!" You wanna throw the poem down, you want to say all kinds of things. It's sometimes at about the fourth revision that you tear it apart, but if you can just make yourself go past that, it will turn a corner later and it will say, "Here I am, come get me." At some time, by the ninth or tenth revision, when you are practically despairing about it, it turns that corner and that is the most exquisite moment when it happens. And all this is worth the days, the weeks, the months you've spent, and then it flows and the rhythm is there, the imagery is there and it's so wonderful. All that process made it happen. Sometimes you put it down for the night and then you pick it up from the bed in the cold light of the morning. When you read it out loud, in the early morning hours when things are clear, the poem becomes clear also. I always maintain that it's revision that makes that poem turn a corner—and you really don't know how it happens.

Wounded Lions and Handgrenades

SS: I love titles. I don't know; they come from some place. I was working on a book called *A Blues Book for Blue Black Magical Women*. It's like a semi-autobiography. It's about black women, the ones who have traveled from the South to the North, that generation who go to university training, went out into the work force, the generation that did political stuff, from civil rights to black power—it's all in there. How we loved, how some of the men left us for younger women. Some of these women were as political as their husbands and just as radical but you didn't know that because of the sexism, but it happened to a number of women that I knew at the time. All of that is in there; there is something about that which is very fascinating to me, so a lot of that I needed to write about. Every night, EVERY NIGHT, I dreamt about this particular woman who was in a tomb and she talked to me. The book is also about the book of the dead, about the book of the tomb.

It led me to read up on Islam, on the masonry and coming to the West. I researched that book probably for a year; then it just fell into place, and then I woke up one morning with the title. *A Blues Book for Blue Black Magical Women*. Blue is the color of mourning in Egypt.

I did one called *Home Coming*, a lot of writers, from Ngugi on, had written a book called "homecoming." We were all coming home, at a certain time, people were coming home to themselves, to their identities, their sense of selves, and that's what happened with me. And then I started playing with words, "We a baad people"—and they didn't understand the terminology, and we had to say, "No, no, no, we be bad, as in good. We the good people, the really hip people." The spelling of all those kinds of things, also for the first times, in the early seventies, I started to notate musically, the sense of a word, how a poem should be read. It first occurred at Brown University and I was asked to read "Poem to Coltrane," which I had not read out loud before. And as I read it, I started to allow the music to enter the words. After that, I began to experiment more with music.

And in the middle of a response she would just close her eyes and give voice to a poem she had written twenty years before as though she had written it yesterday.

Wilson's Story

Does Your House Have Lions? described as an "urban tragedy" is Sanchez's thirteenth book, nominated for the 1998 National Book Critics Award. A work of love for her brother, it tells the story of how he and their father were reunited in the face of AIDS. The story of this journey is told in rhyme royal in four sections, in the voice of her brother, Wilson, their father, the ancestors, and herself. In this seventy-page epic, narrative poem, Sanchez took the brave step of talking openly about gay sexuality with African American families at a time when it was rarely acknowledged or spoken of, even less so during the time when her brother was alive. Wilson left Alabama and, like many African Americans, moved north, where he lost himself in New York's gay lifestyle. He died in his prime in 1981.

SS: I had not written a book in seven years. After *Homegirls and Handgrenades*, I did *Wounded in the House of a Friend* in 1994; it had to do with personal lives and finding balance, you know. Right behind that, two years after, *Does Your House Have Lions?* In fact I had already started *Lions* before *Wounded.* I had already written the first stanza, up to:

> *this was a migration unlike the 1900s of black*
> *men and women coming north for jobs.*
> *freedom, life. this was a migration to begin to*
> *bend a father's heart again to birth seduction*
> *from the past to repay desertion at last.*

So, I'd done that, and I thought there were going to be two more stanzas and that was the poem. And then it hit me. I realized that I was going to tell the story about my brother in my brother's voice, who came north at seventeen; the family that had deserted him. I realized then that I had a voice in this too. Then I said to my father, "I'm going to do a book about Wilson, your son." "Well Sonia," he said, "if you're saying anything about Wilson, you'll have to say something about me, won't you, because you really won't understand Wilson until you understand what happened to me in the South." And I remember thinking, "Whoa, this is more than a thought." That's when I put the book down.

I went back to *Lions* after I sent *Wounded* out to my editor. I often write two books at the same time. I came home from work one day and this man had said something about the ancestors to me earlier and I slowed the car down and I listened very quietly, so by the time I pulled my car in my driveway, the music was already in my head and it shook me. It made me think how one art influences the other, music, painting, in other forms of art, and I thought, "Oh my God, this is a book that I have no control over." I picked up the book and had the ancestors idea in my head and I started writing literally in my brother's voice.

He died at a time when they couldn't figure out what was killing these young men. I was reading the *New York Times* and Wilson was in the hospital and everything they said about AIDS; he had a "classic case" if you call it that. A lot of the men in that generation never came out and they submerged themselves into alcohol, that aggressive rage of having to prove themselves all the time.

I thought that I would have to cut my many questions for Sista Sonia (my West African upbringing still makes me hesitate in calling this matriarch

Sista, too—and so for me, she remained, throughout the interview,
Ms. Sanchez). I wanted to know, why she wrote the last sections of *Lions*,
the Ancestor's voices, in Wolof. With at least eight hundred languages in
Africa, why Wolof? Before I could ask her, she passionately continued
that story.

SS: It came to me in Wolof, Sista Kadija, I can't tell you why that language;
I didn't understand it and I don't know Wolof, so I had to call some friends
who knew people, who knew Wolof. Where I come from, I must have spoken
in Wolof. I thought it must be my spirit, I believe that when we die, we speak
our African languages. I believe that we speak languages that we were born
into. Some people call it speaking in tongues because they don't know it's the
language they were born into. When the ancestors come for us, we begin to
speak in our African languages.

It took me a good year to finish it. I finished that book in Seattle,
Washington, where I had gone to visit a friend. I went back over that entire
book in a week, read it, edited it, especially the part about my father. I called
my father on the phone, just to hear his voice. I went back and honed it
down, and leaned back, and listened to my father's voice. I realized when
I read it that night that I had finished it. The first time I read it all the way
through, as I got to the voice of my father, I nearly broke down, as my father
was not well during this time. It had been over six years, at that time, and he
was dying.

I'm *very* pleased about the way I wrote this book. I'd done ballads,
villanelles, and my own form and this is rhyme royal so I didn't know if
people would read it. I remember the first time I read that book out loud,
it was in an all girls' school, just outside of New York. When I finished it was
so quiet, it was so still. All of a sudden someone started clapping and I knew
it was alright and then a woman stood up and said with tears in her eyes,
"Professor Sanchez, I wish I had that book before my son died. I'm saying it
out loud for the first time, my son died of AIDS and I did not let him come
home to die." I started to cry and I went over and embraced her.

A big-time black politician started calling me on my private line to ask me
to stop talking about it in public because white people were saying that AIDS
came from Africa and that I was perpetuating that myth. But I continued
about my business. I feel very good about writing that book. I explained to
him that anything happens on this planet, we as a Black family are involved

in it. I always say, let your heart be your first teacher, let your heart inform you about your child, your husband, your family, nothing else.

From BAM to Hip Hop

SS: The Black Arts Movement was the most important movement after the Harlem Renaissance. (Morani Sanchez is currently producing a documentary on the Black Arts Movement.) There are people who tried to say it was not a movement, and that nothing happened, that it had no lasting effect. Those people are fools. It began in the 1950s and affected the whole bloody country! There is no time frame; there is cutting off. You saw people begin to write; people were reflecting. We went into the universities; we took it into the classrooms and it made people think that they could become vice presidents of corporations too. The roots of hip hop today harken back to that of the 1960s. I went to the Caribbean and we saw all the things that we had been doing and talking about in the sixties. I went to England in the 1970s and people were writing what we had been writing about in the sixties, so the influence was unbelievable. When Ngugi came to this country, I did a private reading for him in Chicago. He's heard how I read; he'd heard of my book, *Home Coming*. He came late and kind of leaned back on himself, and went, "Whoa, that's what I want to do."

I say in the introduction of *Home Coming* that we took words and sliced them up, resliced them, refocused them, turned the language around, and then put them right back into the middle and said, "Here we is." We didn't come to say, "We'd like to be here"—we are here.

It is the African in Sanchez that chants as she talks, undulates as she relates tales, softens as she recited her poetry, then strikes hard as she recalls incidents and activities throughout African American history.

SS: We taught women about women, that they could get up and read. That's what people don't want to talk about. We were invited to Berkeley and asked by white women, "How do you get up on stage with men and hold your own?" Black women have always done that. It goes back to slavery times. We were equal in the sense, that, whatever the men did, we did. What I'm simply saying is, it's something I learned from my grandmother's time. I was equal on the stage with Baraka, Marvin X, I would be reading next to last. They didn't put me first. They understood the chronology of how I read. That was real. People always talk about the sexism, but we were no more sexist than anyone else. They were all sexists, all races, from the corporations to the organizations, because that's what they knew.

We fought it . . . I fought it, sometimes from the stage, sometimes quietly too. And there were conferences (there still are) that I wasn't invited to because of that. But I still forged ahead and cut corners. Very simply, I wasn't going to take that. The so-called political men, they don't really listen to women unless they can be of some service to them. They would put women sometimes on panels and pretend that they listened. Just the idea of being a woman leader with ideas—they are listened to, but not used.

I remember that from Queen Mother Moore, more than thirty years ago, asking her, "What in the world is reparations?" I used to listen to her a lot. Thirty-five years ago, Mother was a woman in her sixties and they considered her as just an old woman and patted her on her back and said, "Yes mother." They would just listen and go about their business. Reparations is now in the vernacular and is talked about by a civil rights person, to a corporate person, to a student, who all talk about the physicality of reparations and how they can make it a reality. You can't forget her.

An Interview with Sonia Sanchez

Sascha Feinstein / 2003

From *Brilliant Corners: A Journal of Jazz & Literature*, vol. 7, no. 2 (Summer 2003): 77–98. Reprinted with permission of the author.

Sascha Feinstein: When did the crossovers between music and literature fully form in your life?

Sonia Sanchez: I grew up with music. My father was a drummer and a school teacher in Birmingham, Alabama. He was inducted into the Black Music Hall of Fame. And my father taught [the legendary drummer] "Papa" Jo Jones how to play the drums. They had an amazing friendship, and they argued amazingly, sometimes, too. ("Papa" Jo Jones was a cousin of mine and had asked me to do his biography, but when I would come up on weekends to interview him, the door would be open, he'd be gone with a note [saying that] he's at the corner bar—it was an impossible situation. Being an academic, and trying to keep my children in line—whatever—I just thought it had to stop because I couldn't pin him down.)

So I grew up in a house of music. I was probably one of the few children who could recognize [the music of pianist] Art Tatum. I'd walk into people's homes, they'd have Art Tatum on, and I'd say very casually, "Oh, I love Art Tatum." And they'd say, "What do you know about Art Tatum?" They didn't expect children to *know*. But I grew up on musicians. I met [drummer] Sid Catlett. He would put me on his lap while he talked to my father. I met all of the musicians who played down on Fifty-Second Street. My father gave up music when he came to New York City because musicians had to travel, and he had a new wife, and she was saying, "If you go overseas, that's it." My father had to make the decision between a father who would stay home with an ordinary job, as opposed to [a professional jazz musician]. But he still would do gigs in the Village—for years, until he got too old—and he gave lessons. He gave one of his drums—one of the old fashioned drums with the pedal—to Max Roach, and I still have his other drums at home.

155

I'm saying all that as background. Music has been a part of my life for a very long time, and I think music has helped me to survive for a very long time, too. I watched the motion and movement of music as it changed. I remember when bebop came in; my father didn't think it was music [Feinstein chuckles] because music was Duke Ellington, and we, who then began to listen to the new music, looked up at him and thought, "Huh. That's something 'wrong.' That's something *else* that we can be alienated with and about."

I learned about black literature from Miss Hutson—Jean Hutson—at the Schomburg [Library, now the Schomburg Center for Research in Black Culture]. After I got out of Hunter [College in 1955], I needed to get a job, so I answered an ad in the *New York Times*. The ad said the company needed a writer for their firm: "Would you please send a sample of your writing and your CV." I did. And I got a *telegram*: "Report to work on Monday at nine AM" I went down the hallway, knocked on my father's bedroom door, showed him the telegram, and said, "See? See? I *can* get a job as a writer." My father—I will never forget—gave this droll answer: "Well, go try it, but if I were you, I would really prepare to be a teacher." Right? I had *not* prepared to be a teacher at Hunter. I had prepared to go to Law School with no money. (They weren't giving out money at that time.) But being a liberal arts grad, you could always get a job teaching.

Anyway, I go downtown that Monday. I have a blue suit on. Blue shoes on. Blue hat on. Blue purse and white gloves—I *know* I look good. I didn't go on C.P. time—

Feinstein: Oh, you're terrible—

Sanchez: I was there at eight thirty. *Eight thirty.* Nobody was there, so I'm standing outside. Then in comes the secretary/receptionist, and she said, "Yes?" and I showed her this [telegram], and she opened the door. I sat down, and I'm thinking, "This is like really what I—." I mean, can you imagine? "I can make all this money before I go back to school. I have a chance to really write—they like my writing," because I was a closet writer. All of a sudden—they had another entrance there—I saw this face, and I smiled. And another face, and I smiled. And about ten minutes to nine, this guy walks up and says, "I'm so sorry, but the job is taken." I looked at my watch and said, "But I wasn't due to report until nine o'clock. How can I not have a job at ten to nine when I wasn't due here until nine o'clock?" He said, "The job is taken." I said, "But I have the telegram." He looked at it, and he looked at me, and his eyes said, "Whoa, did I make a mistake." He raised his voice— "I *said*, the job is taken."—and he walked away. I turned to the secretary and she looked down; she never looked up. I could see the offices back there, and I said, "You're discriminating against me! I'm going to call the Urban League." The guy turned around to me, like, "The Urban League? So what? What are they going to do?"

I go out, take off my hat, and I get on the train. But I was so angry that I didn't get off at Ninety-sixth and it went all the way to the East Side. I had to get to the West Side, so I said, "Okay, I'll walk across. I won't pay any more money to go back downtown." I get off at 135th Street and start crossing the street. I look up. I'm hot, I'm sweaty now, and I'm angry. And there's this guy standing out on the steps. I said, "*Schomburg*? What is the Schomburg?" He said, "It's a library." I said, "What library?" He said, "Go inside and ask the lady inside." So I walked in and saw that long, long table with all of these men— black, white scholars—sitting down like this [Sanchez bows her head], working at this long table that took up this whole room.

Miss Hutson was enclosed in a glass office where she could look out. She had her back to me, and I knocked. (She used to tell this story to all my students, and I would be so embarrassed. She used to tell it with this very subtle, sly smile.) I said, "Hello?" She said, "Yes? I'm Miss Jean Hutson." I said, "What kind of library is this? I've never heard of this library. I just got out of Hunter College. I've never heard of the Schomburg." "Oh, dear," she said. "This library *only* has books by and about black folk." And I said, at age nineteen and a half: "There must not be many books in here."

Feinstein: Wow . . .

Sanchez: She sat me down, my brother, and she said, "I'm going to bring you some books." And she brought three books: [Du Bois's] *Souls of Black Folk*, [Booker T. Washington's] *Up from Slavery*, and the top one was [Zora Neale Hurston's] *Their Eyes Were Watching God*. She said [Sanchez taps the table]: "Okay. For you, dear." I looked around. These men have not looked up yet. Didn't matter who was sitting where. They were working with all these books spread out. I had this little tiny space. I started reading, and then I got into the black English part, and I was thrown for one minute, but I kept reading. And then, I started to cry.

I inched out, knocked on her door, and said, "How can I be an educated woman and not have read these books?" and she said [Sanchez grins widely]: "Yes, dear. Now go back and read." I inched back in and read some more, and came back out again. I mean, I was *stricken* by this, my brother. Then I sat back down, and one of the scholars said [Sanchez speaks in a gruff voice]: "Miss Hutson! Will you please tell this young woman either she sits still or she has to go!" [Feinstein laughs.] And I sat still, and I read those books. I came back everyday. I stopped looking for a job. I would tell my father, "I'm going to look for a job," but I came to the Schomburg.

I had heard the music of poetry in the black schools of the South— because someone always recited Langston Hughes, Countee Cullen, or Paul Laurence Dunbar. So I knew that existed; I could hear the rhythm. Someone would do Paul Laurence Dunbar's [poem "A Negro Love Song"]: "Jump back, honey, jump back." We had heard that. We had heard the music; this poetry had been planted in our subconscious already and in a sense was ready to come out.

I always heard music as I wrote. I ignored it for a long time, or I would write, "To be sung," on the side. Or, "Clap your hands." I would give all kinds of directions. I heard the music at the base of my skull, but I never, *ever* read any of my poems with music until I was making a trek from New York to Brown University, and we got caught in a snow storm.

Feinstein: When was this?
Sanchez: This would have been in the early seventies.

Feinstein: After you published *We a BaddDDD People* [1970]?
Sanchez: Yes. By the time I got back to New York, I had two books: *Home Coming* [1969] and *We a BaddDDD People*.

So the plane was delayed. The plane circled and didn't have enough fuel to get back to New York, and finally the pilot said, "Well, I guess we'd better try to land now." I was due to read at eight. The students were told what had happened; they had gone out, eaten, and come back. It is now about ten thirty and they're ushering me into this packed auditorium. With introductions and all that, I'm reading at eleven o'clock at night. So I said, "I'll give you a good reading."

I did about an hour and a half—from eleven to twelve thirty—because they had waited, and they were so appreciative. And then someone said,

"Would you entertain a couple of questions, Professor Sanchez?" I'm thinking, *I'm whipped, and I've got to teach a class tomorrow,* but I said, "Yes. A couple." And this young African American man said, "Would you read your Coltrane poem?" I said, "I've never read that poem out loud. I've read it silently, and I read it out loud as I was writing it, but I've never read it out loud." He said, "Yeah, I know—but we waited for you for two and a half hours," and I thought, *Whoa! Okay,* and said, "Give me a minute to look it over."

I had always stretched words out, but that's as far as I would go with the music. I would go, "Ahhhhhhhhh"—merely stretching out the words, in spite of the music that I was hearing, because I didn't trust myself. "I'm not a singer. How can I do this?" In New York, we sometimes would read with musicians and drummers, so my voice was always there, but I had never done a piece like that by myself and made my voice assume all of the instruments, all of the sounds, all of the screams that the [Coltrane] poem encompasses. And when I would read with musicians, I would always be aware that *this* was the poem and *that* was the music.

Well, thank goodness for the Ancestors. And thank goodness for an appreciative audience. When I got to it, I *did* the music. I did Coltrane. The voice did everything. [Sings a brief, rising tone.] It just came to me. And from that point on, I was literally released to do whatever I wanted to do with a poem, with music, with sound. I began to investigate different languages as a consequence. I began to notate more—what should be done, what should not be done. I began the whole process of [thinking about] the poem and the music as one.

Feinstein: You've performed with [tenor saxophonist] Archie Shepp. What was that like?

Sanchez: I started teaching at Amherst in 1973, and Max Roach and Archie Shepp were there, as well as the brother who teaches music—Horace Boyer—and I began to do things with them. We did a gig at Boston University [in 1974] that's on the Black Box series. (Someone recorded it and, afterwards, sold it without our permission.) Anyway, Max said, "Why don't we do something together, Sonia?" I said, "Yeah. You want to rehearse?" (I'll never forget that.) And he said, "Oh, no! Just read a little poem. Something short." I thought, "Oh my God . . ." Not that I hadn't done anything with musicians, but we're talking a huge audience: a thousand people! They said, "You go on stage and start reading. We'll come and join you."

Well, I go out there, and, man, all of a sudden, Archie comes out and starts blowing: *Woooooooooo! Do do do–do do*! And you cannot continue to read as you were reading before. Of course I had to stop, because the audience clapped, and then I had to fit my voice and these lines over that music so they complemented each other. I truly appreciated jazz singers then; I really understood what they did on that stage. You go to a jazz place and you listen to people, and you think, "Okay. She's singing. She stops. He comes in. Simple." But they made me become a jazz singer on that stage— with poetry—and they also made me direct: "Now I'm gonna do it again as he plays"—whatever. I found myself repeating lines, also, in the same fashion that I remembered the jazz singers did. Then I'd let him play. Then I'd dip right back in. So we were doing that, and then all of a sudden, the pianist came in. Archie changed up with him, and I *couldn't* be left out, so I had to change up with the two of them. Then Max came out and started beating. It was an amazing moment.

When I finished, I left and let them play, and when they finished, Max said, "See? I told you it would work," and he threw me up in the air. And you know what it reminded me of? "Papa" Jo Jones. He would come to our house in Alabama for Sunday dinner—he'd come in chewing gum, with that kind of rhythm that he had—and he'd come for us: my sister and I would try to run away. But he'd grab me while talking to my father, throw me in the air, and, at the last minute, he caught me. I just knew he would not catch me, 'cause he was not looking at me. He'd say, "Okay, Sonia! And you know what I think—" and then he caught me. Your heart would be on the floor someplace, and your stomach . . . [Feinstein laughs.] And all the time he was talking, he had his foot moving.

It's only been in the last two years that I've stopped doing that, too— tapping my foot. People would say, "Why don't you stop?" My foot was always moving with a fast beat. When I'd walk with my children outside, I used to walk like my father and "Papa" Jo: *fast*. My children would say, "Ma! Why don't you slow down?' I would say, "Well, keep up!" [Chuckles.] It was always some kind of rhythm that was going on, some kind of beat that I kept with me.

The students at Amherst were so interested in jazz, and I did a lot with the students. They would play and I would read. As a consequence, they began to make the connections between music and poetry, that there was really no separation at all. The college had promised them more professors, and one of the things the students wanted was their own music person there because UMass had Max and Archie. So I contacted [multi-reed instrumentalist] Yusef Lateef and asked if he wanted to teach, and he said yes. The people in the music department didn't care who we got—until they found out who Yusef Lateef *was*. Then the music department started saying, "Well, a man like him should be in the music department." I said, "No! He should be in the Afro American Studies department," because we had different disciplines that made up the Afro American Studies department. Do you know they fought me for that? And Yusef didn't want to get caught in the middle. That's not his aura, you know? I had said to him, "It's not a controversy. Just say that you want to be in our department." But the music department *made* this a controversy, so he didn't come.

At Amherst, the more I listened to this music, the more music would infiltrate the lines of poetry. Now I find myself always, always, always—in each poem—making the music happen. But then I sometimes had a run-in with the music: I would want to be lyrical as opposed to musical. There was a battle that went on. Sometimes the lyrical would take hold. The music came out, however, when I spoke/wrote in Wolof. My brother, as he moved towards death, began to speak Wolof because the ancestors spoke Wolof to him. So I would write "to be sung." I allowed the music to come out in that kind of history, as opposed to interfering with the lyricism of the poem. Because the poem took rhyme royal form, the lines that I had that were infused with music weren't working as well. I had to come in and cut—do you know what I'm saying?—cut the music from them.

I usually do two books at one time because when one's working, the other one's not working. I was doing *Wounded in the House of a Friend* and *Does Your House Have Lions?* I had started *Does Your House* first, but in the middle of this book, there were voices that I heard which were similar to the music. When I say "music"—I would hear music in a different language, and I would call my friends who are African and say, "What is this?" and they would say, "Oh—that's Wolof." I said, "I must have heard someone singing it someplace and picked it up. Tell me how to say this properly. Does this mean what I think it means?" It was a real joy.

When I did a piece for Gerald Penny—one of the young students who drowned at Amherst—I relied a lot on the music. That piece not only had African qualities but Native American qualities as well. I said to someone as I was doing this piece, "In this place it's like *massacres* have been here, so the sounds that I hear I know cannot be African—I know they're Native American," and someone told me about that whole area: "There was a massacre on this spot," and I said, "I know." I mean, I didn't *know*, but I could feel it, feel the chanting.

I believe all of our chants or chanting are the same, anyway. You cannot have people invade—the way the Moors did, get into France, and Italy, and as far away as Ireland—without leaving something behind (part of a language, and music, too). The *cante jondo*—the deep song—is in each one of our cultures. One of the *cante jondo* is the blues. The *cante jondo* that became urban—more modern—is jazz, in my head. At some point, when you hear that wail, that song, that fusion, that movement off the ground into the sky—then you know this is ancient and modern at the same time.

That's what I try to capture when I chant: a combination of what is ancient and what is modern. Sometimes I do the ancient part by incorporating the African language into it, and then the sound. I've done "Middle Passage" [published in *Wounded in the House of a Friend* as "Improvisation"] in the Midwest, my brother, and I have broken down because I have heard the Native American voices. And I've had Native Americans come up to me and give me something, like a piece of jewelry. They'll say, "I heard our voice in there," and I say, "Yes, because it's the same voice." When you travel and you hear the different cultures, then you know this is indeed the same voice. People have just separated our voices and said, "This one belongs over here—in Ireland. This one belongs in Scotland. This one belongs in the Middle East—and it's only a Middle Eastern sound"—and you know that's not true. These people have moved back and forth and have left their chants, their smells, their sounds, and new people have been born and picked up those old sounds and said, "Oh, look—a new sound." But we know it's the same *old* sound. That's why I'm so amazed when I hear flamenco. I stop—because it's an old sound, but a new sound. It's in the mountains, but it's also in a bare, urban apartment in Harlem.

That's what I try to do when I use music: I try to make people hear that which they ignore. I try to make people hear that which they would rather not sing. They'd rather *say* it and get it over with, and I'll say, "No—this is a poem that is to be sung. It is to be hummed. It is to be turned over on its side so you can see the juices inside. Sometimes I dry it off and then give it back to you in a dry fashion, but it is still the song and the poem—at the same time."

Feinstein: Is it okay to talk about Etheridge Knight? [Sanchez and Knight were married from 1968 to 1970.]
Sanchez: Sure.

Feinstein: We were friends, and whenever we were on panels discussing jazz-related literature, Etheridge always mentioned your writing: "Sonia's work *drips* with jazz." How do you think jazz influenced his work?
Sanchez: I think jazz influenced his work in a different way from mine.

Feinstein: Your poems *sound* different.
Sanchez: Yes. Very different. I think the jazz poems Etheridge did were always in *homage* to someone, you know what I'm saying? He made the line become jazz, but I would never say that Etheridge was a Jazz Poet the way that some of us are. Or let me put it this way: to me, his poems oozed of blues, which is very close to jazz but never makes that turn. There is so much pain in Etheridge's work that his poems are always infused with the blues life, the blues style, the blues way of looking at the world. If you do jazz, my brother, you see a win. That's why I love jazz. Jazz musicians, when they play, are saying, "I got it. I see a win."

When I do a blues, and I try to make it "smart" sometimes, I try to infuse an urban style blues, because Bessie [Smith], when she was talking about the rich man in her blues, there was a win there, there was a tartness there, there was a smartness there. And, as much as I loved Etheridge, I think he didn't see a win. He could *record* jazz, but he was not of *jazz*. He could admire all of those people, and listen to the music, but he couldn't *sing* it. Do you know what I'm saying? I don't know if I'm right or wrong on this. But if you listen to him read, he never could jazz it up from the voice. It was always like what I call "the old poetry," like Dudley Randall reading. It was just that kind of sing/song thing. There were times when he wrote lines and you wanted to say, "Whip it. Twist it, turn it. Send it up, and then send it back down." But he couldn't do it that way. That's what I meant [before]: he could write about jazz, and he did write about jazz—he wrote some exquisite poems, wonderful poems with the aroma of jazz—but when you opened it up, it wasn't jazz, it was blues.

Feinstein: Who then—for you—would be among the true jazz poets?
Sanchez: I don't want to say that you have to be in an urban setting to
do jazz. That's not necessarily true. But I do think that the people who really
touch on a jazz motif not only make poems about jazz but create jazz riffs. In
other words, the composition of the poem is jazz, the delivery of the poem is
jazz, and the juice, infusing it, is jazz. [Amiri] Baraka does it well. Quincy
[Troupe] does it well. Jayne [Cortez] does it well. A lot of the younger poets
do it well. Ras Baraka is just like his father on so many levels. Sometimes I
have to close my eyes to try to figure out the difference there. I think Eugene
[Redmond] does it. Slightly.

Feinstein: He thinks of himself much more as a blues poet.
Sanchez: That's what I'm saying—"slightly." He does more what Etheridge
does, that is to say, he will write about a jazz person but he's not in it.

Feinstein: I don't think Eugene would argue with that. He doesn't consider
himself to be a jazz poet.
Sanchez: Some people think they *are*, and I don't want to give my opinion
just to run over people. Some people think that if they're writing a poem
about a jazz person, they are a jazz poet. I've been listening to Eugene
[Redmond]. He will write a poem about a jazz person, but he's not really a
jazz poet per se. I think you're right: he's more infused with the blues.

There were a lot of jazz poets in *Black Fire* [*An Anthology of Afro-American
Writing*, 1968]. You don't see a lot of them now. . . . That was an amazing collection: you saw what they were doing, how they were moving. And that
anthology that you did [with Yusef Komunyakaa, *The Jazz Poetry Anthology*,
1991]: you can see that some of the poets in there are really jazz poets,
because they got it. They not only have the composition of it but I've heard
them deliver it, and they're *into* what a jazz poem is all about—from the riff
on down to what I call the silences between the lines. That's what I try to do
(though I'm not sure if it always works). When you're silent, you let the
music resonate from your voice so people hear it, and then you come back in
on it. That's when you don't have the music with you, so you do it. I try to
make the silences. When I stop, I'm saying to an audience, "Come on. Hear it.
Come back into it." That kind of thing.

I don't always know how one does it, but I know at some point that once
you hear that music then it's all possible. But you have to hear that music

back here, in the base of the skull. I used to ignore it because initially I kept saying, "I can't sing." I thought it had to do with singing, but it doesn't have to do with singing, you know what I'm saying? I was limiting myself. I was limiting myself to a jazz singer, as opposed to a jazz poet. So, when I said to that young man at Brown, "But, I've never read that. I don't sing" (and I had *written* "to be sung"), I was limiting myself. I had to leave that arena of limiting myself to being a jazz singer. As a poet performing with musicians, you sometimes have to go back to that arena because you have to do some of the things that a jazz singer would do. But when you're performing by yourself, you don't have to. You accomplish everything. You pull the horn with you. You pull the drums with you.

Feinstein: What would you consider to be some of your representative jazz poems?

Sanchez: Well, obviously, the Coltrane poem. The first blues poem that I wrote is not a blues poem; it has the sensibility of the blues but it's really, at its core, in its execution, it's a jazz poem. Another jazz piece would be—and no one understands this, but I can hear Coltrane playing behind—"I have walked a long time/longer than death—." The poem for Ella. The poem "Sequences" is a jazz poem; it's a jazz poem with, like, Rahsaan Roland Kirk playing. It's a jazz suite, something like what Langston [Hughes] did in *Ask Your Mama*. At the core of that is the blues motif, but the execution is jazz.

Feinstein: You got your book title, *Does Your House Have Lions?*, from Kirk's CD set [*Rahsaan Roland Kirk Anthology*], right?

Sanchez: Yes. I was so stricken by the Kirk anthology. I thought that was an amazing question—"Does your house have lions?"—in many contexts. And so typical of Rahsaan to pose that question that has so many ramifications. ("You're building a house? Does your house have lions?" "What do you mean?" "You know—*lions.*") All the important buildings—libraries, banks— always used to have lions so you knew you were entering a place that was mighty, that was fortified. But if you go back to the continent of Africa and you talk about lions, you're talking about something else, too—the lion as Juba—so that the lion goes back beyond what we see here in the States. And that's why I thought, "What a title!" and I put it in my journal.

As I was writing this book, which is about my brother [dying of AIDS], I didn't have a title. All of a sudden, it hit me: this is what I've been talking about—the idea of a family having lions, the kind of protection that they should have at some particular point. About a country, too, having that kind of protection. So I knew that was the title.

We did this piece [Sanchez taps the cover of *Does Your House Have Lions?*] with music, did you know that? [Tenor saxophonist] Odean Pope, a percussionist, Khan Jamal, and a dancer, Rennie Harris, who danced the part of my brother. I read. We came on stage all dressed in white. It began with the sister's voice, with the brother at seventeen (the dancer) coming out in a green suit. By the time he was getting ready to die, of course, he'd pulled off his layered clothes and was all in white, also. In many societies, of course, people wear white when people die, or in celebration of life. Odean did all the music.

Feinstein: He's a tremendous musician. There's a reason Max Roach played with him for years.
Sanchez: He *is* amazing. He did the music for that. We were supposed to have a director there at the theater, but he was away in California and came back only two days before. Odean looked at me and I looked at him, and we said to each other, "We'd better do this ourselves and plan this ourselves, 'cause this guy's going to come in and do lighting, but we're going to have to do the actual work" [chuckles]. So we ended up directing ourselves.

Feinstein: That's smart—to make sure that it's done the way that you want it to be done.
Sanchez: We had a chance to try it out before we did it on stage. I had a gig someplace up in Pennsylvania, and I told the people, "You have to send a big car for me," and we had this limo where we could put all the instruments in. So, lo and behold, I came into this place with "my posse" (like I told you yesterday, those students were "my posse" last night), and we heard what was not working, what was working, on stage. That was really very good for us, and when we did it again at the theater, it really came together. It was what music and theater could be, what poetry and dance could be.

Feinstein: What was it like to be one of the relatively few female voices to represent the Black Arts Movement of the late 1960s?
Sanchez: [Laughs]: It was amazing. People complain and say that Black Arts was sexist. I say to people, "*America* was sexist." All the political organizations

were sexist, so that was not just part of Black Arts. But: they weren't sexist on stage. Baraka, Ed Bullins, Marvin X, Larry Neal—I was the only woman on stage with them, and they did not treat me differently. They didn't make me go first, for example, which would have been the completely sexist thing to do.

I always tell this story about Baraka and myself: when we went out to California [in 1965], we thought we were some *baaad* people, know what I mean? And we did our first reading at San Francisco State—just the two of us, right? We did this reading where he read something and I read something—we did like a jazz thing. He did something and I answered him; he looked at me, and I answer him with a poem. He said, "Ta doo da doo doo," and I was, "Ta doo da dee dee," and he said, "Ra tuh ta ta," and I was "Dada tatata"—I mean, you loved what you were doing on stage and you understood what the stage was about. And then someone raised a hand and said, "Could you do that again?"—I remember being so taken aback—"You did it so fast. We didn't understand it." Whoa! (I think about the rappers today—talk about *fast* fast.) And we went, "Okay." And so he read, and then I read, but we were self-conscious.

That was an amazing moment for me. It was the first time I understood the difference between the East Coast and the West Coast, the first time I understood that when you're in different places you have to read things in a different fashion. And it got to be tricky, sometimes, because you always hear the rhythm. You know how you're going to read something, and all of a sudden I heard myself slowing it down 'cause I looked at the audience. "Where are you? Where are you off to?" You had to slow down the beat, just a little bit.

I remember a concert called ToBu—Towards a Black University—down at Howard University, where we honored Sterling Brown in a big gym. I'm trying to remember if there was another woman poet on that program; I don't think so. It was Baraka, Haki [Madhubuti], Larry [Neal], some other poets, and then Sterling at the end. I read right before Baraka—[Sanchez chuckles] I *always* read right before Baraka—and then Sterling came on and the place exploded. And Sterling said [Sanchez deepens her voice to sound more formal]: "These young poets right here used to scare me."

He was like Dr. Arthur P. Davis—remember that seminal essay where he called us "The Poets of Hate"? (This is an aside but I think it's important because I think that people can change.) I had gone to Howard to do a reading, years later, and there, with his hand up, is Dr. Davis. And I said,

"Oops . . ." [Laughs.] "How you doing, sir?" He said [Sanchez imitates an exceedingly self-conscious tone]: "My name is Arthur P. Davis. I was here at Howard for forty-odd years, and I wrote an essay called 'The Poets of Hate.'" Then he said, "I was wrong." It was an amazing moment. We became very dear friends. During the time when he was ill, I used to take the train and read to him once a week. In fact [taps the cover of *Does Your House Have Lions?*], I started that book during the time when he was ill, and I would read to him, and he said to me, "That is a great book." He said, "The thing that I realize is that you have exemplified people starting at one point and continuing to evolve and grow. What I said about all those poets . . . What they were saying, they *had* to say in that way."

No one would have heard us if we had said, "I am a poet. I am here to read you a poem." You had to come out and go, "*Ahhh ah ah!*" because *then* everyone looked up. There was no ready-made audience for poetry. Young people think, "Oh, I wish I had been back there with you." We had to *make* the audience. And you make an audience by learning how to walk a stage: if I came out and stayed right in the middle of the stage, people would look and then look away, but if I came out and moved on that stage, they followed you. People would wonder, "What is she doing?" And if you used a curse word, people would go, "*Oh* . . ." [Feinstein laughs.] But you'd never use another curse word, because you'd grabbed them, you'd brought them in. You needed all sorts of techniques to bring people into that arena because people were not interested in poetry.

Baraka probably won't tell this story, but Ed Bullins organized a program for us [in the late 1960s?] and there were, at most, twenty people there. We got on stage and started to read, and someone leaned over and said, "What they doing?" Some guy says, "They reading poetry." "I thought they were gonna sing—let's go!" [Sanchez laughs.] The whole first row got up and left. But all they did was make us hone our skills, more and more. Hone the music. Made us appreciate what we were doing. And it also made us, initially, change to make it slower and then speed it up again. We brought them back with us. We said, "Okay. I gave you a chance to hear it, now come on—ride this way." And then, it made them do what we did: they came at it at another level, at our level. It was an infusion of the East Coast on the West Coast. We were privileged to be a part of the Black Arts on the East Coast, and then the Black Arts West in San Francisco. We were there with the Black House when Eldridge Cleaver came out of jail—but I *never, ever* liked that man. I went on record from the very beginning. I mean, the Panthers came to talk to me because I said, "He's not a revolutionary," and a lot of people said, "Well, you don't understand." *That's* when a lot of the sexism came out: "Well, you know, Sonia, you don't understand. You just a woman," and I said, "No. No no. I might be just a woman, but he is no revolutionary." Haki [Madhubuti] brought me *Soul on Ice* [to review for *Negro Digest*], and—I'll never forget—I stayed up and read that book. The next day, I got up and said, "Haki, when I write this review, the first line will be, 'Eldridge Cleaver is not a revolutionary. He's a hustler.' I come from New York. I've seen many a hustler." I don't know where that review is; back then, you'd send stuff off with no copies 'cause you just knew they were going to print it. But they never printed it.

Many of us were so political that they banned us from teaching in New York. We challenged the universities with the stuff we were teaching in African American Studies. I taught [W. E. B.] Du Bois and [Marcus] Garvey and [Paul] Robeson out at San Francisco State, and the FBI knocked on my door with my landlord and said, "You should put her out. She's out there teaching Du *Bwah*." [Feinstein laughs.] This was 1966 or '67. People can teach Du Bois and Robeson now, but they were on the banned list then. America said they were Communists; that was what that was all about. But we were such innocents. Young people think of Black Arts and say, "Oh, you knew everything." No! I was a real *inocente*.

Feinstein: Certain qualities to your work have carried over throughout the years, but your poetry, of course, has changed, and your politics seem to have changed as well. I mean, I don't see you writing "a/coltrane/poem" at this point in your life.

Sanchez: You're right, but I use Coltrane in my music. That's the difference. Let me put it this way: when you truly are a jazz poet, you don't have to mention Coltrane; people will hear it. I carry the improvisational part of him into what I do. Coltrane is very much a part of "Middle Passage," but it's done in a different way. The music is in the beat, in the repetition.

Feinstein: What about the very conscious fusion of Coltrane and politics, which was a common element of many Coltrane poems from the late 1960s?

Sanchez: This music *is* political. Although Coltrane never came out and said, "I am a political man," he did some music that was political by the very nature of the time and the nature of what he said.

Feinstein: In titles—

Sanchez: In titles. But even when the titles aren't there, the music is still political, because all music, like poetry, is political; it either maintains the status quo or it talks about change. You see, when I first started to write, we had just found out that we'd been enslaved and no one had told us. So coming out of that we had to say something about being black. If we hadn't done that, we would not have understood our motion and movement. So you had to say, "Wow! I'm a black woman!" "Whoa! They didn't tell us we'd been enslaved!" "Oh my God! These people *did* this to us!" You had to come out slamming everybody and their mama. You had to do it. You had to exorcize that. But in the 1970s, if I happen to still be doing that, there was something wrong.

You meet people. You travel in the world. You read different poets. You get up on stages with people. One of the most important people I met in the late sixties was Paul Blackburn. He was a dear friend. I used to call Paul when he was ill with cancer, and we would talk and hug over the phone. Paul also had that great jazz sensibility—

Feinstein: "Listening to Sonny Rollins at the Five-Spot"—

Sanchez: Oh, yes. Paul loved that [kind of] poetry. And I looked up to him. And he once said, "I know you're not talking to me when you're calling people 'honkies'—" [Feinstein laughs.] I said, "But you have to give voice to these people—you gotta call them *something*," and he said, "But you limited it in your poetry." And I did—it was in, like, two poems that I did, and they were mean poems. So we were laughing about that. But some people came with preconceived notions and they were surprised if you didn't take crap. I would say to some poets, "I come to you as an equal. I'm no flunky. Don't treat me like a flunky." That was the difference, and sometimes people didn't like that. But Paul treated me as an equal, and as a friend, and I read Paul's poetry in my classes. No one's heard of him.

Feinstein: He's just not taught.

Sanchez: I suggested to a couple of students [at Bucknell] that they should really read him. I teach him in every class that I teach because I think he's such a fine poet and fine human being. That's a case of the good ones being taken early, you know what I mean?

Feinstein: There's a long list for that.
Sanchez: A *long*, mighty list for that.

Feinstein: Can you talk a little about your poem for Ella Fitzgerald?
Sanchez: Oh, yes. You know, I was going to perform that last night, but something happened to me last night: Every time I got ready to read something, the page flew open to something [else]. I'm serious. It happened three times, and you have to play that; something was happening.

I've done that Ella Fitzgerald piece on the Academy of Music stage—not with any musicians. I chose that piece because it was a celebration of Ella, and I love that piece because I try to make my voice at the end—[Sanchez sings three notes, the last rising until it's out of her vocal range]. The Philadelphia musicians who were there were like, "Whoa! We would have come out there with you if we had known you were going to do that," and I said, "Well, I never know how I'm going to do that with her." I just thought it was so important to celebrate that woman.

And I've got to do a Sarah [Vaughan] poem. (I don't have it yet; I've done parts.) Ella was very much of this earth. She never left this earth. She was given a voice like no other voice; her voice could travel but, as high as it got, it always stayed earthbound. The beauty of it was that it went *inside* the earth, then came up and out, and then came back down. But *Sarah* left the universe sometimes. Sarah sang so that you would close your eyes and move out of this world into another world. Sometimes she sounded ancient: she went back—really went back—back to Africa, back to India, back to the Middle East, back to Spain. Ella couldn't do that.

Feinstein: Do you have a preference for early or late [recordings of] Sarah?
Sanchez: Well, I told you I grew up with music, and I remember when I heard Sarah for the first time, my father said, "She does too much with her voice. It's too rich," and then he said, "When she gets older it'll get better." I remember that. Sarah didn't know what to do with what she had in her early years. She'd go: [Sanchez scats briefly]. And when she got older—my God. The richness. The layers. So many layers. See, she was just an American voice in her early years. Then she became an international voice. She became a universal voice. She became Indian, African, Spanish, Mexican. She became Jewish; she became Palestinian. She went down in *there*—beyond her gut to her womb. Amazing. Much later, I said to my father, "You were right," and he

said, "I know." He didn't ask what I was talking about. [Feinstein laughs.] My father always had something to say about something. But he was right.

I was working one night, and [the radio station] WRTI started playing this Brazilian album that she made. Actually, there are three [*I Love Brazil, Brazilian Romance,* and *Copacabana*], but there's one ["Empty Faces/Vera Cruz," from *I Love Brazil*] where she starts doing this chant that's African/ Jewish/Indian/Native American . . . I sobbed. I just sobbed. Then I bought the album. It is *amazing.* It does what every artist attempts to do.

I studied [at New York University] with a woman named Louise Bogan—

Feinstein: Sure—

Sanchez: Bogan was right about the poet being a universal person, and I began to understand what that was about. I didn't have to change my skin to become universal. The moment you pull out and you give out this sound, this lyricism, these lines that might be talking about my experience in Harlem, or my experience—wherever—someone will pick it up and say, "Oh, yeah. I had a similar experience."

That's what happened when we went out to San Francisco: we left in search of ourselves—our history and herstory in the black studies—and we found everybody else, hidden. I mean, I'd be in a classroom and someone would pass by and say, "Sonia, here is a picture. We think this is of a concentration camp for Japanese. You have a couple of Japanese students; bring it up in class." That was how we were teaching. And the students got *mad* at me: "*I don't know anything about that, Sonia!*" They really got pissed. But I said, "At least ask your parents about this." My brother, these eighteen year olds came back to class that Tuesday with tears in their eyes. Their parents had told them that they had been *in* the concentration camps, but they had kept it a secret. That's what happened to us: we went searching for ourselves and we discovered other people hidden, too. Japanese. Chinese. Motion and movement. You couldn't teach this and stay in one place. You had to go out.

Bogan was an interesting woman [chuckles]. Very aristocratic woman, right? There were a couple of things she said that were amazing, that have held true. She's the reason I'm so strict in class. A lot of students don't understand that. The other day, I walked in when some students were throwing candy across the table, and I turned and said, "Stop it. . . . You wouldn't do that in another class." I was saying to them, "This is creative writing. This is holy to me. Come make it holy." Some of the students are really privileged and spoiled; they're not accustomed to anyone saying anything like that, being strict. In a history class, or a science class, they wouldn't behave that way. But in a creative writing class, they're like, "Hey . . ." They *say* they want to write, but, my brother, they really don't. It's too casual. It's not what it means to you, or to me, or to Yusef [Komunyakaa] or someone else. I'm serious about that. In the classroom, I'll kid around—but you can't demean the atmosphere. Sometimes in private schools, creative writing is just like, "Oh, yeah, yeah. One credit—I'll get it. Whatever. I'm gone."

Bogan was strict, too, and I know that that's how I teach because she was my teacher on many levels. I'll never forget asking her, "Do I have any talent?" She said [Sanchez imitates a slow, haughty delivery]: "*Many* people have talent, Sonia." [Feinstein laughs.] I said, "Well, yeah—but I'm not talking about many people. I'm talking about *me*." I wanted to know, should I invest something in this? And she said, "It depends. What do you want to do with it?" And I said, "Well, you just informed me about this, and I don't think I know what to do with it—" and she said, "Yes, you doooo." As I look back on that question that she posed, it might have been a double-layered question because she's looking at me, and I was the only black in that class, right? But in that class, I was the first poet who got published—because Bogan would make you send your work out. And I do the same thing. (I started doing it with this class at Bucknell but they weren't interested.) I'm always coming to my classrooms saying, "There's an anthology . . ." And I've always had students get into anthologies. I say, "Send stuff out. Mention that you're in my class—whatever." So I've had students included in books such as *Confirmation* [*An Anthology of African-American Women*, 1983] on down to *Bum Rush the Page* [*A Def Poetry Jam*, 2001]. I tell my students, "Send stuff in," and they're *in* there, you know? Because this is what this business is about, at some point.

But I'm also amazed by the people who don't have that kind of energy toward this thing that we do called poetry. I teach people who have such egos at such a young age. I say to those people in my class, "You will never, ever *move* with that ego. You've got to drop it." One way to do that is to work with musicians, 'cause you will drop your ego real fast—[Feinstein laughs]—if you're in there for about thirty minutes. They say, "Okay. Show me what you got," and you say, "Oh my God." You're going to get out in front of a whole bunch of people, two hundred people, and you're thinking, "What am I *doing*?"

At the Painted Bride in Philadelphia, where they have readings and music and dance, we did an evening of poetry and music—[vibraphonist] Khan Jamal, Odean, and a bass player [Tyrone Brown], and it was really nice. I had given them the poem, and we played with it a great deal and had a lot of fun on stage. When we finished, the people said, "No. You can't get off the stage." We were tired. We had done about an hour. (An hour by yourself is tiring, but an hour with music—you're very much aware of whom you're dealing with.) But musicians are amazing people, let me tell you. Khan and Odean said, "Come on back, Sonia. Let's do something," and they started playing. [Sanchez sings musical lines in the spirit of Odean Pope.] And then Odean came and stood there right next to me. And you can't look at an audience and say, "I don't have anything written . . ." It got to be funny, so that's when I started with the laughter: [laughs with a staccato sound] and Odean went [sings with a similar rhythm]. That's why when I read "Middle Passage" I start off with laughter. [Sanchez laughs again, then reads very quickly from "Improvisation" in *Wounded in the House of a Friend*]: "It was It was It was It was / It was the coming that was bad." I hear nothing but music in that.

The Ancestors. Thank God for the Ancestors. The Ancestors came in and helped me out. That's what they put in my mouth. "It was / it was the coming that was bad." Of course, I added stuff later on, and that's when we started moving on the stage. And Odean really pushed me. He pushed me to such a point that on stage I actually got down to my knees.

I did this piece down in Atlanta with—what's his name?—the jazz singer out of Chicago—Brown—

Feinstein: Oscar?

Sanchez: Oscar Brown. We did a set together. He sang, and then he went off stage, and I read some blues pieces and then "Middle Passage" with some of his musicians. And these brothers were so subtle at first, so quiet, and then they started pushing me until I almost had to give up. Again, I literally got down on my knees to do that piece.

But Odean has pushed me to a place deeper than I have ever been. I have done the piece in other ways, but every time I do it, I hear Odean. That's what I meant about Coltrane, and what musicians will do: they cause you to make the word respond to the music until it becomes the music.

Feinstein: I appreciate what you're saying about the poet and musician inspiring each other, but, in general, don't you think musicians tend to inspire writing more than writing inspires music? I mean, I've published a lot of pieces by writers on music, but very few by musicians on literature. It seems to be predominantly in one direction.
Sanchez: That's so true.

Feinstein: Why do you think that is?
Sanchez: I don't know. I think that they probably don't see themselves necessarily as writers, or, if they are writers, they don't feel the need to talk about it. I think if you're a musician, and people can't write what you want, you probably have to write what you need to play, or to hear played, or you have to write what you're feeling at some particular point. Nobody else is going to do that for you. I think that is what you see—that writing became an extension of the music. And I think it takes a little genius to do that— a little extra genius to do that: "Now let me sit down and write this, too."

Feinstein: I think music will always have the edge on literature. There are things that I can feel and understand through poetry that I do not understand so absolutely, perhaps, through music—either as a listener or a player—but there's an immediacy to music that literature can only aspire towards.
Sanchez: That is so true. I mean, that is *so* true. Sometimes you try to make the poem *do* all that, and when I read from *Does Your House Have Lions?* I repeat, I go back, like a musician would do. I'll do it three times. There's a section where I break the form in *Does Your House Have Lions?* where my brother talks about being touched. (I had gone down to take care of my brother and whenever I touched him, he said it hurt. You know, with AIDS patients every time you touch them it hurts, right?) Although I had written the passage three times, I had never read it three times:

> hold me with air
> breathe me with air
> sponge me with air
> whisper me with air
> comb me with air
> brush me with air
> rinse me with air.

And I didn't realize until I read with Odean that it needed that repetition. Isn't that something? I mean, that subconscious is a mutha, you know what I mean? [Both laugh.] It is a *mutha*. . . .

I changed to sound like Odean, like his horn. I broke it up and repeated the lines. People hear the sweet lines, and all of a sudden you don't *want* people to hear the sweet lines. You want them to know how horrific it is, on many levels.

The first time I performed the piece, I tried to stay true to the line, because that's what you do if you're a writer: you don't want to change that line. But if you're working with musicians, you *have* to change it. That's why collaboration with musicians is something else: it changes the poetry so much. But also, the poem can change the music. I would say to Odean, "I hear how you're playing it, but that's not how I hear it." I'd read it, and he would hear what I meant. We both came with an idea of what that book was about, and then we collided—in a nice fashion—and we listened—in a most wonderful fashion—and then it became something else, something completely different. That's what's so wonderful about working with musicians.

Interview with Sonia Sanchez:
Poet, Playwright, Teacher, and
Intellectual Activist

Joyce A. Joyce / 2005

This interview was conducted in Ms. Sanchez's home on March 20, 2005, and April 9, 2005.

Joyce: In an early interview with Anita Cornwell, you said that your Aunt Sarah kept the twins while you worked in New York City and Amherst, Massachusetts. Who is Aunt Sarah? I don't remember other references to her.

Sanchez: My Aunt Sarah was my father's sister, my grandmother's daughter who took care of me and my sister after my grandmother "Mama" died. She would some years later come and live with me to take care of my twins for a couple of years when I taught in New York City and at Amherst College in Amherst, Massachusetts. And so a very important part of my life was this woman who took care of me when I was a child.

Joyce: You once said to me that in the 1960s and maybe you included the 1970s that publishers were more interested in protest than they were in imagery like some poems in *Under a Soprano Sky* that have quite a bit of imagery. This comment reminds me of the fact that Black male writers of the Harlem Renaissance, such as Hughes and McKay, had more opportunities for publishing and have been more historically taught in universities than Black women poets of the Harlem Renaissance, such as Georgia Douglas Johnson and Mae Cowdery. Can you please comment on how who and what is published determine the characteristics of a particular literary period?

Sanchez: I think I had at some point talked about the period that we were writing in and the kinds of poems that were probably prevalent at that particular time. And many of the poems that I wrote were poems that spoke to what was happening in America. So many [of these poems] were, perhaps, protest poems. However, if you read my Malcolm poem, it is very gentle, loving, and generous in imagery. I wrote some poems that were full of imagery at the same time that I wrote poems like "Definition for Black Children" that used the jargon of the day. I tried to mix both. I was aware also of how poetry was selling at the time. And I think that how poetry was selling at the time was that many of the people saw us as poets who were very much interested in the things that had a big bang, a big noise to it. An urban smartness. So the poems I did about the Supremes and "Revolutionary Pimp" were poems that were said in the language of the day. And I think what we were trying to do and trying to show, in a sense, was this language that people spoke, the masses spoke, the workers spoke, the revolutionaries spoke, the students spoke was also language that should be considered poetic. Just as Sterling Brown took the language of workers and Black folks and used their Black English, I tried to do the same thing with urban Black English.

The Black English that we spoke in the streets of New York City, I also put that into my poems and said, "See, look at it. It exists. It be." And so, I very consciously wrote the language that people and I spoke. And so, I wrote within the context of this urban language, because that's what this was—this urban, this northern urban language that many of us were using at some point. It was similar to Black southern speech, but it had a different kind of rhythm, a different kind of movement, you know, a different kind of urgency, a different way of looking at the world. We were Malcolm's daughters and sons, you see. We were his children, because this language was that very hip, modern, humorous, urban language, and our poetry reflected that also. And so a lot of the imagery that you find in *Under a Soprano Sky* was in poems that I had written in my journal. And in that book, I decided, just as I decided for the first time in *Love Poems*, the first book of love poems I did, I decided to put in my haiku. I had been writing haiku all along, but I had never published them. Because I didn't think the haiku would sail under the skies, under the sixties skies that we were sailing under. I thought that at that particular time, it was not a sky for a haiku to ride under, to be on top of. But it was a different kind of sky we were riding. It was a Black sky. And Japanese haiku were not sailing under that sky. But you see that doesn't mean you're not writing different kinds of poems. And at some point, I think that it's important for you to be on time as we were on time in the sixties. But also, it is necessary to check on oneself, to keep looking back at time so time doesn't pass you by. So I published my haiku so I could be on time with this necessary form. I also wrote *A Blues Book for Blue Black Magical Women* because it was time for me to do a longer poem about Black women in the struggle.

At the time I was writing *A Blues Book for Blue Black Magical Women*, I was reading *The Book of the Dead*, a book on masonry, *A Book of the Beginning*, the Koran, the Bible, and Anacalypsis. The book was just infused with all of that. At the time that I was writing *A Blues Book*, every night I had the same dream. And the dream was that I was in this tomb with my mother, who was Egyptian and dressed in blue. And I went back to the same place where she was buried and in some miraculous way I was in the space with her, and she talked to me, sang to me, and said, "I will protect you." These dreams helped me to complete the poem because each time I came out of the dream, I would literally sit down to write. After I had finished the book, I asked Ademola to do the cover. I told him that what I remembered about the dream is that my mother wore blue, and he brought me the blue of Egypt and the pyramids and a royal woman surrounded by her story. It is a beautiful cover. I haven't told many people about that experience except in an interview with Gloria Hull.

Joyce: Akasha Gloria Hull?
Sanchez: Gloria Hull. It was her book on spirituality.

Joyce: I have that. It is called *The New Spirituality of African American Women*. In the dictionary of symbols blue is the color for spirituality.
Sanchez: At this time I knew that I would use all the different forms that I had learned under Louise Bogan at NYU. At this time I knew that I would write what I wanted to write. I think I answered that right?

Joyce: In your interview with Claudia Tate, you talked about the systemic plotting, whose aim was to disintegrate the political activities of the 1960s' revolution. How does this disintegration manifest in contemporary Black culture in Africa and in the Diaspora?
Sanchez: Well, I mentioned that many of us were teaching in something called Black Studies. And we all looked at some point and realized that people had been sent into our classes to report on us. I think that

I mentioned to you before that I was home one day from school on a day that I was not teaching, and my landlord came and knocked on my door and said, "These two men want to talk to you." And the guy took out his FBI badge, and he screamed at me, "You are teaching Du Bois, Hughes, Garvey, Robeson." And I said, "Yes." How dumb and naïve I was. I said, "Yes, you cannot teach Black literature without all these people." That's how dumb I was. This man stared at me, and he turned to my landlord and said, "You should put her out. She is one of those radicals on the campus, and she needs to be put out!" I didn't understand his anger, for I was teaching Black lit at that time thematically. At that time I did not teach the sociology, history, herstory, and economics of literature. This agent was so mad at me. The other agent stood still as stagnant water, while his partner performed and got red in the face, and said again screaming at me, "You're teaching Du Bois, Garvey, Hughes, Robeson." Finally, I realized how useless this all was and said goodbye as I closed the door.

Joyce: Why do you think, perhaps, professors were far more engaged in political activism in the sixties and seventies than they are today?
Sanchez: I think professors knew the reason why they were in that university was because of students. I came into the university system because of students, because of the student movement at San Francisco State. The students sat down and said simply that we're going to have this and open enrollment. So at San Francisco State, you had Jerry Vernado, Jimmy Garrett; you had all of these young brothers and sisters in the Black Student Union. The sister actually did all the hard work of this organization. How courageous! How brave! What vision they had when they declared, "We'll going to have Black Studies at San Francisco State College." And we the professors knew that we were in that struggle together. It was a struggle that involved students and the students involved us, so it was an involvement of a community. To come back to your question is that what happened was the student activism died down and also the activism in the streets of America had died down. As a result, you had people who came into the university who didn't understand, didn't know about the activism of students or didn't care, or they came through being educated in other places. So they didn't feel any responsibility to students. They didn't necessarily feel that they were there because of students. They thought that they were there because they had gotten a Ph.D. some place. So that's what you see sometimes now in universities. There are still

people like you and Professor Bracey, Professor Elaine De Lancey, Chinua Achebe, Ngugi wa Thiong'o, Toni Morrison, and Amiri Baraka who maintain a responsibility to students.

I would also include that entire group at the University of Massachusetts. I like that Black Studies Program at UMass; it's a good program, and they're good people there, and they're progressive people, too. They are teachers still, but they know at some point that they had come into the university system via students, you know, via the activism of students, who demanded Black Studies. And so you come in under that and look up and understand that you have a grand responsibility, a great responsibility to make sure they get their information, to make sure that they study, to make sure that they have a consciousness that they continue, to make sure that they learn. It's a grand responsibility that you have. But you know it's a reciprocal kind of thing that I always felt; I knew I was there because of them, because of their needs and their interests at that particular point. And I think, as I said, that some people have been taught by people who do not necessarily demand that they be politically engaged, okay? And so, you have people who come in and say, "I have a Ph.D. I have a right to, to just be here." And that's true. No one is saying they don't have a right to be there. So they see themselves just as a professor. And my point is that I don't see myself just as a professor.

Joyce: Would you comment on what you see as the factors behind the high visibility of a few Black women fiction writers and the low visibility of Black women poets and poets generally? Always without exception in my classes, when I ask students to give the names of contemporary fiction writers, after they give Toni Morrison and E. Lynn Harris's names, they end the list.

Sanchez: Right. Well, that has a lot do with the whole fact that many students are not taught any literature before they get to the university, okay? We're blessed to have a Toni Morrison, of course, you know, who is a brilliant writer/thinker. I was so happy that her books were chosen for Oprah's show. So you got this great writer whose books are chosen by a woman who is one of our great communicators. And a great thing happened there because you got great literature to a mass audience.

The first time I walked into my Black lit class at San Francisco State, I was in a classroom of forty or fifty people. Then I had people practically sitting on windowsills. I had people sitting on chairs outside who were not registered. Honestly, Joyce, it was an amazing moment. And in this classroom, there were blackboards all the way around the room. So, I decided I was going to write on the boards some names, similar to the question that you ask now in 2005, right? But mine was not a question, and I started writing all these names on the boards. They were all writers. The only two writers they recognized were Malcolm X and Martin Luther King. Not Richard Wright. Not Georgia Douglas Johnson. Not Paul Robeson. Not Maria Stewart. Not Margaret Walker. Not Gwendolyn Brooks. Not Du Bois. Not Langston Hughes. Not Sterling Brown. My students said, "We never heard of them. We never knew about them." When I used to come into the classroom, they would be sitting there waiting. Every time I walked in, there were more people. There were more chairs outside the door. People just came in because they realized that they had not been taught this literature, and they wanted to learn. It was an amazing moment in history.

Joyce: Do you agree that there is a high visibility today of fiction writers compared to a low visibility of poets?
Sanchez: Well, I think that probably the thing goes in cycles, that in the sixties and seventies, the high visibility of writers were poets and playwrights.

Joyce: Yes, yes.
Sanchez: And then around the mid and late seventies, you began to see a shift, and the shift came because Alice Walker also started writing fiction. Toni Morrison begins to publish. Toni Cade Bambara, June Jordan, Amiri Baraka, Ishmael Reed were publishing essays and fiction as well. In my classroom, I taught fiction, poetry, and plays. It is important to teach all three. And I did not have emphasis on one more than the other because it is important for students to study all three of these genres. But the point is, I think, the country looked in a very serious way at poets and said that there had been disruption with this thing called poetry and therefore it should be controlled. And so, then you saw the disintegration of Broadside Press. You saw the constant struggle for survival of Third World Press, Haki Madhubuti's press, and Africa World Press. The closing down of Third Press in New York City occurred also.

So what I think that part of your question was speaking to is that we were not highly visible any more. But the interesting thing is that not only did we continue to publish, but we continued to gain an audience. There's always been an audience for poetry. Now they're saying that the audience has just started again, because of the hip-hop movement. I say to you that that is true because the hip-hop movement has grabbed this new younger generation, but when the hip-hop movement turned around and looked over its shoulder, they saw the Black Arts Movement. I brought Chuck D to Temple to speak to students. He got up onstage and said, "Well, you know, I'm indebted to Sanchez and Baraka, and the last poets and that group of people, because my parents gave me their books." And so he and others understood from whence they came. The same thing that Mos Def, Talib, Common, Kanye, Toni Blackman, and Ursula Rucker understand.

If I can elaborate further, I know, very well, what this country is capable of, and I know that this country will attempt to "whiteball" you if you appear to be too potent, too powerful, and will put every little thing in your way. But the country always underestimates the PEOPLE. The people in spite of the country will get to you, will invite you some place. The point is that my work has continued to sell over the years and I hope will continue to sell over the years, because at some point, there have been people I've influenced by being in the university, by teaching workshops and by staying on that circuit, and I think that's important.

There has always been a legacy of poetry. And so Russell Simmons, Danny Simmons, Bruce George, and Stan Latham tapped into that legacy. And we have Def Poetry Jam on television, coming out of the sixties, the seventies, and the hip-hop movement.

Joyce: In 1970, you taught a course on the Black woman at the University of Pittsburgh. Choosing writers to teach is always a difficult process, particularly when we've had so many good ones. Whom did you teach, and why?
Sanchez: It was not in 1970; I think it was 1969. I came home to New York. So in '69, I really, really did not have any writers per se other than those people who had done essays and a lot of the poets. I used Margaret Walker's *Jubilee*. But a lot of things were excerpts that I had accumulated in 1969. We looked at many short stories, African history, and the Moynihan report.

Joyce: In anthologies?
Sanchez: Anthologies, right. There was an African woman professor who taught at the University of Pittsburgh. I asked her to come in and teach the

classes on Africa and the African woman. She was excellent. I set the course up to deal with Africa, the South and slavery, freedom, the Civil Rights Movement, and the Black revolutionary movement. During the semester, we discussed matriarchy and patriarchy because the Moynihan Report had been published. The heated discussions made me search for another term that would describe the discussion that we found ourselves in. I said at the time that our survival in America was not really patriarchal or really matriarchal. What many of us truly had was a diarchy, that is in some of these Black families you had a mother and grandmother, a mother and an aunt, a mother and uncle. And the family survived.

Joyce: Could you talk a little about your friendships with Audre Lorde and Margaret Walker? I asked you this question because these two poets have such varying personalities. They began their literary careers in such different historical periods, and their poetry is strikingly different.
Sanchez: I love Audre Lorde and Margaret Walker. I've always loved Audre's poetry and prose. Her work is very complex, very layered with mythology, very direct and full of exquisite imagery.

And above all, she's always been an honest poet. So, I've always loved her poetry—the density, the politics of it, the "womaness" of it and the honesty. She says, "This is who I am. I am a lesbian, a warrior for justice and social change. Here is a poem about men, women, children, sexism, love, cancer. Here is a poem about a man loving a woman, a woman loving a woman."

And at the same time in a class I would teach Audre Lorde's books, I would teach Margaret Walker's books. Margaret is a woman who came at a different period from us. She was our teacher and mentor. She gave us a seminal book called *For My People*. She was a woman, who is a little short woman with a large mouth and an opinion about everything on the planet, a woman who gave us *Jubilee*, one of our greatest novels. This book talks about a Black woman being enslaved. This book comes out of the Black women's freedom narratives. I never call these books slave narratives.

They're freedom narratives because they're all about freedom. And so, she gives us this *Jubilee*, and we read it to learn not only about Black women and Black men being enslaved, but also about the psychology of the enslavers, both male and female. At the beginning of the novel, we see the master visiting his slave as she prepares to die, a slave that he raped as a young girl, who had been given to him by his father as property. We see this slave woman and

we see her death because the women who attend her know that there
is death in the womb. And Margaret Walker, by saying in the beginning of
this novel that there is death in her womb, is also saying there is death in the
womb of all enslaved people, in all Africans in this Western hemisphere and
for the Whites who enslaved Africans. They share a mutual death. If she
had written no other books than these, her place in Black literature would
be secure.

Joyce: I find that too many of my Black women students resist thinking of
themselves as feminists and that they are not as politicized around feminist
issues as I wish they were. I would appreciate some advice on how I can
approach this issue of feminism and feminist consciousness raising in my
classes.
Sanchez: If you scratch the surface of any woman of color, you know
she's a womanist already. She's had to struggle with men. She had to
struggle with her own identity. She's had to struggle in a house, just to be
herself. She has to struggle against rape, incest. She's had to struggle to go to
school. People have attempted to destroy the power of the word *feminism.*
That's why I like "womanist" so much. I like what Alice Walker did with that
word. You see if I'm a "womanist," I love myself; then I love other women
and I love men also. I love my people too. I can't be on this earth without
all of these loves. We see Black women in homes, churches, schools, hospitals.
So one of the things that I think you need to talk about is the places they
see Black women or women of color. What does it mean to be a woman in
a place of power or authority? What does it mean for you to work in some
of these places and not be passive. In fact, tell them to really check out
their mothers and their grandmothers and they will see a womanist
looking the world straight in the eye surviving, exerting their power in
every arena.

Joyce: Sonia, what would be the nature of a Women's Studies Department
that you create for people of color?
Sanchez: That question was asked a number of years ago. And if I remember
correctly, there was some discussion with sister Audre Lorde and sister
Barbara Smith, addressing the need for a Black Women's Studies Department
or Program. I'm not in academia at this point, and I haven't thought about
it for a while. But it seems to me you would have to have a chairperson and

an assistant chairperson, and you would have to have a number of faculty people who could very well be involved in other departments like English, political science, sociology, history, film, dance, and languages. And I think that at some point, one would have to frame this idea of an introduction to Black women, chronicle African women as they came from Africa to the Americas, their experience here under slavery and their experience out of slavery, their experience as sexual objects of masters and of men under slavery, which actually no one ever talks about. So Black women were really the sexual objects of everybody. A Black Women's Studies Department should also chronicle Black women's experiences in the post-slavery days and in the movement north. Some things can be done as they are done in Black Studies Departments. Some people would ask why not just put two women's courses or a woman's course in Black Studies and then go with that. I think not because it's much more complex than that. I think that people have got to understand that we have not done the kind of research one needs to do on African American women. We have just skimmed the top of what it means to be an African woman in the Diaspora, what it means to be the lowest person on the totem pole that has White men, White women, Black men, and at the bottom Black women. What it means also to deal with issues of economics, issues of education, issues of culture, issues that speak to the health of Black women, most especially today all over the world. There is so much to be done in terms of this African woman that you could probably have two departments, one that would speak to the issues of what it really means to be an African American woman, an African woman in the Diaspora, and a woman of color in the Americas. What we need to deal with is Black women's psychology.

What was the psychology of being an African woman being enslaved on the plantation? What did it really mean to be an African woman constantly tied up with another man, a Black man, as she negotiated the master's rapes? What does that do to the psyche? So it means that we have not done the scholarly work that we need to do. We've been looking at the surface stuff that we see on the idiot box about how Black women dress, if they get their hair fixed, their derrières fixed, their noses fixed, or their cheeks fixed. So the Black women that they want us to think are beautiful are some of the women on the idiot box who have all the characteristics of White women. So we need to discuss what is beauty in a sociology class. And we need to understand that it comes to the point we need to thrash those things out, talking about Black beauty, White beauty, Latina beauty, Asian beauty, Native American beauty.

What I'm saying is that we've just scratched the subject matter of a Black Women's Studies that would talk about women's politics. We need to have a course for the International African woman. How does the African American woman compare with the Afro-Brazilian, Afro-Cuban, Afro-Britain, Afro-Caribbean, the continental? What are the commonalities? What are the differences? So if anyone has a question about Black women or women of color, the person directs the question to the Department of Black Women's Studies. But I'm talking about having a consolidated place for the study of people.

Joyce: The next set of questions has introductions to them, because I want to place the questions inside of a context.
Sanchez: Okay.

Joyce: Something that is affecting students, graduate students particularly, very seriously in the academy today is the issue of theory. I have actually been told by some graduate students that they've been asked theoretical questions in job interviews and that if they didn't have a particular answer to these questions, they felt like there was a problem. They also felt that if they studied under certain people, who were not theorists, that they didn't feel they were very competitive for the job.
Sanchez: I see.

Joyce: So, because you are someone who has been a writer for a very long time and a teacher for a very long time, I want to ask you some questions that address the concept of theory in the academy.
Sanchez: Okay.

Joyce: I have said before in some of my work that the poets and the aestheticians of the Black Arts Movement made a number of comments about the relationship between the reader and the audience, long before reader-response criticism became a focus in the academy. In the book *Reader Response Criticism: From Formalism to Post-Structuralism*, Jane Tompkins cites Stanley Fish as the first critic to propose that if literature is what happens when we read, its value depends on the value of the reading process.

In your interview with Danielle A. Rome, you say that writers are manipulators of words and language and language images. You say that poetry is a subconscious conversation and that it is as much the work of those who write as it is those who listen. Despite the fact that on the surface, it appears that you and Fish are saying the same thing, I believe that you see a value in literature that leads to social change. Can you please respond to my rather lengthy inquiry?

Sanchez: Well, you know maybe some people think that when one reads lit that it is a very private occasion, a very private endeavor. But quite often the way that I found this literature and my family did in the South is that it was a very communal activity. Someone read the lit out loud, and we listened to it. Therefore, we knew that it was not necessarily the private, the private movement of a person. I said in defining poetry that poetry was what I call subconscious conversation. It was as much the work of those who write it and read it out loud and those who listen and say Amen, Awoman. I understand in a sense, perhaps, that the role of literature is not necessarily to make us become engaged readers and then bury all that knowledge in our brain and in our heads. The kind of literature we were talking about in the sixties and the seventies and the eighties and the nineties and two thousand is that you read it and it goes into the brain, and, perhaps, it resonates there for a while, but within the literature that we're talking about we see that it begins to make a movement, and it makes a movement into the bloodstream, down to the heart, down to the hands, down to the stomach, and down to the feet and the knees (is the flesh tender where the knees weep?). And you begin to understand that it is those words that will make you move. It's those words that will make you live and become a part of some kind of action that responds to being human.

These words are humanized. This literature makes us better human beings; that's why I think we have the writers. When I truly began to teach literature, I began to try to make connections towards human actions and connections with the world. For me and this includes everything: literature, religion, architecture, music, and film, everything you could possibly include. The whole idea of going to church and listening to a preacher talk about our work as human beings and of being holy is that you walk out of the church—or even before you walk out of the church—to hug somebody and go out then to do work. If I'm a landlord, I cannot maltreat people. I cannot exploit. If I'm a capitalist (and this is a hard one), I must not exploit people in this country, or if I am a CEO, I cannot rob people and take all their money and then leave them with nothing. To me, this literature humanizes us. It makes us human beings, and, therefore, when I write, I want someone to read it out loud preferably and then look at it and say simply, "Okay, this has helped me to survive and be. This has helped me to be a better person. This has quieted down this activity that is in my body that makes me want to be violent. This has opened my eyes to the beat of the world so I can go outside and look at a tree and not want to cut it down because I want to build some buildings or factory some place."

That's what I'm talking about. It is to me, the theory of life. The theory of being human supersedes any other theory that you can look at in academia. So what does this literature do? We will be remembered if this earth survives for this language that we speak and this language that we write. We speak. We communicate, and what are we communicating? What this country allows us to communicate now via the idiot box or even the radio is, "Say anything you want to say about anybody you want to, and we'll laugh at them, and we will mock them. Don't say anything that will, perhaps, make us think and think about why a person would do what she has done." So I think that for me literature is sometimes to show what happens in the world and certainly to get people to think about the issues of what it really means to have drug houses in Black communities. What does it really mean to have a young girl named Norma whose life in a sense was wasted by drugs? What does it mean then to be a country called America in which you are willing to waste the life of children and of large numbers of people of color so you can continue in a system that denies humanity. But on some level, I know that there is a tie up between language and audience, and the tie up is maybe a bureaucracy of sorts. It is appealing to the intellect for learned people to deal with ideas. But then there's an appeal to action. So it is that bureaucracy in this democracy that demands the true lover of literature to read and listen and act, if that makes sense.

Joyce: It makes sense. Thank you for that. I was really intrigued by a comment you made about one of your students' poems in a workshop class. I want to tie what you said to the student in the workshop class to Roland Barthes's comments in *The Pleasure of the Text*. In this workshop class on playwrighting, mentioned also in your interview with Rome, you asked students to bring in a piece of dialogue. One student brought in a dialogue of his parents' arguing and separating. He had heard this dialogue as a child. When he read the piece, he was the only one in the class who cried, and he was surprised that the rest of you did not cry. He was surprised that the rest of you were not involved in his story. He said that the story happened just as he had related it. You told him that he needed to use his imagination more effectively, that he needed to lie a little bit. I would like for you to discuss this idea, your response to the student in the context of the poststructuralist distinction between a text and a work. In his *The Pleasure of the Text*, Roland Barthes contends that a text is a structure of language and that it produces meaning independent of the author and that our old-fashioned ideas of meaning, closure, and authorial intentions are not applicable. He says that the text interacts with the reader, and the reader produces the text. A work, on the other hand, is a closed system, which we have traditionally thought reflected the author's thoughts in a world outside the poem or the novel. Will you connect Barthes's idea of a text as an open system and a work as a closed system. Do you see a connection between Barthes's idea of a text and your telling the student that if he related the story about his parents exactly as he had experienced it that he was not using his imagination effectively and that he needed to lie a little bit?

Sanchez: So you are asking if his relating the story just as it happened, right, is a work or a text?

Joyce: I'm suggesting that, perhaps, his relating the story just as it happened was a work and that you were suggesting that he needed to think more about how his language would be received by and interact with the reader.

Sanchez: Yes, I remember. It was a playwrighting class that I was teaching at the University of Pennsylvania. One of the first assignments was to get them to do a dialogue about people who were close to them. And this young man did this piece about his parents who were arguing, and as he read it he gave us the language of the argument. As he read it, he started to cry, and we sat and watched him cry, and then when he finished, he looked up, and I think he expected us to be in tears, too. We were just sitting looking at him. We were not involved with it at all, because he had told the story of his parents, not our parents. He had not made his parents our parents. And I think when we write about a grandmother or a husband or a child, we make our children their children, our grandmothers their grandmothers, our lovers their lovers. You don't do that by completely staying within the context of your own experience—meaning this Black experience. You've also got to have something that speaks to a larger experience. He asked what was wrong and said that he wrote the story just as it happened. But it was boring, uninteresting, and the point is not that you write it just as it happened. The point is that you write it so that, therefore, we believe that that is just as it happened, and there is a difference there, you see. And he asked, "Well, how do you do that, Professor Sanchez?" And I said, well, one's writing is about imagination. It's not about hearing just what is said.

And there is another magical part that goes in there and that is lying, the thing Sterling Brown was referring to when he would say, "Now, I'm going to read you some of my lies." I remember the first time I heard him say that and my head jumped back and I said to myself, "I've read his work. Those aren't lies." I realized that he was saying simply that none of this stuff happens just as is written. The writer, the poet, is what I call the instigator, an instigator of events, an instigator of eruptions and so you might write down exactly what your parents said, and you read it out loud and you say simply, "Do those words make me cry or is it what lies underneath those words that makes me cry?" The student was not just listening to the words and the herstory of that house. He was listening to the history and herstory of his parents. He was listening to the inflections; he was listening to the venom. He was listening to all the things that made up those words, and unless the words reflect all that, then his piece will not work. The words must reflect the house, the day, the darkness, the absence of life. The words must reflect the pain of a child, listening to parents he loves saying things to each other, even things they thought the child doesn't understand. He hears the terror in those words. That's what I'm talking about, and I said that he had to change those words so that they will show all of that.

Joyce: One of the reasons why I find your response to your student's play intriguing and helpful is that the idea in the academy now, one idea is the more we read a text, the further and further that we get into it, the more contradictions we encounter. And as long as we encounter these contradictions, the text does not reflect a reality outside of itself. What we have are words on a page that have a relationship to each other. Through this reading, the transformative agent of the text becomes ineffective. I think that this is a position that is actually antithetical to the tradition of African American literature. Can you comment on this idea?

Sanchez: Well, I think it's antithetical to the whole tradition of being human. For everything that we do on this earth there is a reaction. There is instigation. There is a result. There is interaction. And, therefore, we cannot separate words and make them stagnant in a sense or inactive. You and I know that words have great action and great energy involved with them. And when they are spoken or written on a page, they can spirit up mankind, womankind, and everyone to some action; and if not to some action, at least to some thought that will lead to action or thought that will lead to a better way of looking at the world, or to a thought that says simply, this will make me want to be more human. There are some novels that are full of contradictions. There are some poems that are full of contradictions. But the point is that it's interesting that you can recognize the contradiction. It doesn't mean that you don't act. Contradictions are not to make us stay and remain in a state of stasis. Contradictions are just a point of information, something that we note as we note other things. If all we note are the contradictions and not the things that make the contradictions viable in a piece, then there's something wrong with us as we look at the world. This world must be sustained and supported by people who look at this literature not in a box and not as something that is cute or to be noted, to be played with, to be petted, to be deconstructed and then reconstructed and then deconstructed again until you come down to a pin and you say this is all that is left. And if that's all that is left, then it's unimportant and you can't do anything with it. That's word masturbation. That's a way of looking at the world and a way of looking at people that show some disdain for people and some disdain for the beauty of words and, not only the beauty of words, but the power of words. The notion is if you can't do it, then you can destroy it. If you can't do it, then you can "destruct" it.

But the point to me is that a work can be looked at from a point of beauty, from a point of availability, from a point of workability, from a point of humanity, from a point of non-humanity, from a point of structure. Writing is not just about constructing a piece; it's about ringing a sound of hope from a point of herstory or history, from a point of its place in time. It's all those things that you would bring to the thought and process of how in the world this book came about. How in the world did we get *The Bluest Eye* after the guidance of Linda Brent [Harriet Jacobs]? How did we get *The Bluest Eye* after we read *Maud Martha*? How did we get *The Bluest Eye* after we tasted *Their Eyes Were Watching God*? So, therefore, you can't look at something just as an entity without looking at the forces of nature, the forces of the words that have come before. We have to look at the sounds and the lines and the words of other books that have come before. *The Bluest Eye* is not just one book standing alone. It's standing on the shoulders of other people, of other books that have gone before, and also it's standing on the books of the blood of a country that has produced it.

Nothing just comes out all of a sudden and says, "Well, here I is; I just grew." To me there's a master-slave relationship here. The book is the slave and the critic is the master, and the critic thinks let me now cage you and make you submit until there is only the "grease" that is left behind, and none of the juice and none of the potency and none of the saving grace, not even the screams. Everything gets deconstructed to a point. I hope I'm making some kind of sense here. I think that some current criticism is an easy way for us not to deal with the sociology of a book, the economics of a book, the humanity of a book, the positioning in time of that book, the progression of a book in time, you know, all of that. I think it's just a way that now we can say, in a sense, this literature right here, can go no further. This literature cannot advance any further so let's just empty our cups right now. Let us deconstruct it, and say, "By golly by gee, not only does it not work, but what purpose does is serve"? And I think that the purpose that is served is that we begin to understand the history and herstory of language and words. To me literature engages not disengages.

Joyce: In your comments in other interviews you indicate that you are quite proud of having published some of your earlier books with Dudley Randall's Broadside Press in Detroit. Broadside has such an undeniably essential place in the history of Black poetry, publishing poets who had political perspectives that White presses would not touch. I am proud of having published two books with a historically Black press, Third World Press in Chicago, which has published the works of such intellectuals as Gwendolyn Brooks, John Henrik-Clarke, Frances Cress-Welsing, Askia Touré, and Amiri Baraka as well as yourself. While publishing has always been a problem with Blacks seeking tenure and promotion in White liberal arts colleges and research universities, the politics of tenure and promotion have become so elitist now that I advise young Black scholars to try to

publish their books with the most prestigious White university presses and
not to publish with Black presses before they have achieved both tenure and
promotion if they want to compete in research universities. Will you please
comment on this dilemma?

Sanchez: Well, I think that probably it might be more of a dilemma for
essayists or critics than for poets. I think when I came up for tenure, I had
published most of my books with Black presses. I had published one with
Bantam books and one with Thunder's Mouth Press. Maybe in terms of
academe and the whole sense of critical essays and not with novels as such, it
may be necessary to deal with established presses or university presses or big
presses. So I can understand your telling young academics to try to get their
first book done with a mainstream publisher, okay? And then maybe later on
when they have a couple books and are tenured, then they can go and support
some of the smaller presses or alternative presses that exist. So, I don't know.
I think the other part of that equation though is that it [the publisher]
depends on how it [the book] is also distributed. I mean it is possible for them
to do a book with a small press, an alternative press, or a Black press and the
distribution could be very miniscule. The manuscript might not even be sub-
mitted for awards that are out there. I think that a smaller press or a Black
press does not have the mechanisms to do all the things that a big press has.
A lot of real political books or a book that speaks to non-traditional issues
that exist out there have trouble finding publishers. Some of the big presses
are owned by these big conglomerates. I think that it's really important for all
of us to support some of the presses and then understand the losses, understand the games, understand how it benefits us, understand also how publishing with a specific press might not help us and then make that choice to
support those alternative presses that must stay alive in this country. These
publishing companies are really big huge animals and just like the newspapers, my sister, are not necessarily amenable to what many of us are trying to
say at this point.

Joyce: Thank you. Please comment on what drew you to Alexander Pushkin
and Pablo Neruda, and in your comments, please place their poetry in the
context of their times.

Sanchez: Well, one of the librarians in New York City when I was a little girl
began giving me poetry. I don't know why, because I never told her I like or
wrote poetry. She was a librarian at 145th Street, New York City. I used to go

to the library when I was twelve and thirteen and fourteen to get the "good" books, the books that had a good part, the good sex parts. And so I would bring home books like *Forever Amber* and stuff like that. And I'd just read them overnight, getting into the good part. I used to just check out all these books, and one day I got to the counter, and she handed me an anthology of what was called Negro poetry, and she gave me Pushkin, and I brought them home and I was just so happy and startled to see all those wonderful poets, Black poets in there. And she told me that Pushkin was an Afro-Russian. And I realized later on that that was a leftist. I didn't understand a lot of Pushkin at that time, but I read him for the musicality. I read him out loud for the musicality of it and also just for some of the lines that were understandable.

I was drawn to Neruda by reading all kinds of poetry. I guess it was in the 1970s or mid-1970s that I discovered Neruda in some of the anthologies, and then I started collecting the books of this brilliant, brilliant writer. So I began this great, fantastic journey to Neruda, reading some of the translations by Robert Bly. One of the very political brothers at Amherst, a Latino, gave me a book on Neruda's poetry that he had translated and I was just mesmerized by it, and also that's how I discovered Nicolás Guillén. So I started reading a lot of poetry of our brothers and sisters in Latin America and the Caribbean and just was mesmerized by the way they wrote about this country and about their own country. I was mesmerized by the chances that they took with language. It's just like I met a kindred soul. So that was one man I wanted to meet. I met Guillén when I went to Cuba in the seventies, and I met Antonio Paz, the Mexican poet when I went to Oslo, Norway, the year of the MOVE bombings here in 1985. And Langston Hughes was the other person who had translated many of these poets, these Latin-American poets, these Cuban poets.

And the joy, the great joy for me, is to have Black and Latino students and White students write haiku because I've been teaching that since before I went to Temple. I've always taught that form, because I fell in love with that form when I was studying with Louise Bogan at NYU, and she told us all to go find a form, choose a form and study it, and, perhaps, imitate it. And I found a haiku book down in the Village, and just really found my voice in an interesting way. The Japanese haiku counts sounds, and we don't count sounds. We count syllables that approximate the sounds. I found my sound which was interesting.

Joyce: Your comments here are interesting because my next question addressed the haiku, and you just answered it. Yet, I have another part to my question: Would you talk about your conception of the sonku, which, of course, I totally identify with you.

Sanchez: Sonku is my form. I always tell my students, after I teach the haiku, the tanka, and the cinquain, to make up their own syllabic verse and name it. You can't make it up without naming it. I told the students that that's all the Japanese poets did in the courts at first. What they first wrote was not the haiku. They first wrote the tanka with five lines, and then they had these three lines left over and that's how the haiku came into existence. Isn't that amazing? I tell my students that this thing called creative writing means that you can create something, besides just learning other people's forms, and it takes you to another place when you can create your own form. When you create your own form, then you can say that you really have a handle on this thing called poetry.

Joyce: I see creating your form takes you away from imitating. You are friends with Chinua Achebe and Ngugi wa Thiong'o. Can you talk a little bit about the influence of their relationship, their art, and their essays on your work?

Sanchez: Well, certainly, just meeting the two of them and seeing what they're writing about I've learned about Kenya; I have learned about Nigeria. I think the importance of brother Achebe and brother Ngugi for me is that they have allowed me as this African American to see two cultures that were removed from us. They both allowed me to make grand distinctions between a Nigerian writer and a Kenyan writer. It is a valuable experience to read especially Ngugi's essays on writing and literature, the politics of literature, and the politics of writing in one's own language.

But I think more than anything with Chinua what really compels me is the conversation that we have about language, about politics, about the country, about what really happened on the continent of Africa, and what is happening now on his continent. Our conversations pose the question for us all: What does it mean to be human in the midst of greed and dislocation? How will we as Africans in the Diaspora continue to survive?

Joyce: I would like now for us to move to a discussion of your new CD, *Full Moon of Sonia* [Sanchez's musical stage production of her poetry]. I have several questions regarding this artistic production, but first, I think we should debunk this notion that poets like you, Baraka, Touré, Cortez, and others are performance poets. I'm interested in this idea because historically, those trained in universities studying Marianne Moore, T. S. Eliot, et cetera, have a very westernized, narrow definition of poetry. Will you please describe or define the performance poet and then explain what you see as the difference between performance poetry and the kind of poetry you write and read?

Sanchez: Well, I think that quite often when it comes to poets of color that what has happened is that they've come up with the idea of performance poetry, which I think attempts to keep us out of the arena of being poets. Some of the younger people today say they are performance poets. They feel very happy with that, and I don't disagree with it. I let them just go ahead and say that, but I always tell them very gently that the most important word in there is *poet*. But I think that it is very difficult in this country, if you're Black or a person of color, to be considered seriously as a poet. For instance, before sister Gwen Brooks died, there was an attempt to give her a major award in New York City. Lucille Clifton was on the board that challenged Ms. Brooks's right to get an award. Gwen was in her eighties, and they were questioning this woman with a Pulitzer Prize and numerous awards, which means they didn't like the idea and thought she didn't deserve the Pulitzer at all. So it's on that level that you truly understand how we are really regarded as poets. If you really don't think that we are poets, then the interesting way to limit us is to call us performance poets.

Joyce: Would you explain what you see as the continuum between the Black Arts Movement agenda and your production of *The Full Moon of Sonia*?

Sanchez: Well, I think *The Full Moon of Sonia* engages a lot of genres: blues, love songs, ballads, political rap. My poetry responds to the jazz that is being played, and so, therefore, what you see is a complete connection to what we were doing in the sixties with our craft called poetry, with our presentation of poetry with jazz. Our poetry was an eye on the world. Our poetry was an eye on the people. Our poetry was an eye on music. This is what we do with *The Full Moon of Sonia*, and we add many ingredients to it from jazz to rap, to poetry that speaks to issues that are going on and that's what our poetry had always done coming out of the sixties up until 2000. And another ingredient in *Full Moon of Sonia*, as it related to today, is we have young people engaged in that CD. The drummer who plays the piece for Tupac [Shakur] is a hip-hop drummer, and the sound resonates with a hip-hop urgency. We have the gospel component in there, and we juxtapose this gospel sound with an urban sound that happens as a woman takes her child into a crack house and the plaintive cry of the singer reflecting the plaintive cry of a crack addict as she leaves her child in a crack house. All of those things have been brought together for us to look and see and taste along with that constant beat of hip-hop to blues to jazz to gospel to all of the sounds that emanate from an urban city, and all of the stars that emanate also from a celebration of people. We celebrate Langston Hughes and we celebrate Tupac, two people looking at each other from different generations. They are two people, very much involved with the people. Langston the poet, the poet laureate, the laureate of New York and Pac, the laureate of the world, the young peoples' laureate of the world.

Joyce: Thank you. We have so few autobiographies and biographies of African American writers. I think the memoir that you are currently writing is an essential contribution to African American intellectual history. Please describe what you are doing in your memoir that is in progress.

Sanchez: I don't know. I'm doing so much I think I'm overwriting. And I think I'm going to end up having to cut, but I felt like the only way I could talk about myself probably was to overwrite. So this memoir is one that is very close to my heart right now as I write it, and I really hesitate talking about it a lot, because I notice that if you talk about it, you don't write. But it is going to be about at least three major movements that I participated in: the Black Arts Movement, the Black Studies Movement and the peace movement, women's/peace movement. I think it's important for young people to know that we have involved ourselves in a peace movement and a Black Studies Movement and a Black Arts Movement. And I am not disregarding other periods, but those are interesting because a lot happened.

Joyce: I would like for us now to turn to just a few questions about your drama.

Sanchez: Okay.

Joyce: Though very talented writers usually write in more than one genre, it is common that we critics and teachers limit our attention to one specific genre by a particular writer. For example Baldwin is as much a skillful novelist as he is an essayist.

Sanchez: And playwright.

Joyce: And playwright, thank you. You have written a number of plays, and stylistically, they are very different from each other, but let's begin with what you see as the difference between the art or craft of poetry and the craft of drama? Do you see a difference between those two?

Sanchez: I'm not so sure I see a difference. I see a different product, okay. But I don't think it's by chance that many poets are playwrights. You go back to Baraka, from [Bertolt] Brecht to many people who write poetry and who also write plays. And I think that's because of how we deal in a sense with the dialogue sometimes in our poetry. I think writing poetry is almost a natural movement into this genre of the writing of plays, where you take the lines and make them spoken lines that are also lyrical. You know what I mean? So, my plays have come about because I'd been writing some poems, and the poems didn't say all that I wanted to say and it spilled over into dialogue. Then I realized the dialogue should be put into a play because I was not writing a poem.

And *The Bronx Is Next*, my first play, was something that just came out. I did that play in New York City and that play came out of something that I read in the newspaper about a cop chasing a kid down the street, 125th Street. And the young person said, "I was just running because it's my street; it's my street." It's a Harlem kind of a response. And this cop went, "Yeah, right!" Okay? *The Bronx Is Next* is a play that Dr. Arthur P. Davis called one of the best plays that he had ever read in the twentieth century. Anyway, he loved that play; he kept publishing it. But I wrote that play because I wanted to show how urban cities were killing Black folks, how death permeated our souls as it is in these ghettos, in the tenements, in these houses that people didn't care about, and I wanted to show also how the possibilities of organizing people to take them South where they had come from and to begin to rebuild. There's some way that you have to leverage what people are doing to you. You just can't keep on the status quo of hopelessness. You've got to leverage. You've got to make something happen, so therefore, something else will happen. And so the point was that they were going to evacuate Harlem and burn Harlem down. And so, it's almost similar to the play that was written years ago about when all the Blacks disappeared?

Joyce: *Day of Absence.*
Sanchez: Yes, that's it. I've seen the *The Bronx Is Next* done on many occasions, and I've seen the energy that young actors have put into their performance. The most moving part comes with the White policeman and the Black man. It speaks to issues that are still resonating now with the police. Part of the training for policemen should be role reversal. They should take that little section there and have a policeman pretend to be a Black man and run down the street. And then let a Black man pretend to be a policeman and come up and say, "Where are you going boy? Where are you running to?" When I was up for tenure, I had three committees: one for my poetry, one for my prose, and one for my plays. One of the men who was on the committee for my plays came up and said, "You really write well, Sonia, but you know this thing in *The Bronx Is Next* about a Black man running down the street in Harlem and being stopped and pushed up against a building just does not happen." Low and behold, I read later in the *New York Times* a very similar incident and when this professor later came into my office, I sat there and read to him that this young man in Harlem had been running down the street at 2:00 a.m. in the morning, and he was beaten as he screamed out, "But I am just running in my Harlem. I ain't doing nothing wrong." It's amazing how art imitates life and life imitates art, right? Maybe some Whites choose not to understand that you could be running down your own street doing nothing with nobody chasing you, but you are just feeling good and hot and young, you know? And someone grabs you and beats you up and drags you to jail. The professor went out of the office and that was it. Yeah.

Joyce: I think that *Dirty Hearts* is a very strange play. In the play, we have what you refer to as the first man, the second man, Shigeko, Carl, and a poet. The first man and second man are waiting for Carl to join them so that they can play cards. Shigeko is also with them. Carl finally arrives, and they begin to play cards, but the play seems to be about something far more subtle than the characters' interaction with each other during the card game. The language seems to be rather stylized. Is the message pessimistic? The poet has a long speech in which he says, "I write about old things, past things, perhaps dead things because I am dead and at ease with my contemporaries. I no longer write about you." Speaking to the second man, Shigeko, or Carl, the poet says, "You are the world's painful propaganda." Can you please explain your conceptualization of this play? Why do the first man and second man not have names?

Sanchez: Because it was unimportant for them to have names. They're like every man out there who, from businessman to activist to worker, are united in their destruction of Carl. They're united in their destination of Carl. They're united in being empathetic towards Shigeko, and they are united in their disgust for the poet who is nonproductive and weak.

The purpose of this card game called *Dirty Hearts* is not to get the Queen of Spades and any hearts. And what I wanted people to recognize is that there was not a Black woman there. The Black woman only surfaces as the bad card that no one wants. So there was Shigeko because Hiroshima had happened. I met a Shigeko who had come in to get her face repaired from the bombing of Hiroshima. And the poet, like some of them at that time, is not writing about issues. So this play was a take-off of the many things that were happening at that time in America. You know, people doing disclaimers, people talking about wanting to be a Black capitalist. We do have capitalists now, you know. People wanted to be Black capitalists, whether they were or not.

Joyce: Thank you for that. It's a very complicated play. What you just explained about *Dirty Hearts*, I think, relates to another of your plays called *Uh Huh: But How Do It Free Us?* I want to ask you to comment on the style or arrangement of that play. It is interesting to me that rather than dividing the play into scenes, you have what you refer to as groups. You have three groups. In the first group, you have the interaction between Malik, Waleesha, and Nefertia. In the second group, we have the sister whore, the White whore, three brothers, and one White man, and another brother. And in the third group, we have a Black woman, a Black man, and a White woman. The Black woman is pregnant and lives with the Black man. The White woman is the Black man's lover. Can you comment on what you want the reader to get out of each of the character's interaction in each of these groups and on how the groups are interrelated?

Sanchez: Well, the groups are only interrelated in the sense that these were about three separate things that were going on in the Black movement, the Black radical movement or the Black Power movement. What you failed to mention is that I also had dancers, and at the conclusion of each section, the dancers danced, which was a re-telling in dance of the observations of the dancers who are stretched out on the floor down stage, responding to everything that happened. They laugh and point at each other and the characters they become.

The first one is a commentary on the idea of polygamy. That's why the title is *Uh Huh: But How Do It Free Us?* So, how is polygamy going to free us. And this young brother is in school; he has two sisters, who lived with him, and ostensibly, they are getting along. One was pregnant; one was not. But we find out that they both are pregnant later on. This man has two women, and he doesn't have a job. He's just in school. And so the whole point of living in the United States, the whole concept is wrong, you know. And because he turns and asks one of the sisters, "Do you have your welfare check?" He wants her to endorse the check and give it to him, so he can go cash it and get some money. So he's really living off these sisters, and they're just as meek and mild and whatever. The moment he leaves they fight, talking about who loves whom the most, and who's pregnant, and when I have his son, I will consolidate my relationship with Malik, and you'll be out. I mean all of that occurs in that first section. Women were at each other because they had not been prepared for polygamy. It was not a cultural thing. It was like something you implanted in an apartment or in houses. It had not come out of the culture, the culture of that society. It was doomed to failure. So the dancers were amazing. This dancer got up, a male dancer, and danced like a cock, like a rooster. And the two women were walking behind him straight as robots. And he'd stop and they'd stop. I use dance to back up what I am saying and to show how dancers interpret things.

The second group was about drugs in the Black community. We see the reduction always of the Black woman in any society. We have in this play the movement of a Black man, a White man who is a floater, and other assorted characters. This group is about the drug culture that came about during that period, a very crucial period in the movement. It was on purpose and so all these good minds were just enmeshed in drugs and could not move and could not be helped or help any one because that's all they were doing.

The last group was another thing that happened in the movement, which is that some, but not all Black men had a White woman. And when the movement becomes more prominent, the White woman recognizes that the Black man is going to be a leader, so she tells him he needs a Black woman.

And a Black woman comes three thousand miles unaware that this is happening. This Black man is juxtaposed between the two of them. And this situation harkens back a little bit to slavery days, when the Black woman and White woman were antagonistic because of the White master. Now coming full circle to the sixties, the Black woman and White woman are antagonists because of a Black man.

And so you see, that's what I was trying to show. This Black woman is the only one who survives. So it's a play that spoke to the issues. And I got flack for that play because people were seeing themselves up there on stage, which is what I wanted them to do. It's a Brechtian kind of play, because I wanted people to see themselves and then to correct themselves, and to see how they were really killing themselves and others.

Joyce: How many of your plays were performed?
Sanchez: All I think were performed.

Joyce: All in New York or some in L.A.?
Sanchez: Some were performed at Northwestern University. I've never seen *Dirty Hearts* performed. I saw *Malcolm Man/Don't Live Here No More*, because I wrote it for the Black schools in Pittsburgh. *The Bronx Is Next* was performed downtown in the Village. *Sister Son/ji* was performed from the University of Buffalo to New York City, at the Joe Papp's Theater to Washington, D.C. I received many letters from sisters who said they received scholarships for performing *Sister Son/ji* to go to graduate school. It's a very hard play to do. One of the last plays I did was a play called *I'm Black When I'm Singing, I'm Blue When I Ain't.* And that play is about three women who are in the music business, a woman who might be Billie Holiday, a woman who might be Bessie Smith, and a woman who might be Nina Simone.

It's done in verse. When the play opens this woman is sitting on a toilet in an asylum. She gets up off the toilet; she picks up what she's done, and she starts to eat it. And the audience gets grossed out, and then she looks at the audience and says, "What's your problem?" And then she laughs at the audience, and she looks around at the audience and she says, "Yeah, that's me. It's me." And then she says, "Yeah, it's me; I'm the one. You used to see me on stage before when I sang." Then there are what I call the chorus, who are the attendants, who come in to make the changes with her, and they come announcing things. And like all attendants and all choruses, they announce bad news quite often. Into this arena of madness comes the doctor and what we discover is that this woman has a multiple personality. And that's how I'm able to bring in Billie and Bessie. I did a lot of research on these singers. With Bessie Smith, I found out that she had lived in railroad flats because hotels didn't rent rooms, even to great Black singers.

Quite often Bessie got drunk in the railroad flats and passed out on the floor and the same people who had cheered her earlier with I love you, I love you watched her with amusement. I think there is something that people don't like about artists. There is something about their greatness that intimidates, even as they cheer them on. So instead of protecting her from those inquiring eyes and putting her to bed, they participate in the destruction of the artist.

And there's Nina. Her motion and movement showed how she really never loved herself. The psychiatrist knows that she is two people. It is she Nina who is telling the story, and then there is also Bessie and Billie. All of a sudden she has a slip of the tongue and says, "That bitch." The psychiatrist says, "What bitch, whom are you talking about?" And he realizes there's a third character, and the third one is a singer who has gotten it together in terms of who she is. She is like some of the younger jazz singers singing today. Nina says, "She thinks she's going to get me, but I'm in charge."

And so there is this whole thing where there is a fight between this modern-day singer who really has looked at the world and really has the world in tune to this Black aesthetic that she has. She has this sense of herself as a human being, and she's saying to Nina and her ghost, "Okay, we going to retire you. You must rest now. Thank you for all that you have given us." A battle takes place on the stage between the two of them. I wrote all the lyrics for the play.

Joyce: *I'm Black When I'm Singing, I'm Blue When I Ain't*, the play you just finished discussing has not been published, am I correct?
Sanchez: No, it's now in production in a collection at the University of Alabama Press.

Joyce: Your home base has been in Philadelphia for well over twenty years. You recently received a very distinguished Avatar Award here in the city, and an Avatar is an exemplar or an embodiment of a known model or category.

You also received some years ago, the Lucretia Mott Award here in Philadelphia. Would you comment on the city of Philadelphia's reception of you as a poet?

Sanchez: I am also the recipient of a mayor's medal and received the Governor's Award for Humanity, a PEW Fellowship in the Arts, and a Leeway Foundation Transformation Award. Philadelphia has been a good place for me to work and write and raise my children. I taught some amazing students at Temple University. It's been a wonderful twenty-nine years in Philadelphia.

Index